THE FRANCO-GERMAN
RELATIONSHIP IN THE EUROPEAN
UNION

'Engine', 'motor', 'vanguard', 'axis', 'couple', 'pair', 'entente', 'partnership': all of these labels applied to their relationship indicate that France and Germany together play a critical – if not dominant – role in the European Union and the European integration process. But little is actually known about the intensity of the two governments' relationship, nor the extent of their influence on EU policies and decisions. This book illuminates this important bilateral relationship in the EU, showing how its intensity and impact vary significantly across different issues and policy areas.

The contributors cover policy sectors ranging from the 'high political' issues of economic and monetary union, the EU's East European enlargement, foreign affairs and defence, to normally more mundane issues of electricity and telecommunications liberalisation, research and technology, agriculture, social affairs and immigration. Collectively, the sectoral analyses reveal an extremely variegated picture of the closeness and intensity of the Franco-German relationship in the EU, and of the two states' impact and influence on EU policy.

Differences in the intensity of the relationship appear to be explicable in terms of the political salience of the issues to each government, and the strength and longevity of the EU's competences, the level of multilateral interaction in the sector. This suggests that with the deepening of the integration process, the bilateral relationship becomes increasingly institutionalised, crisis-resistant and less vulnerable to changes of government and political leadership in Paris and Bonn.

The Franco-German Relationship in the European Union provides much needed empirical data and analysis on a significant topic for which, until now, there has been very little information. It will be a vital resource for political scientists, or anyone concerned with European public policy or EU governance.

Douglas Webber is Associate Professor of Political Science at INSEAD (European Institute of Business Administration), Fontainebleau, co-author of *Hostile Brothers* (Clarendon Press, 1990) and has published extensively on German and European politics.

ROUTLEDGE RESEARCH IN EUROPEAN PUBLIC POLICY
Edited by Jeremy Richardson
Nuffield College, University of Oxford

1 THE POLITICS OF CORPORATE TAXATION IN THE EUROPEAN UNION
Knowledge and International Policy Agendas
Claudio M. Radaelli

2 THE LARGE FIRM AS A POLITICAL ACTOR IN THE EU
David Coen

3 PUBLIC POLICY DISASTERS IN WESTERN EUROPE
Edited by Pat Gray and Paul 't Hart

4 THE EU COMMISSION AND EUROPEAN GOVERNANCE
An Institutional Analysis
Thomas Christiansen

5 EUROPE'S DIGITAL REVOLUTION
Broadcasting Regulation, The EU and the Nation State
David Levy

6 EU SOCIAL POLICY IN THE 1990s
Towards a Corporatist Policy Community
Gerda Falkner

7 THE FRANCO-GERMAN RELATIONSHIP IN THE EU
Edited by Douglas Webber

8 ECONOMIC CITIZENSHIP IN THE EUROPEAN UNION
Employment relations in the new Europe
Paul Teague

9 THE EUROPEAN AUTOMOBILE INDUSTRY
Multi-Level Governance, Policy and Politics
Andrew M. McLaughlin and William A. Maloney

Other titles in the European Public Policy series:

European Union *Jeremy Richardson*; Democratic Spain *Richard Gillespie, Fernando Rodrigo and Jonathan Story*; Regulating Europe *Giandomenico Majone*; Adjusting to Europe *Yves Meny, Pierre Muller and Jean Louis Quermonne*; Policy-making in the European Union *Laura Cram*; Regions in Europe *Patrick Le Galès and Christian Lequesne*; Green Parties and Politics in the European Union *Elizabeth Bomberg*; A Common Foreign Policy for Europe? *John Peterson and Helene Sjursen*; Policy-making, European Integration and the Role of Interest Groups *Sonia Mazey and Jeremy Richardson*

THE FRANCO-GERMAN RELATIONSHIP IN THE EUROPEAN UNION

Edited by Douglas Webber

London and New York

First published 1999
by Routledge
11 New Fetter Lane, London EC4P 4EE

Simultaneously published in the USA and Canada
by Routledge
29 West 35th Street, New York, NY 10001

Routledge is a member of the Taylor and Francis Group

Typeset in Garamond by
HWA Text and Data Management Ltd, Tunbridge Wells
Printed and bound in Great Britain by St Edmundsbury Press,
Bury St Edmunds, Suffolk

British Library Cataloguing in Publication Data
A catalogue record for this book is available from the British Library

Library of Congress Cataloging in Publication Data
The Franco-German relationship in the European Union / edited by
Douglas Webber
p. cm. — (Routledge research in European public policy ; 7)
Includes bibliographical references and index.
1. European Union – France. 2. European Union – Germany.
3. France – Foreign relations – Germany. 4. Germany – Foreign
relations – France. I. Webber, Douglas. II. Series.
HC240.25.F8F73 1999 98-53737
327.43044–dc21 CIP

ISBN 0-415-17065-6

CONTENTS

List of illustrations   vii
List of contributors   viii
Series editor's preface   x
Author's preface   xii
List of abbreviations   xiv

1 Introduction   1
   DOUGLAS WEBBER

2 Monetary union: economic competition and political negotiation   20
   JONATHAN STORY

3 France, Germany, the IGC and Eastern enlargement   41
   PATRICK MCCARTHY

4 Mastering differences: the Franco-German alliance and the
   liberalisation of European electricity markets   58
   SUSANNE K. SCHMIDT

5 From high to low politics in Franco-German relations: the case
   of telecommunications   75
   VOLKER SCHNEIDER AND THIERRY VEDEL

6 Integration with a Spluttering Engine: the Franco-German
   relationship in European research and technology policy   93
   BURKARD EBERLEIN AND EDGAR GRANDE

7 Agricultural policy: the hard core   111
   DOUGLAS WEBBER

CONTENTS

8 An awkward alliance: France, Germany and Social Policy   130
   MARTIN RHODES

9 Franco-German co-operation in foreign affairs, security
   and defence: a case study   148
   AMAYA BLOCH-LAINÉ

10 France, Germany and immigration policy: a paradoxical convergence 159
   PATRICK WEIL

11 Conclusion   167
   DOUGLAS WEBBER

   Index   183

ILLUSTRATIONS

Figure 4.1 European electricity prices 1992–96   60

Table 5.1   Summary of French, German and EU
            Telecommunications Policy   82

CONTRIBUTORS

Amaya Bloch-Lainé is a Research Associate, working on European security, at CREST-École Polytechnique, Paris. Her research is focused on the security and defence identity of the European Union (EU), particularly in the light of the EU's prospective enlargement to include the countries of Central and Eastern Europe.

Burkard Eberlein is Assistant Professor of Political Science at the Technische Universität München, Germany. His current research interests include the political economy of regulation in Europe, regional governance in the EU, comparative regional innovation and research and development policies.

Edgar Grande is Professor of Political Science at the Technische Universität München, Germany. His current research interests include German and European technology policy, European integration and the political economy of public regulation. He has published widely on various aspects of German and European politics and public policies.

Patrick McCarthy is Professor of European Studies at the Johns Hopkins University Bologna Centre, Bologna, Italy. Among his most recent publications is the edited volume, *France-Germany 1983–1993: The Struggle to Cooperate* (Basingstoke and London: Macmillan, 1993).

Martin Rhodes is Research Professor at the Robert Schuman Centre of the European University Institute, Florence, Italy. His main research interests include Italian politics, comparative public policy (labour markets and welfare states), European social policy and globalisation and change in contemporary capitalist societies.

Susanne K. Schmidt is Research Fellow at the Max Planck Institute for the Study of Societies, Cologne, Germany. Her recent publications include *Coordinating Technology*, co-authored with Raymund Werle (Cambridge, USA: MIT Press, 1998) and *Liberalisierung in Europa: Die Rolle der Europäischen Kommission* (Frankfurt am Main: Campus, 1998).

Volker Schneider is Professor of Political Science in the Faculty of Public Policy and Management at the Universität Konstanz, Constance, Germany. His current research interests include theories of the state, policy studies, network analysis, and telecommunications policy.

Jonathan Story is Professor of International Political Economy at INSEAD (European Institute of Business Administration), Fontainebleau, France and has written widely on European affairs. His most recent publications are *The Frontiers of Fortune* (London: Pitman, 1999) and, with Ingo Walter, *Political Economy of Financial Integration in Europe: The Battle of the Systems* (Manchester and Cambridge, USA: University of Manchester Press and MIT Press, 1997).

Thierry Vedel is a Research Fellow at the National Centre for Scientific Research (CNRS), Paris, based at CEVIPOF (Centre for the Study of French Political Life), a research centre of the National Foundation for Political Science. His research deals with public policies for new communications technologies. He is the co-author of *La télévision de demain* (Paris: Armand Colin, 1993) and is currently working on a book entitled *L'euphorie technologique*.

Douglas Webber is Associate Professor of Political Science at INSEAD (European Institute of Business Administration), Fontainebleau, France. His main research interests include the Franco-German relationship, EU agricultural politics and German politics.

Patrick Weil is Director of Research at the National Centre for Scientific Research (CNRS), Paris and works at the Centre for Research on the History of Social Movements and Trade Unionism at Université Paris 1 (Panthéon-Sorbonne).

SERIES EDITOR'S PREFACE

One of the most common and persistent assumptions made about the European integration process is that it is shaped or driven by a special relationship between France and Germany. This putative relationship is often resented by other member states, not only by the United Kingdom, but also by smaller EU member states fearful of being subordinated to a Franco-German hegemony or *directoire*. At the same time, however, Franco-German co-operation is often regarded as essential to enable decisions to be reached and the integration process to advance. Bilateral summit meetings, the issuing of joint communiqués on EU issues, 'breakfast' and other meetings between French and German leaders on the 'margins' of European Council sessions – these are just a few of the indicators that are typically used to highlight the special role that the two states are alleged to play in the EU.

Despite the significance so often and widely attributed to it, the Franco-German relationship in the EU has been the object of very little systematic and careful analysis. Not even the 'intergovernmentalist' theorists of European integration who emphasise the predominance of the governments of (usually) the (biggest) states in the EU decision-making process, have devoted much energy to divulging its inner workings. Consequently, very little is actually known about the extent, intensity, nature and consequences of co-ordination between the two governments on EU issues. Do the two governments co-ordinate their positions on EU issues more closely than with other member governments? To what extent do they succeed in mediating their conflicts? Do they typically try to act jointly in EU organs? How influential are the two governments when they act in tandem? And to what extent, and how does it matter if and when they do not? To these questions, the existing political science literature on the EU gives relatively few answers.

Insofar as the Franco-German relationship has been studied by political scientists, their focus has been very much on the role played by the French President and the German Chancellor. The Franco-German relationship tends thus to be reduced to that of Chancellor Adenauer and President de Gaulle in the late 1950s and early 1960s, to that of Chancellor Schmidt and President Giscard d'Estaing in the 1970s and to that of Chancellor Kohl and President Mitterrand in the 1980s and the first half of the 1990s. Albeit the heads of government and, in the French case, of state, have undeniably exercised a powerful influence on the relationship, the relationship's relative continuity, sporadic 'crises', such as that concerning the presidency of the European Central Bank in 1998, notwithstanding, indicates that the Franco-German 'tandem' is a phenomenon that continues to transcend individual political leaders.

The principal objective of the present volume is to compare and contrast the functioning and impact of the Franco-German relationship across different issue and policy areas in the EU. The case studies reveal that the reality 'on the ground' in Brussels is more complex than most of the public discussion about the Bonn–Paris 'tandem' suggest. They show that there are wide variations both in the intensity of the relationship and its impact, positive or negative, on the policy-making process and policy outputs. There is no single Franco-German relationship, but a number of Franco-German relationships, close or distant, depending on the issue or policy area; there is no Franco-German *directoire*, but rather some issues and policy areas in which the two governments form something akin to a 'hard core' of the EU and others where France and Germany are far from exercising a preponderant influence. The picture that the studies collectively portray is also one of a relationship that, in parallel with the integration process, has solidified and, if anything, grown stronger over time. It would therefore be dangerous to assume, on account of momentary 'crises', that, overall, the Franco-German relationship is going to become a less significant factor in EU politics in the twenty-first century than it was in the second half of the twentieth.

AUTHOR'S PREFACE

The project of which this book is the product was not conceived in France or Germany, but rather in Italy, on the hills overlooking Florence at San Domenico di Fiesole, location of the European University Institute (EUI), where, as a Jean Monnet fellow at the Robert Schuman Centre (RSC), I spent one and a half unforgettable and intellectually enriching years from October 1995 to April 1997. The idea that inspired the project was quite simple: a great deal is written, said or thought about the Franco-German relationship in the European Union (EU), but little is in fact known about its actual functioning and impact on EU policy decisions. This book is intended to contribute to our knowledge of these two questions. The Robert Schuman Centre and my 'home' institute, INSEAD (European Institute of Business Administration), enabled me to stage a conference on this topic at Florence on 6 and 7 February 1997. Most of the scholars who were invited to participate in the conference are specialists in the analysis of public, especially EU, policy. My hope in inviting mainly scholars with this profile rather than those whose expertise is in the analysis of the Franco-German relationship itself to contribute to the conference was that the former would provide fresh views on and insights into the workings of the Franco-German relationship in the EU. It is for the reader to judge whether and to what extent this hope has been fulfilled. Of the contributions to this volume, all but one – that written by Susanne Schmidt on electricity supply liberalisation – were originally presented at this conference. Papers were also given at the conference by Elie Cohen on the internal market and Adrienne Héritier on environmental and road haulage policies. Among my former colleagues at the EUI, Yves Mény, director of the RSC, Roger Morgan, formerly Professor in the Department of Political and Social Sciences, Amy Verdun, fellow of the European Forum, and Andrea Lenschow, Jean Monnet fellow at the RSC, also contributed as discussants of the papers presented respectively by Adrienne Héritier, Amaya Bloch-Lainé, Jonathan Story and myself. As a general discussant, Wolfgang Wessels, Professor of Political Science at the University of Cologne, also took part in the conference.

I should like to thank all of the above colleagues, in particular the contributors to this volume, for their having helped to realise this project. I should also like to express my thanks to the staff of the RSC who organised the Florence conference, notably Monique Cavallari, to Beatrice Otto, for her work in making the individual contributions suitable for publication, and my secretary at INSEAD, Dominique Greitzer, for her help in preparing the final manuscript.

I am above all grateful to INSEAD and to the RSC for having financed the Florence conference and to Yves Mény, for the moral and practical support that he gave to this project.

Douglas Webber
Fontainebleau, November 1998

ABBREVIATIONS

BMFT	Bundesministerium für Forschung und Technologie (Federal Ministry for Research and Technology
CAP	Common Agricultural Policy
CDU/CSU	Christian Democratic Union/Christian Social Union
CEEP	Centre européen des entreprises à participation publique (European Centre of Public Enterprises)
CEPT	Conference of European Post and Telecommunications Administrations
CFDT	Confédération Française Democratique du Travail (French Democratic Confederation of Labour)
CFSP	Common Foreign and Security Policy
CGT	Confédération Générale du Travail (General Confederation of Labour)
COST	Coopération Scientifique et Technologique (Scientific and Technological Cooperation)
DBV	Deutscher Bauernverband (German Farmers' Association)
DGB	Deutscher Gewerkschaftsbund (German Trade Union Federation)
DM	Deutsche Mark
EC	European Communities
ECB	European Central Bank
ECJ	European Court of Justice
ECU	European Currency Unit
ETUC	European Trade Union Confederation
EEC	European Economic Community
EdF	Electricité de France
EFTA	European Free Trade Association
EG	Europäische Gemeinschaft (European Community)
EIPA	European Institute of Public Administration
ELRO	European Launcher Development Organisation
EMF	European Monetary Fund
EMI	European Monetary Institute
EMS	European Monetary System
EMU	Economic and Monetary Union
EP	European Parliament

EPC	European Political Co-operation
ERM	Exchange-Rate Mechanism
ESA	European Space Agency
ESI	Electricity Supply Industry
ESRO	European Space Research Organisation
EU	European Union
EUI	European University Institute
EURATOM	European Atomic Energy Community
EWG	Europäische Wirtschaftsgemeinschaft (European Economic Community)
FCC	Federal Communications Commission
FDP	Freie Demokratische Partei (Free Democratic Party)
GATT	General Agreement on Tariffs and Trade
GDP	Gross Domestic Product
IGC	Intergovernmental Conference
IMF	International Monetary Fund
ITU	International Telecommunications Union
MLF	Multilateral Force
NATO	North Atlantic Treaty Organisation
OECD	Organisation for Economic Cooperation and Development
OSCE	Organisation for Security and Cooperation in Europe
PAC	Politique agricole commune (Common Agricultural Policy)
PTO	Public Telecommunications Operator
PTT	Postal, Telephone and Telegraph Administration
QMV	Qualified Majority Voting
R&D	Research and Development
RFA	République fédérale d'Allemagne (Federal Republic of Germany)
RSC	Robert Schuman Centre
RWE	Rheinisch-Westfälisches Elektrizitätswerk
SCGI	Sécrétariat général du comité interministériel pour les questions de coopération économique européen (General Secretariat of the Interministerial Committee for Questions of European Economic Cooperation)
SDI	Strategic Defence Initiative
SEA	Single European Act
SME	Small and medium-sized enterprises
SOGT	Senior Officials Group of Telecommunications
SPD	Sozialdemokratische Partei Deutschlands (German Social Democratic Party)
TPA	Third party access
UCPTE	Union pour la Coordination de la Production et du Transport d'Electricité (Association for the Coordination of the Production and Transport of Electricity)

UNICE	Union of Industrial and Employers' Confederations of Europe
VDEW	Vereinigung Deutsche Elektrizitätswerke (German Electricity Suppliers' Association)
WEU	West European Union
WTO	World Trade Organisation

1

INTRODUCTION

Douglas Webber

It is a commonplace that there is, in some sense, a 'special' relationship between France and Germany and that these two states somehow play a 'special' or central role in the European Union (EU). The idea that there is a 'special' Franco-German relationship is expressed in numerous labels applied to it: link, tandem, couple, pair, entente, axis, alliance, friendship, partnership or 'privileged' partnership, etc. For the role played jointly by the two states in the EU, the concepts or ideas of the engine, motor, locomotive, pacemaker, vanguard, core, hard core, or indeed, as in a famous or notorious German Christian Democratic paper on European policy, 'the core of the hard core' have been used (CDU/CSU Parliamentary Group: 1994).

Much – less in English than in French and German – has been written about the Franco-German relationship. However, in what sense or in what respect the relationship between 'Paris' and 'Bonn' differs from bilateral relations between other states is seldom clearly defined. The literature on the role played by the two states in the European Union is much less voluminous than that on their relationship as such. Here again, however, what exactly is meant by the terms such as engine, motor, locomotive or (hard) core is not normally made very explicit. Moreover, that France and Germany play such a role in the EU is more often taken for granted or simply asserted than demonstrated by careful empirical research.

This volume was conceived as a contribution to closing this 'gap' in the literature. It is not a study of the bilateral Franco-German relationship in all its facets and dimensions, of the history of Franco-German relations or of the foundations of the relationship and the motives which have led the two states to engage in it. Rather, it brings together a number of analyses of policy sectors and issues with the goal of improving the state of our knowledge on the extent to which the two governments co-ordinate their policies and strategies on EU issues and on the role played and influence exercised by the two states in the EU and European integration process.

The Franco-German relationship: distinctive traits

What is it that scholars of Franco-German relations mean when they describe the relationship between the two states, as they typically do, as 'special', 'privileged' or indeed 'unique'? First and foremost, they are referring to the volume and the degree of institutionalisation of communications and exchange between the governments of the two states. One striking indicator of the intensity of communications between the two sides is the number of meetings between the German chancellor and the French president, of which, in the decade from 1982 to 1992, there were allegedly 115 (Boyer 1996: 243).[1] Beneath the level of heads of government or state, there are also regular and frequent bilateral meetings and consultations between the French and German foreign and – less or much less often – other ministers.[2] Meetings of joint Franco-German councils, such as for defence and security and economic and financial affairs, represent 'only the tip of the iceberg of a close network of consultation and co-ordination. Nearly every day there is a Franco-German meeting on the agenda in Bonn and Paris' (Klaiber 1998: 38). The Franco-German relationship has also become meanwhile a 'matter of routine involvement of administrators' (Middlemas 1995: 323). In one view, it pervades 'all levels of the administration' in the two capitals and has become 'second nature for many civil servants' (interview).[3] As well as being relatively intensive, communications between the two governments are also highly institutionalised, that is to say that they have indeed become 'routine' and are governed by formal and informal rules, norms and expectations that define such a level of exchange as normal or necessary. It is mainly to this dimension of intensive and highly institutionalised communications that scholars and practitioners of the Franco-German relationship are referring when they refer to its 'unprecedented level of intimacy' (Boyer 1996: 241), when they describe it as the 'closest possible of bilateral alliances' (de Schoutheete 1990: 109) or when they argue that 'no two other countries in the world have developed such close co-operation' (Klaiber 1998: 38), that the relationship between Chancellor Kohl and President Mitterrand was closer than between any other heads of government or state, past or present (Védrine 1996: 575) or that the intimacy of the relationship between their predecessors Schmidt and Giscard was 'unique' among the leaders of the principal states in their era (Giscard d'Estaing 1988: 124).

The other less frequently identified dimension of the Franco-German relationship that arguably makes it unique relates to the purpose of bilateral communications or exchange. It is the shared norm that, at least on issues which the one or other or both governments regard as important, they should ultimately mediate their conflicts and reach a joint or common position. To be sure, such efforts have not always been successful or even always undertaken but, by and large, the two governments are more concerned not to fall out with each other than they are not to fall out with any other EU member states. Already the 1963 Elysée Treaty stipulated that the two governments should consult with each other on all important foreign policy issues with a view to 'reaching, as far as possible, a common position' (Elysée Treaty, published in Ménudier 1993: 87). In fact, the two foreign ministries had begun to try to develop 'concerted positions' on EU issues right from the start of the EU in 1958 (Couve de Murville 1971: 241–42). If the norm was not followed after Adenauer's replacement as German Chancellor by Erhard in 1963, it was resurrected during the period from 1974 onwards by Chancellor Schmidt and President Giscard d'Estaing, who agreed to develop – and, according to Giscard, succeeded in developing – a common position on all issues that they regarded as 'essential' so as to avoid a situation in which their differences would be arbitrated by other European states or the USA (Giscard d'Estaing 1988: 130).

The Franco-German relationship: its role in the EU

It is on EU issues that, as the above remarks suggest, France and Germany have been most concerned to consult each other and to co-ordinate their positions. To the extent that the very purpose of the 'special' relationship was to forge a Europe so closely integrated that war between its constituent states would no longer be feasible, this is not surprising. If anything, over time, Franco-German co-operation has become increasingly preoccupied with the handling of EU issues (Bocquet 1997: 5; Deubner 1997: 17). It is not an exaggeration to argue that it is 'impossible' to separate the relations within the partnership from EU affairs (Leblond 1997: 130).

Certainly it is less contentious to argue that the EU and the European integration process have been at the heart of the Franco-German relationship than to argue that the Franco-German relationship has been at the heart of the EU. The analogy of the 'motor' or 'engine' implies that these two states have supplied the power or momentum which has driven or propelled the integration process. Whether the 'motor' or 'engine' has a reverse gear that may drive the process towards disintegration is not normally discussed. Equally, it is seldom made clear whether the Franco-German 'motor' only supplies the power or momentum for the process or whether it also steers, that is to say, determines the direction of, the process. Although the concept of the 'motor' or 'engine' does not necessarily imply that the 'motor' or 'engine' steers the process, it is clearly the belief of most of those who attribute such a role in the EU to the Franco-German relationship.

Those – apart from political practitioners, they are mostly scholars of international relations – who argue that France and Germany jointly do constitute the 'engine' or 'motor' of the integration process normally do so because, in their view, the two states have exercised a decisive influence on the most important integration decisions or projects, such as the creation of the European Council, the European Monetary System (EMS), the Single European Act, and the Maastricht Treaty, with its provisions for a common foreign and security policy as well as for monetary union (Bocquet 1997: 5; Mazzarelli 1997; Klaiber 1998: 39; Moravcsik 1991). There is by no means a consensus, however, that France and Germany together have played an 'engine' role in these episodes. In respect of the Treaty of Rome, the initial impetus was supplied by the Benelux states, although the treaty may not have been agreed but for some late conflict mediation between the German Chancellor Adenauer and the French Prime Minister Mollet (see Küsters 1982: 324–30; Gerbet 1990: 78–83; Anderson 1997: 56–7). Several interpretations of the Single European Act, for example, have attributed more important roles in its adoption to supranational actors such as the Commission and transnational business interests such as the European Round Table than to the French and German governments (Cowles 1995; Armstrong and Bulmer 1998: 13–42; Sandholtz and Zysman 1989). Moreover, not even the most fervent proponents of the idea that France and Germany form the 'engine' of the integration process could argue that they have always played this role (see, for example, Guérin-Sendelbach 1993: 12–13). The failure of the European Defence Community (EDC) on French parliamentary opposition in the 1950s and De Gaulle's temporary boycott of the EU institutions in 1965–66 are two of the best-known cases in which the Franco-German 'engine' did not ignite and the integration process, far from being boosted, was braked. It is crises such as these – and their (negative) impact on the integration process – that have nourished the argument that 'wherever Germany and France agree, Europe makes progress; wherever they are divided, Europe marks time' (Giscard, quoted – approvingly – in Schmidt 1990: 288). In other words, whether functioning as engine or brake, the impact of the Franco-German relationship is in any case decisive for the fate of the integration process.

Irrespective of the role played by France and Germany in the conflicts over the EU treaties, scholars who emphasise the two states' 'engine' role are criticised for their too exclusive focus on the 'high politics' of the integration process. Even if France and Germany have exercised a strong influence on the big intergovernmental agreements in the EU's history, it is argued, this does not mean that they play a similar role in the day-to-day politics of the union. This perspective on the Franco-German role in the EU is widely shared by political scientists whose background is in the subdiscipline of comparative politics rather than international relations and who tend to regard the EU not as an international organisation, but rather as a political system that does not differ qualitatively from that found in nation-states.

France and Germany in European integration theory

The distribution of power between national governments and supranational actors and its evolution over time are the issues that lie at the core of the theoretical debate about the European integration process and the nature of EU politics. In terms of the significance attributed to the role of the national governments, including the French and German, a distinction may be drawn between intergovernmentalism, which, as the term connotes, sees the national governments as the most powerful actors in 'Brussels', and other approaches or models, which relativise their centrality.

The *intergovernmentalist* model, which has its roots in the realist theory of international relations, is the one which attributes the greatest importance to the role of France and Germany. For 'intergovernmentalists', national governments are not only the most powerful actors in the EU, but there is also a clear hierarchy of power among them. Hence, for Moravcsik, the EU, since its inception, has been based on 'interstate bargains between its leading member states'. Having initially consisted of bilateral agreements between France and Germany, the bargains now 'consist of trilateral agreements including Britain' (Moravcsik 1991: 25–6). Bargaining in the EU converges towards the lowest common denominator of large state interests, whereby if two major states 'isolate the third and credibly threaten it with exclusion', such a threat may facilitate a more far-reaching agreement (Moravcsik 1991: 26). Whereas large states exercise a de facto veto over fundamental changes in the EU, small states can be 'bought off with side payments' (Moravcsik 1991: 25). In respect of the Single European Act, there was no 'central initiative' that was launched or vetoed by the other member states (Moravcsik 1991: 49). Apart from his reference to the usage of side payments (which suggests that economic potency may be as or more significant a determinant of influence as the sheer size of a state), Moravcsik does not explain why the three large states should be able to exercise a dominant influence over decisions taken at an intergovernmental conference where, formally, every member state has a power of veto.[4] It is clear, however, that, for Moravcsik, France and Germany were the 'engine' behind the Single European Act, as, where the preferences of the 'big three' states diverged, they were the two who combined to isolate the third, Britain, and threaten it with exclusion. Nonetheless, as, on most issues, lowest common denominator outcomes prevailed, the overall result corresponded most closely to the preferences of the government that was most hostile to changes in the status quo, namely the British (Moravcsik 1991: 49). In an otherwise similarly intergovernmentalist analysis of the Single European Act, Garrett concludes that the outcome was most strongly influenced by France and, especially, Germany. They could recruit the Benelux states as allies for their project because of their structural dependence on the French and German economies and the poorer, southern member states by promising them side payments. The threat of forging closer economic integration on a bilateral basis and with the Benelux states in the event of the project's failure was used to secure the acquiescence of Britain (Garrett 1992).

In contrast to intergovernmentalism, the *neo-functionalist* theory of European integration predicted, as a consequence of economic and political 'spillover' processes, the development of increasingly legitimate and powerful supranational organs and a waning of the influence of national governments. Although early neo-functionalist theorists did not give any concrete idea as to how long this process would take, they would probably have expected that, by the end of the century, the EU member states would be political units with a role and powers comparable to those of the states in federal polities such as the USA and, in any case, less influential in the decision-making process than supranational organs such as the European Commission, the European Parliament (EP) and the European Court of Justice (ECJ). To the extent that the national governments were condemned to increasing impotence, the role of France and Germany and their relationship in the EU would seem to neo-functionalists to be an increasingly irrelevant issue. Not only were unstoppable socio-economic processes forcing national governments to accede to the transfer of decision-making competences to the European level, but their functions at this level were also increasingly to be usurped by supranational actors.

Similar to neo-functionalism, the *transnational exchange* theory of European integration posits that growing volumes of cross-national transactions and communications create inexorable, but, by policy area variable, pressures for supranational governance: 'the competence of the EC to make binding rules in any given policy sector' (Stone Sweet and Sandholtz 1997: 297). Proponents of this theory admit that it does not 'tell us what specific rules and policies will emerge' and that transnational exchange 'cannot, in and of itself, determine the specific details, or the precise timing' of EU decisions (Stone Sweet and Sandholtz 1997: 299, 310). However, in their view, the expansion of transnational society, the pro-integrative activities of supranational organisations, and the growing density of supranational rules 'gradually, but inevitably, reduce the capacity of the member states to control outcomes' (Stone Sweet and Sandholtz 1997: 299–300, 306). Larger states 'command greater resources' and tend therefore to 'wield greater influence' on policy outcomes than smaller states, but in as far as intergovernmental bargaining remains a 'ubiquitous feature of supranational governance', the EU simply resembles many federal states (Stone Sweet and Sandholtz 1997: 314). Thus, while transnational exchange theory recognises that the member states still play a more or less important role in EU decision-making and that some are more influential than others, their collective influence is argued to be diminishing. Like their neo-functionalist colleagues, transnational exchange theorists would be unlikely to regard the role played, and influence exercised, in the EU by France and Germany as a worthwhile issue for investigation.

In *neo-institutionalist and historical-institutionalist* models of EU politics, the distribution of power between the member states and between the supranational organs and the member states is a more open question than in the neo-functionalist or transnational exchange models. Institutionalist models do not presuppose any particular 'teleology of development' (Armstrong and Bulmer 1998: 54). Essentially, the balance of power between different actors in the EU is a function of the configuration of institutions, which may encompass not only formal institutions but also 'informal institutions and conventions; the norms and symbols embedded in them; and policy instruments and procedures' (Armstrong and Bulmer 1998: 52). Institutional configurations may vary across policy areas, but not necessarily, as in transnational exchange theory, according to the volume of transnational exchange. The significance of institutions lies in the fact that they 'structure the access of political forces to the political process, creating a kind of bias' and can develop their own 'endogenous ... impetuses for policy change that exceed the role of mere institutional mediation' (Armstrong and Bulmer 1998: 52). The 'institutionalist' theorist's answer to the question concerning the role played and influence exercised by France and Germany would thus be that it 'all depends on the institutional configuration'. It is clear, however, that, for institutionalists, the EU is not a merely intergovernmental organisation or system and the supranational organs such as the Commission and the ECJ (may) exercise an independent impact on policy decisions and outcomes. Moreover, a number of factors or forces, including national governments' restricted time horizons and changing preferences as well as the unintended consequences of past decisions that are extremely difficult to revoke, have eroded the governments' capacity to control the EU (Pierson 1996). Although member states remain 'extremely powerful', the EU possesses 'characteristics of a supranational entity' that is no longer firmly under the states' control and in which their influence is 'increasingly circumscribed' (Pierson 1996: 158).

A similar analysis to Pierson's is developed in the *multi-level governance* model of European integration. The proponents of this model 'do not reject the view that state executives and state arenas are important or that these remain the *most* important pieces of the European puzzle' (Marks, Hooghe and Blank 1996: 346; original emphasis). But while national governments are 'formidable participants in EU policy-making, control has slipped away from them to supranational institutions' (Marks, Hooghe and Blank 1996: 342). In the multi-level European polity, decision-making competencies are 'shared by actors at different levels rather than monopolised by state executives', individual state executives experience a significant loss of control (thanks not least to the extension of qualified majority voting). Direct linkages have developed between supranational and sub-national actors, such that national governments no longer have a monopoly of the representation of national interests vis-à-vis 'Brussels' (Marks, Hooghe and Blank 1996: 346–7). The capacity of the national governments to control supranational actors, in particular the Commission, is curtailed by their relative disunity, mutual distrust, informational asymmetries and the unintended consequences of past institutional decisions, which can be rectified only if the states agree unanimously to revise the treaties.

Compared with other models, *policy networks* approaches to the analysis of EU politics draw a strong distinction between the 'high' and 'low' politics of the union (Peters 1992; Peterson 1995). While the 'high' politics of the EU, as represented by the meetings of the European Council or the treaty revision conferences, may be intergovernmental, the character of day-to-day policy-making is quite different. Everyday policy-making is functionally segmented, decentralised, bureaucratic and technically rather than politically oriented (Peters 1992). At this level, national governments may be far from being unitary actors. Rather, the different parts of national administrations are more like 'quasi-autonomous actors with their own goals', which may conflict with those of other actors from the same state (Peters 1992: 115). The relative weakness of central co-ordination of EU policy and the relatively high degree of functional differentiation of EU policy-making enable policy networks consisting primarily of officials from Commission directorates-general and national ministries to exercise greater control over the EU policy process than over that in the member states (Peters 1992: 80–81). Within these networks, the Commission, with its technical expertise, agenda-setting powers and greater flexibility, has 'an increasing number of weapons and apparently a growing influence' (Peters 1992: 119; Héritier 1993).

In contrast to models of European integration that diagnose a growth in the influence of supranational actors and decline in that of the member states, the *fusion* model (Wessels 1997) sees a trend towards 'interlocking politics' (*Politikverflechtung*) akin to that observed in federal polities such as the Federal Republic of Germany (see Scharpf 1988) . The distinctive trait of 'interlocking politics' is the simultaneous extension of the competences of the 'federation' (in our case, the EU) and the scope for participation in the decision-making process by the federation's constituent units (the member states). The EU member states have agreed to the extension of the EU's competences in the face of 'growing demands for welfare … and public services … on the one hand, and increasing European interdependencies and strong trends towards globalisation on the other hand' (Wessels 1997: 273). Like the above models, the 'fusion' model regards the EU institutions as 'actors in their own right and with their own weight' (Wessels 1997: 274). However, the 'fusion' model emphasises the 'comprehensive and intensive participation of national governments and administrations in all phases of the EU's policy cycle, also and especially in those areas of decision preparation and implementation which were originally earmarked as prerogatives of the Commission … The considerable and increasing role of EC institutions … is not leading to the substitution of national actors' (Wessels 1997: 280).

Overall, the theoretical literature on the EU and the integration process pays very little attention to the issue of the relative power and roles of different member states. Logically, as this model attributes the greatest influence to the member states, the intergovernmentalist model is more preoccupied with this question than the others. That the other models should neglect it to the extent that they do is nonetheless surprising. While, except for the fusion model, they posit a decline in the influence of the national governments vis-à-vis the supranational institutions, none goes so far as to claim that the latter have become the most powerful actors on the Brussels stage and their proponents are typically at pains to emphasise that there is a great deal of 'intergovernmental bargaining' in the EU and the national governments are still more or less important or significant actors in the policy process. As for the intergovernmentalist model, as represented by Moravcsik, it is relatively silent on the issues as to why the big member states should be able to exercise a stronger influence on policy decisions and outcomes than the smaller ones and whether the same pattern of the predominance of the 'big three' member states is replicated in day-to-day EU policy-making. None of the models addresses very explicitly the issue of the implications of collective Franco-German governmental action in the EU, although there are plausible reasons for thinking that it might make a difference to policy decisions and outcomes if and when co-ordination of policy and strategy takes place between two member states which together command 20 votes – close to a blocking minority – in the Council of Ministers, represent over 40 per cent of the EU GDP (1991) and the biggest markets for almost all the other member states, and finance, in net terms, almost three-quarters per cent of the EU budget (1994: Germany 62 per cent, France 12 per cent).

France and Germany in existing literature on the EU

The existing empirical literature that explicitly addresses the role of France and Germany and their relationship in the EU is also relatively sparse. In as far as it exists, it suggests that, although the Franco-German relationship is indeed closer than any other bilateral relationship between the member states, the degree to which the two governments co-operate on EU issues and their role in the policy process tend to be exaggerated or overestimated.

Thus, in his analysis of the EU's 'subsystems', de Schoutheete argues that France and Germany form by far the closest bilateral relationship among the member states (de Schoutheete 1990: 111). Citing the EMS, the origins of the Single European Act and the 'Eureka' high-technology programme (see Chapter 6 by Eberlein and Grande) as examples, he observes that 'over the years Franco-German initiatives in fields of such fundamental importance as monetary policy, diplomacy, research and defence have been at least partly successful in the European framework' (de Schoutheete 1990: 109). However, these projects were adopted in part at least because they could count on and met with the support of several other member states. De Schoutheete concludes that, although France and Germany together have exerted a 'significant influence on the development of European affairs', the idea that EU decisions are 'to a large extent predetermined by bi- or trilateral arrangements is unsupported by any evidence' (de Schoutheete 1990: 121).

In her studies of bilateral and trilateral relations and negotiations in the EU, Helen Wallace reaches broadly comparable conclusions to de Schoutheete, but identifies important changes over time in the role played by France and Germany (Wallace 1986a, 1986b, 1990). In the original six-state EU, 'any strong disagreement on an issue between the French and German governments could effectively prevent any broader EEC consensus' (Wallace 1986a: 157). Under Schmidt's and Giscard's leadership, Franco-German co-ordination intensified:

> There was signal evidence of close bilateral co-operation and consultation before, during and after EC negotiations. At the top of the pyramid the relationship was intimate, intense and often disdainful of other, less serious partners … Further down the governmental pyramid the reflexes for consultation, fostered by the long-term investment of the Elysée Treaty, began to pay off across the EC policy agenda and across ministries … By the end of the 1970s, it had become more or less automatic in

national co-ordinating meetings on EC business to ask explicitly what was the known position of the other partner and to look for ways of accommodating it.

(Wallace 1986a: 161–2; see also Wallace 1986b: 139–45)

The pattern of 'bilateral empathy' between Paris and Bonn began to 'structure the expectations of other partners and of the Commission ... If a Franco-German deal could be stitched together even on issues difficult for one or both, the other participants in the negotiations would generally fall into line. Often this would encourage French and German negotiators to prepare bilaterally the side-deals which would permit a broader compromise to emerge' (Wallace 1986a: 162).

Thus, in the 'old Community and even during the 1970s the intimate Paris–Bonn relationship often played a preponderant role in defining the agenda and identifying solutions for Community action' (Wallace 1990: 146). However, as a consequence of successive enlargements and the expansion of the range of policy issues dealt with by the EU, the Franco-German relationship no longer provided a 'sufficient condition of further steps toward European unification ... a Community of Twelve cannot be dominated by a Bonn–Paris tandem. The coalition patterns of the EC are more diffuse and more variegated' (Wallace 1990: 145, also 146–7). Of the major decisions reached in the EU between the late 1970s and late 1980s, including the Single European Act, 'only the EMS provides clear-cut evidence of a Franco-German impulse' (Wallace 1990: 153). France and Germany 'singly and in combination' continued to exercise a 'special influence' on the EU, but without possessing a monopoly of influence and initiative (Wallace 1990: 153–4). The two governments having recognised that 'operating à deux' was unlikely to be an effective means of shaping EU policy, the relationship had actually become 'much less exclusive' in the first half of the 1980s (Wallace 1986b: 154).

In his analysis of interstate co-operation and alliances in the EU, Middlemas also argues that the Franco-German relationship became more consolidated and institutionalised – 'densely resilient' – in the 1970s (Middlemas 1995: 323; see also Bocquet 1997: 5). Nevertheless, then and later, it remained an 'act of political will', based on the respective political leaders' mutual understanding that 'both their states had much to lose if things were not resolved according to their preferences' (Middlemas 1995: 324). The Franco-German 'entente' functioned as a motor in a 'more limited sense' than often assumed, by helping to 'set many of the details of agendas before the European Council and before some Councils of Ministers' and being responsible for some 'pivotal innovations', such as the EMS and aspects of the Maastricht Treaty (Middlemas 1995: 327). Even in this 'more limited sense', it could only play this role as long as other member states acquiesced to it. The Franco-German 'link' 'does not determine how the [other] member states will react' and it is 'certainly not in the inherent interests of any other member state' (Middlemas 1995: 328). Rather than being a kind of fait accompli presented to the other governments, Franco-German accords resemble the 'core around which other member states could, if they chose to cluster, produce effective majorities if not always unanimity' (Middlemas 1995: 324). Middlemas agrees with Wallace that the power of the Franco-German 'entente' has been diminished by the EU's enlargements (Middlemas 1995: 689).

Overall, these analyses paint a picture of a relationship whose intensity has varied over time, which has exercised a variable, but, on the whole, less than dominant influence on EU policy, and whose role has gradually diminished as the EU has enlarged. This picture does not differ greatly, in turn, from that which emerges from collective Franco-German studies of the relationship and its role in the EU. The contributions to a volume on 'Franco-German bilateralism and European integration', written in 1988, produced a 'predominantly sobering picture of the Franco-German "motor" and its role in the EU decision-making process that does not really correspond to the ambitious claims and expectations produced by the two governments' (Picht, Uterwedde and Wessels 1990: 29). 'Every case study' in a more recent volume and 'almost every analysis of the overall political debate in the two countries show ... that there is hardly one area in which the respective interests and goals and, even more so, the world-views, concepts and approaches of the two sides are so closely aligned that they correspond to notions of an ideal partnership and ... could provide a solid foundation for joint European action' (Kolboom and Picht 1995: 352). Not all the recent empirical research on the topic, however, relativises the Franco-German role and influence in the EU. Thus, having compared the conflicts over monetary union, the GATT Uruguay Round, military intervention in former Yugoslavia and institutional reform in the first half of the 1990s, Wood concludes that 'Franco-German relations remain at the core of the post-Maastricht EC, and the shape of the European Community continues to bear the imprint of bargains and trade-offs rooted in perceptions of their national interests' (Wood 1995: 238). Franco-German agreements were not always sufficient to solve conflicts in the EU: 'Nevertheless, France and Germany set the outside limits of policy, and their combined weight allows them jointly to steer the process of integration' (Wood 1995: 239).

The predominantly sceptical tone of most of the empirical research on the role of the Franco-German relationship in the EU also contrasts strikingly with the significance attributed to it by the principal actors involved in the relationship over the last two decades. Hence, Giscard argues that 'all progress in the European construction has started from joint Franco-German initiatives. If one day there would no longer be these common efforts ... Europe would no longer progress' (quoted in Boyer 1996: 247). Similarly, for his counterpart as German Chancellor in the 1970s, Schmidt, all the steps taken towards closer European integration in the three decades up to 1990 were only possible as a consequence of the close co-operation between Paris and Bonn (Schmidt 1990: 288). From the Fontainebleau European Council in 1984 to Mitterrand's re-election as French President in 1988, according to one of the president's closest collaborators, the Franco-German 'entente' was 'decisive at every stage, at every Council' (Védrine 1996: 403). The same pattern prevailed during the Italian Council presidency in the second half of 1990, when the Franco-German tandem set the pace 'more than ever' and the decision to launch the Maastricht treaty negotiations was taken (Védrine 1996: 458). The French and German foreign ministers of most of the 1980s and early 1990s convey the same image of an EU more or less entirely dependent for progress on the Franco-German 'motor' (Genscher 1995: 367–95; Dumas 1996: 327–51).[5] Their respective superiors, Kohl and Mitterrand, had a similar conception of the role and significance of the Franco-German relationship.[6] To be sure, Kohl, for example, took pains to emphasise that there was no Franco-German 'directorate' running or dominating the EU: 'A Europe with a Franco-German hegemony cannot work. That would not be a common Europe and no such thing will ever emerge' (Kohl 1996). However, he and Mitterrand may have regarded their role and influence in the EU as greater than they demonstrated or proclaimed publicly. This, at least, is the gist of a conversation between the two leaders that reportedly took place during the controversy over the British contribution to the EU budget in 1984 (Attali 1993: 642):

Mitterrand: We must avoid saying that we are jointly running Europe.
Kohl: You're right. If we are suspected of that, then that's the finish.
Mitterrand: We have a dominant role, but we must never impose anything, we must be modest.

The contributions

The above survey of the views of leading French and German political 'practitioners', theorists of European integration and more strongly empirically oriented scholars yield an unclear picture of the Franco-German relationship and the role it plays in the EU. Among political leaders on both sides of the Rhine, it is undisputed that the two states play a key role in the EU, that they form its 'core'. In the theoretical literature, the role played by France and Germany and their relationship in the EU and the European integration process is contested. The intergovernmentalist model emphasises the dominant role of the 'big three' member states, including also Britain, but, in the work of the model's leading exponent, there is a little analysis of the Franco-German relationship as such and the determinants of the purportedly strong influence of the two states. Proponents of the other models, which see the role and power of the national governments as in decline, do not address these issues, although they generally concede that the national governments remain significant or important actors in EU politics. More empirical analyses of the Franco-German relationship and the role that it plays in the EU also come to different conclusions, although the predominant view appears to be that it is far from constituting the kind of 'directorate' feared by the smaller states and that, as the EU has grown larger, its influence has diminished. Most of the non-theoretical literature on the Franco-German role in the EU has, however, an 'overview' character and does not rest on a strong empirical foundation. In particular, there is a virtually complete absence of studies of the relationship and its role and influence in day-to-day EU policy-making, on those issues and in those policy areas and sectors that may be roughly categorised as belonging to the realm of 'low politics'.

The paucity, not to say non-existence, of such research is important because it cannot simply be assumed that the degree of intensity and the role and level of influence of the Franco-German relationship in the EU does not vary by issue or policy area. The degree to which Paris and Bonn strive to co-ordinate and succeed in co-ordinating their positions and strategies may vary, for example, according to the significance that one or the other or both governments attach to the issue on the agenda or to the policy area in general or to the degree to which their preferences on the issue or in the policy area converge or diverge. The level of their collective influence, the extent to which they succeed in 'multilateralising' whatever bilateral agreements they do reach, may vary, for example, according to the institutional configuration of the issue area – to formal decision-making rules and procedures or more informal 'rules of the game' – or to the pattern of cleavages in the Council, to the extent, that is, that the joint Franco-German position corresponds to the preferences of other governments.

The present volume is designed to address the deficit in our empirical knowledge described above, to produce at least a first impression of the inter-issue and inter-sectoral variations in the closeness and role and influence of the Franco-German relationship in the EU and to account for the observed variations. It includes contributions on issues and sectors that belong indisputably to the realm of 'high politics' (monetary union, Eastern enlargement, foreign and security policy) and others that rarely make political headlines or preoccupy heads of government and foreign ministers (telecommunications and electricity liberalisation and research and technology policy).[7] It includes contributions on sectors and policy areas that are highly 'Europeanised', in the sense that the EU has substantial decision-making competences and the powers of supranational actors such as the Commission and the ECJ are extensive, such as telecommunications and electricity liberalisation, and others that are only weakly 'Europeanised', such as immigration and foreign and security policy. It also includes policy areas in which the two governments have had at least partially convergent preferences (for example, research and technology and social policy) and others – apparently more numerous – in which their preferences are more often divergent (as in electricity liberalisation, agricultural or monetary policy).

The first two chapters deal with the principal issues on the EU agenda in the late twentieth and early twenty-first centuries, namely monetary union, the Central and East European enlargement and institutional reform. Both are issues where the EU could or can proceed only with the approval or acquiescence of all the member states. In his analysis of the politics of monetary union (Chapter 2), *Jonathan Story* quotes approvingly a Bundesbank council member who describes the conflict over the single currency as being about 'power, influence and the pursuit of national interests', especially French and German ones. Monetary union is a French project conceived to combat German economic and monetary dominance in Europe. The final agreement, facilitated and accelerated by German unification, represented a trade-off between the two states. With their 'conflicts and partial accords', France and Germany have 'dominated the agenda of monetary union'. *Patrick McCarthy's* account of the politics of Eastern enlargement and institutional reform (Chapter 3) stresses, like Story's analysis, the divergent interests and preferences of the two states. In contrast to monetary union, however, no radical agreement has been possible between France and Germany or within the EU as a whole. Rather, although their conflicts have diminished and they have 'drawn closer together' on these issues, they have not been able to do more than reach compromises that 'permit, but slow down, Eastern enlargement and minimise institutional reform'. Compared with the single currency issue, precisely because of the incapacity of the two states to reach anything more than 'weak agreement', other member states and the Commission appear here to have exercised a stronger influence on EU policy.

The contributions by *Susanne K. Schmidt* (Chapter 4) and *Volker Schneider* and *Thierry Vedel* (Chapter 5) focus on issues and sectors in respect of which, a priori, thanks to treaty provisions, the European Commission enjoys considerable autonomy vis-à-vis the member states and has broadly comparable powers, rooted in the competition policy articles of the Rome Treaty. In the conflict over electricity liberalisation, analysed by Schmidt, the opposition of the member states to the Commission's proposals was softened by the threat that, in the absence of a Council agreement, the European Court of Justice (ECJ) would arbitrate the conflict between the Commission and the member states. Although France and Germany were at opposite poles of the conflict, they managed nonetheless to reach a compromise which was 'critical' to the agreement finally reached in the Council and which was less radical and more 'flexible' than the Commission's original proposals. A notable feature of the electricity liberalisation conflict was also the relative weakness of pressures for change from electricity suppliers (actual and potential) and consumers. This situation was very different to that which prevailed in telecommunications, where, as Schneider and Vedel show, the Commission mobilised support among large firms to overcome member states' resistance to its liberalisation and deregulation strategy. Gradually, as a consequence of the changing structure of the industry and the need for international co-operation and alliances, the governments abandoned their opposition to telecommunications liberalisation. Given the important role played by the Commission and its big firm allies in this sector, telecommunications politics cannot be described as purely intergovernmental. Nonetheless, national governments remain the central actors in the sector, since most EU decisions are 'agreements at the intergovernmental level' and 'pre-suppose some Franco-German understanding'.

The same pattern of a strong alliance between the Commission and big – indeed, mostly French and German – firms is observed by *Burkard Eberlein* and *Edgar Grande* in Chapter 6 on EU research and technology policy. In this policy area, French and German preferences have been partially convergent and partially divergent, with the major cleavage running between big, economically strong states, such as these two, and smaller and poorer members. Franco-German co-operation – hostile to an expansion of the EU competences – has not been a 'motor' of European integration, but rather a brake on it. However, national governments' opposition to supranational integration was eroded by the 'trans-national co-operation of private economic actors' and the 'entrepeneurial role' played by the Commission; so the Franco-German brake did not function. Thus, the case of research and technology policy seems to contradict two widely shared assumptions about the role and impact of the Franco-German relationship in the EU: that the two states are 'motors' of closer integration and that decisions can not be adopted against their joint opposition.

Compared with Eberlein's and Grande's analysis, *Douglas Webber*'s study of agricultural politics (Chapter 7) reaches far more orthodox conclusions concerning the role and influence of the Franco-German relationship. He examines two series of major agricultural policy conflicts in the EU, the first over the creation of the Common Agricultural Policy (CAP) in the early 1960s and the second over CAP reform and GATT agricultural trade negotiations in the early 1990s. France and Germany have normally occupied opposite ends of the spectrum and been the chief protagonists in these conflicts. When they have found a common position on a given conflict, this position has typically been adopted as EU policy; when they have remained divided, the decision-making process has been deadlocked or crisis stricken; when they have agreed to oppose a given project, their opposition has been insuperable. There is no strong sign of the Franco-German role in agricultural policy-making having been eroded by treaty changes or successive enlargements. In agricultural policy, Webber argues, the EU has a genuine Franco-German 'hard core' that, in view of the conflicts of interest between the two states, has developed a striking capacity for bilateral conflict-mediation.

Chapter 8 by *Martin Rhodes* describes an 'awkward alliance' between France and Germany on EU social policy. Although, as the most expensive production location in the EU, Germany might seem to have the strongest interest in exporting high 'social standards' to other member states, it has often been ambivalent on or opposed to social policy projects, partly because of conflicts between different federal ministries and governing coalition parties. It is France that has acted as the vanguard of social policy innovation. In any case, EU social politics have not been shaped exclusively by France and Germany or even, collectively, by the member states as a whole. The Commission (especially under the leadership of its French president, Jacques Delors) and organised interests, notably the German trade union movement, have also been influential actors. Hence, unlike, in Webber's view, agricultural policy, EU social policy is not wholly susceptible to a purely 'intergovernmentalist' explanation.

Chapter 9 by *Amaya Bloch-Lainé* on foreign, security and defence policy and Chapter 10 by *Patrick Weil* on immigration policy deal with policy areas that belong the second and third 'pillars' of the EU and in which the powers of supranational organs such as the Commission and the ECJ are relatively restricted, increasing the likelihood that they will be shaped by the interactions and conflicts of the national governments. Weil shows how historically very different French and German immigration policies have gradually converged, thanks to the progressive institutionalisation of international norms in both states since World War II, and how Franco-German co-operation has grown, leading to the signature of the Schengen accords, abolishing border controls between the signatory states. He interprets these accords as a 'bargain between France and Germany, a model of intergovernmentalism'. Bloch-Lainé attributes a similar leading role to the Franco-German relationship in respect of the foreign and security policy provisions of the Maastricht and Amsterdam treaties and the creation of the Eurocorps. She notes that, following France's withdrawal from the NATO, Franco-German military co-operation was revived in the 1980s. However, the 'operational and military credibility' of the bilateral relationship is weak and seen to be such by other states. Hence there is no Franco-German 'hard core' at the centre of European foreign, security and defence policy. The EU has been marginalised as an actor in this policy area by the growth of ad hoc groups of big states formed to deal with crises such as that in Bosnia-Hercegovina (and led, it should be added, not by France and Germany, but by the USA).

Collectively, the case studies reveal an extremely variegated picture of the closeness and intensity of the Franco-German relationship in the EU and two states' impact and influence on EU policy. In some sectors, the relationship is close and intense, in others it is barely existent. In some sectors, the Franco-German impact on policy outcomes has been strong, whether in facilitating or preventing the adoption of policy proposals or projects, in others the role and influence of the 'tandem' have been marginal. In the conclusion, *Webber* attributes inter-sectoral variations in the intensity of Franco-German co-ordination to such variables as the political salience of issues or issue areas, the roles of ministries in the political division of labour, and the degree to and length of time for which the EU has exercised decision-making competences in the sector. Franco-German influence varies according to the dominant decision-making logic in the sector – intergovernmental or supranational – and to the degree to which their own respective preferences on a given issue coincide with those of one or the other group of other member states. Paradoxically, the greater the divergence between French and German preferences on a given issue, the more likely it is that, if a common Franco-German position is developed, this will be 'multilateralised' and taken over by the EU as a whole. The conclusion also assesses the interim impact of German reunification on the Franco-German relationship. Webber contradicts those who argue that reunification, by destroying the pre-existing balance of power between Paris and Bonn, has undermined the foundations of the relationship. Not least thanks to the EU and the European integration process, the relationship has reached a high level of institutionalisation that renders it very resistant to geopolitical earthquakes such as the end of the Cold War.

Notes

1 Védrine (1996: 425) refers to Kohl and Mitterrand having met on 40 occasions between 1982 and 1989 – 'without counting messages, letters, telephone conversations, [and] contacts between advisers'.
2 Guérin-Sendelbach (1993: 27) quotes a source stating that the two foreign ministers in the early 1980s, Genscher and Cheysson, phoned each other around 1000 times – that is to say, almost once a day – over a period of three years.
3 For a brief overview of the interaction between different levels of the governments in Bonn and Paris, see Guérin-Sendelbach 1993: 24–8.
4 In his later work , Moravcsik argues that, other things being equal, large member states are more influential than small ones because they are more indispensable to the formation of winning coalitions and economically more self-sufficient, so that they are less dependent on trade liberalisation and can afford to be 'more discriminating' about the terms of any agreement (Moravcsik 1993: 500–3).
5 Whereby Genscher stresses that the 'idea of a directorate of the big [member] states would destroy' the EU. 'Franco-German co-operation was never so conceived, as a motor – yes. Our friends in the other founder member states have always perceived that this co-operation benefited everybody and was never at others' expense' (Genscher 1995: 395).
6 On the evolution of Mitterrand's attitude and policy towards Germany, see Bender (1995). For the former French president's own account of his policy, see Mitterrand (1996).
7 It should be noted that the French and German foreign ministries played an instrumental role in the launching of the 'Eureka' high technology programme. See Genscher (1995: 376–9) and Dumas (1996: 332–3). The role of the political salience or perceived political importance of an issue in determining the intensity or closeness of Franco-German co-operation is indicated by Giscard's remarks concerning his collaboration with Schmidt in the 1970s: 'If the question posed was of secondary importance, we decided to retain a margin of flexibility. But, if we judged it as essential, we decided to reach a common position' (Giscard d'Estaing 1988: 130).

References

Anderson, Perry (1997) 'Under the sign of the interim', in Peter Gowan and Perry Anderson (eds), *The Question of Europe*. London and New York: Verso, 51–71.
Armstrong, Kenneth and Simon Bulmer (1998) *The Governance of the Single European Market*. Manchester and New York: Manchester University Press.
Attali, Jacques (1993) *Verbatim I 1981–1986*. Paris: Fayard.
Bender, Karl-Heinz (1995) *Mitterrand und die Deutschen: Die Wiedervereinigung der Karolinger*. Bonn: Bouvier.
Bocquet, Dominique (1997) 'France and Germany: a second wind', in *The Future of the Franco-German Relationship: Three Views*. London: Royal Institute of International Affairs, Discussion Paper 71, 1–14.
Boyer, Yves (1996) 'France and Germany', in Bertel Heurlin (ed.), *Germany in Europe in the Nineties*. Basingstoke and London: Macmillan, 241–6
CDU/CSU Parliamentary Group ('Schäuble/Lamers Paper') (1994) *Überlegungen zur Europapolitik*. Bonn: CDU/CSU-Fraktion im Deutschen Bundestag.
Couve de Murville, Maurice (1971) *Une politique étrangère*. Paris: Plon.
Cowles, Maria Green (1995) 'Setting the agenda for a new Europe: the ERT and EC 1992', *Journal of Common Market Studies* 33:4, 501–26.
De Schoutheete, Philippe (1990) 'The European Community and its sub-systems', in William Wallace (ed.), *The Dynamics of European Integration*. London and New York: Pinter, 106–24.

Deubner, Christian (1997) 'The Franco-German relationship: from Europe to bilateralism', in *The Future of the Franco-German Relationship: Three Views*. London: Royal Institute of International Affairs, Discussion Paper 71, 15–34.

Dumas, Roland (1996) *Le Fil et la Pelote*. Paris: Plon.

Garrett, Geoffrey (1992) 'International co-operation and institutional choice: the European Community's internal market', *International Organization* 46:2, 533–60.

Genscher, Hans-Dietrich (1995) *Erinnerungen*. Berlin: Siedler.

Gerbet, Pierre (1990) 'Le rôle du couple France-Allemagne dans la création et développement des Communautés Européennes' in Robert Picht and Wolfgang Wessels (eds), *Motor für Europa. Deutsch-französvischer Bilateralismus und europäische Integration*. Bonn: Europa Union, 69–119.

Giscard d'Estaing, Valéry (1988) *Le pouvoir et la vie*. Paris: Compagnie 12.

Guérin-Sendelbach, Valérie (1993) *Ein Tandem für Europa? Die deutsch-französische Zusammenarbeit der achtziger Jahre*. Bonn: Forschungsinstitut der Deutschen Gesellschaft für Auswärtige Politik.

Héritier, Adrienne (1993) 'Policy-Netzwerkanalyse als Untersuchungsinstrument im europäischen Kontext: Folgerungen aus einer empirischen Studie regulativer Politik', in Adrienne Héritier (ed.), *Policy-Analyse: Kritik und Neuorientierung*. Opladen: Westdeutscher Verlag, 432–47.

Klaiber, Klaus-Peter (1998) 'Europe's Franco-German engine: general perspectives', in: David P. Calleo and Eric R. Staal (eds), *Europe's Franco-German Engine*. Washington D.C.: Brookings Institution Press, 37–46.

Kohl, Helmut (1996) 'The Chancellor of Europe' (interview), in *Time*, 30 September 1996, 44–6.

Kolboom, Ingo and Robert Picht (1995) 'Handeln für Europa', in: Centre d'Information et de Recherche sur l'Allemagne Contemporaine (CIRAC), Deutsch-Französisches Institut, Forschungsinstitut der Deutschen Gesellschaft für Auswärtige Politik (DGAP), Institut Français des Relations Internationales (IFRI) (eds), *Handeln für Europa: Deutsch-französische Zusammenarbeit in einer veränderten Welt*. Opladen: Westdeutscher Verlag, 352–64.

Küsters, Hanns Jürgen (1982) *Die Gründung der Europäischen Wirtschaftsgemeinschaft*. Baden-Baden: Nomos.

Leblond, Laurent (1997) *Le couple franco-allemand depuis 1945*. Paris: Le Monde-Editions.

Maillard, Pierre (1995) *De Gaulle et l'Europe: Entre la nation et Maastricht*. Paris: Tallandier.

Marks, Gary, Liesbet Hooghe and Kermit Blank (1996) 'European integration from the 1980s: state-centric v. multi-level governance', *Journal of Common Market Studies* 34:3, 341–78.

Mazzarelli, Colette (1997) *France and Germany at Maastricht: Politics and Negotiations to Create the European Union*. New York and London: Garland.

Ménudier, Henri (ed.) (1993) *Le couple franco-allemand en Europe*. Asnières: Institut d'Allemand d'Asnières.

Middlemas, Keith (1995) *Orchestrating Europe: The Informal Politics of the European Union 1973–95*. London: Fontana Press.

Mitterrand, François (1996) *De l'Allemagne, de la France*. Paris: Odile Jacob.

Moravcsik, Andrew (1991) 'Negotiating the Single European Act: national interests and conventional statecraft in the European Community', *International Organization* 45:1, 19–56.

—— (1993) 'Preferences and power in the European community: a liberal intergovernmentalist approach', *Journal of Common Market Studies* 31:4, 473–524.

Peters, B. Guy (1992) 'Bureaucratic politics and the institutions of the European Community', in Alberta M. Sbragia (ed.), *Euro-Politics: Institutions and Policymaking in the 'New' European Community*. Washington DC: Brookings Institution, 75–122.

Peterson, John (1995) 'Decision-making in the European Union: towards a framework for analysis', *Journal of European Public Policy* 2:1, 69–93.

Picht, Robert, Hendrik Uterwedde and Wolfgang Wessels (1990) 'Deutsch-französischer Bilateralismus als Motor der europäischen Integration: Mythos oder Realität?', in Robert Picht and Wolfgang Wessels (eds), *Motor für Europa? Deutsch-französischer Bilateralismus und europäische Integration*. Bonn: Europa Union, 17–31.

Pierson, Paul (1996) 'The path to European integration: a historical institutionalist analysis', *Comparative Political Studies* 29:2, 123–63.

Sandholtz, Wayne and John Zysman (1989) 'Recasting the European bargain', *World Politics* 41, 95–128.

Scharpf, Fritz W. (1988) 'The joint-decision trap: lessons frm German federalism and European integration', *Public Administration* 66:3 (Autumn 1988) 239–78.

Schmidt, Helmut (1990) *Die Deutschen und ihre Nachbarn: Menschen und Mächte II*. Berlin: Siedler.

Stone Sweet, Alec and Wayne Sandholtz (1997) 'European integration and supranational governance', *Journal of European Public Policy* 4:3, 297–317.

Védrine, Hubert (1996) *Les mondes de François Mitterrand: A l'Élysée 1981–1995*. Paris: Fayard.

Wallace, Helen (1986a) 'Bilateral, trilateral and multilateral negotiations in the European Community', in Roger Morgan and Caroline Bray (eds), *Partners and Rivals in Western Europe: Britain, France and Germany*. Aldershot and Brookfield VT: Gower, 156–74.

—— (1996b) 'The conduct of bilateral relationships by governments', in Roger Morgan and Caroline Bray (eds), *Partners and Rivals in Western Europe: Britain, France and Germany*. Aldershot and Brookfield VT: Gower, 136–55.

—— (1990) 'Institutionalized bilateralism and multilateral relations: axis, motor or detonator?', in Robert Picht, Hendrik Uterwedde and Wolfgang Wessels (eds), *Motor für Europa? Deutsch-französischer Bilateralismus und europäische Integration*. Bonn: Europa Union, 145–57.

Wessels, Wolfgang (1997) 'An ever closer fusion? A dynamic macropolitical view on integration processes', *Journal of Common Market Studies* 35:2, 267–99.

Wood, Pia Christina (1995) 'The Franco-German relationship in the post-Maastricht era', in Carolyn Rhodes and Sonia Mazey (eds), *The State of the European Union. Vol. 3: Building a European Polity?*. Boulder CO: Lynne Rienner and Harlow: Longman, 221–43.

2

MONETARY UNION

Economic competition and political negotiation

Jonathan Story

Introduction

There is little cause for surprise at the motives informing French and German relations through the 1980s and 1990s. Economic competition and political negotiation between the two states were etched into the bargaining and the deals done 'in Europe's name' (Garton Ash 1993). The peculiarity of their negotiations over a new monetary regime for Europe rested on the scope of the interests at stake, and the determination both parties displayed in achieving their goals. The EU's internal market programme, launched in the years 1985–87 to lower non-tariff barriers among member states, was cause enough to arouse interests. But the negotiations concerning a new monetary regime were bound to stir passions.[1] French disquiet at Germany's growing preponderance in Europe became evident in the late 1960s, when the Deutsche Mark (DM) began its ascent on the back of widening trade surpluses to replace sterling as the world's second reserve currency after the dollar. The Bundesbank was seen as Europe's de facto central bank, and chief financial officer of the German financial and corporate sectors.[2]

A perennial dilemma in post-war politics has been how to reconcile France's desire to bind Germany into the EU and the Atlantic alliance with French ambitions to build an economy equivalent to Germany's. In its domestic economy, France hesitated between policies that would harden its own mercantilist practices, and liberalisation policies to accommodate German competition in more integrated world markets. In international monetary negotiations, France alternated between promoting a climate for economic growth in Europe, and meeting German demands for stability oriented policies and performance as a prerequisite to a new currency regime. Its preferred vehicle for reconciling growth and stability was a 'common currency' jointly managed by a confederation of interdependent states. The Bundesbank's steel grip over interest and exchange rate policies in Europe would be loosened if they were decided by a wide coalition of states, including Britain or Italy, that diluted Germany's influence.

The German government had no such hesitations. It regularly presented France with two choices: accept the Bundesbank's unilateral decisions in favour of stability as a junior partner, or make them more multilateral on Frankfurt's terms in a 'hard core' of states, where German preferences would be paramount. In the latter case, its preference was for European Monetary Union (EMU) on a federal model, whose achievement required the convergence of economic policies and performance. This formula enabled the German government both to present an ambitious European project which assured a monopoly over monetary policy for the Bundesbank, if the terms could not be met by other states, or for a European Central Bank (ECB), modelled on Bundesbank lines, if they could. The burden of proof thus rested on others; if the DM remained, it would not be by Germany's design, but on account of the failings of EU member states.

'The present controversy over the new European monetary order', the Bundesbank Council member Wilhelm Nölling as quoted in Connolly (1995: 98) has written, 'is about power, influence and the pursuit of national interests.' These interests, and the bargaining and deals they inspired, are analysed in the following sections on German and French monetary relations in the broader security context of the Atlantic alliance, Germany's emergence as Europe's prime industrial and monetary power, France's challenge to the DM as a result of President Mitterrand's decision (with Chancellor Kohl's support) to accept Germany's conditions in order to achieve a maximal French objective of abolishing the Bundesbank, and the resulting struggle in the course of the 1990s either to preserve the DM or to assure its final demise within a more federal EU.

The Atlantic context

The permanent context of repeated European efforts to fix currencies or to establish monetary union has been provided since the 1940s by the USA as the world's banker. Initially, the dollar was exchangeable by other central banks at the official International Monetary Fund (IMF) price, and Congress ensured that the IMF statutes included no practical measures against chronic surplus countries, the USA being the only candidate for that condition in 1945. But by the 1960s, the US external deficit widened while continental states and Japan moved to trade surplus. Dollar credits accumulated in central bank reserves and irrigated the nascent offshore dollar markets in London.

In 1967 Germany was forbidden to convert dollar reserves into gold, and an arrangement was made whereby the Bundesbank dollar reserves would in part be reinvested in US Treasury bonds, thereby helping to finance the US federal government deficits and to sustain US growth. The whole edifice was brought down in August 1971, when President Nixon announced the dollar's non-convertibility into gold. In March 1973, the Bundesbank followed suit by ending the purchase of surplus dollars and moving the DM to a free float. The dollar–DM axis subsequently became the pivot of intra-European exchange rates, with the shots being called by the world's key currency. The dollar's fall in the winter of 1977 prompted Chancellor Schmidt to establish a stable exchange rate regime in partnership with France. In winter 1994–95, the dollar plunged against the DM following the Mexican debt crisis and the Kobe disaster in Japan, prompting cries from German industrialists for accelerated moves to monetary union in the EU.[3]

German exporters' aspirations to take shelter from dollar turbulence within an EU currency regime were one reason for the choice of money as the route to closer European union. Another lay in the transformation of European security. Since 1967, North Atlantic Treaty Organisation (NATO) policy on nuclear deterrence had hinged on the concepts of 'forward defence' and 'flexible response'. This meant that Germany was to be defended as far forward as possible, but that the allies were to respond to attack by escalating from conventional to nuclear force.

Political support for such a policy began to dry up in Germany during the scare over the installation of nuclear missiles in the early 1980s, prompting Foreign Minister Genscher to introduce security policy into EU deliberations and to vigorously promote détente, as less likely to alienate a frightened German electorate. The end of the nuclear stand-off in central Europe came in December 1987, when the US and USSR leaders signed the Washington Treaty leading to the removal of intermediate-range nuclear weapons in Europe. The deal in effect deprived Germany of credible nuclear cover, and marked the de facto end of the Cold War, of which the fall of the Berlin Wall in November 1989 was a consequence. French diplomacy sought to breathe life into the dormant West European Union (WEU), and to revive the military provisions in the 1963 Franco-German Treaty by setting up the Franco-German Security Council in January 1988.

Foreign Minister Genscher, sensitive to the significance of the Washington Treaty and the need to assuage French concerns over Germany's western orientation, responded favourably (Genscher 1995: 375). With Mitterrand's re-election to the Presidency in May, French EU policy moved in Germany's direction, and at the Franco-German summit of May 1989, Mitterrand picked up on Bonn's initiative to reassert the common objectives of a 'social Europe' and European monetary union. By contrast, French military policy remained firmly national with regard to nuclear weapons (Dominique 1989: 316–26). France's nuclear doctrine of massive retaliation was confirmed in the defence programme presented to the National Assembly in September 1989. Nine regiments, posted on France's eastern frontier, were to be equipped from 1992 on with the Hades nuclear missile system, with a range of 450 km. Bonn was not consulted (*Die Welt*, 15 September 1989). Relations between Paris and Bonn deteriorated sharply as Kohl led Germany to unity. Only the USA stood consistently by Germany.

Indeed, as Zelikow and Rice argue (1995: 365), Maastricht was the tribute paid by Kohl to French dismay and frustration, and a sign to the French of German credentials as good Europeans. The EU's importance for France's embrace of Germany was underlined when Kohl and Mitterrand proposed political union in April 1990. Their common message to the Irish EU presidency called for the intergovernmental conferences to include the establishment of common foreign and defence policies. At the Dublin summits of April and June 1990, political and monetary union talks were set to begin in December, and to end one year later under the Dutch presidency in December 1991. The German government clearly understood political union as a synonym for a common foreign policy, extensive majority voting, and more powers to the European Parliament.

Negotiations at Maastricht yielded a German commitment 'irrevocably' to abandon the DM in January 1999, but without adequate compensation in the form of political union. Security in Europe and for Germany hinged first and foremost on a continued US presence. This implied keeping defence policy within the domain of the states, and therefore of NATO. The USA was Germany's prime ally in the maintenance of the new and wider European balance. A wider Europe introduced further areas of discord between France and Germany over EU institutional forms, relations between the EU, the WEU and NATO, opening to eastern trade, the pace and method of EU enlargement, and the balance to be struck between the demands of the countries of Central–Eastern Europe, and those of the southern Mediterranean.

These differences greatly complicated EU internal deliberations, and were accompanied by much closer security co-operation between Paris and London (Croft 1996: 771–87). France, under President Chirac, rejoined NATO with the ostensible aim of 'Europeanising' the organisation. But the redefinition of NATO's security tasks in a changed Europe at the Berlin Atlantic Council summit in June 1996 in effect consecrated NATO as the prime organisation responsible for European security, and the USA as undisputed leader of the Western alliance (Cornish 1996: 751–69). It was not at all evident that the USA would welcome a fully fledged European currency to challenge the dollar's hegemony as a reward for its pre-eminent role in keeping the European peace.

German primacy in Europe

Monetary union had been an integral part of the federalist cause for a united Europe, but the signatories to the Rome Treaty had made no reference to it in the texts on the grounds that the subject was too sensitive politically. Their premonitions were amply justified, as subsequent EU proposals were regularly whittled down to modest accords on exchange rate co-ordination. Commission suggestions of monetary union and a single capital market had received short shrift from France and Italy in the 1960s. The EU then launched a second and more serious attempt at monetary union, sketched in the Werner Report, presented to the Council in October 1970 (EC Commission 1970). The report proposed the creation of a single European currency, complete liberalisation of capital movements, freedom of establishment for financial institutions, a common central banking system essentially modelled on the US Federal Reserve System, and a centralised EU economic policy body, responsible to the European Parliament. The report also suggested a three stage move to union.

Such aspirations were undermined by divergent ideas on means and ends. Germany argued that it would not be possible to align exchange rates more closely in the absence of convergence in economic policies and performance. France argued that the member states should fix their exchange rates, which would then force them to achieve convergence in their economic policies. These differences cloaked incompatible objectives. Germany's emphasis on economic convergence implied a slowdown in French growth to the German norm. France's proposal to fix exchange rates faced the Bundesbank with the prospect of capital inflows, stimulating inflationary growth, and providing buoyant markets for French, or other, producers. This was not acceptable to the Bundesbank, which decided in March 1973 to float the DM.

The Bundesbank's subsequent tight money policies at home propelled producers on to international markets. Between 1970 and 1993, Germany trade surpluses amounted to over DM1,420 billion (OECD, Series A). One half of total exports was accounted for by 100 of Germany's largest companies (German Monopolies Commission 1987: 15), 88 of the largest companies were run as joint stock companies; and their most frequent shareholders were the three large banks and the insurance giant, Allianz (ibid.: 153). Collective wage bargaining ensured that wage rises lagged behind increases in productivity. Trade unions were given positions of equality with shareholders on the boards of large German corporations. The converse side to this 'model Germany' was the surge in public debt from 18 to 46 per cent of GDP between 1973 and 1993, making the DM bond market the third largest in the world. The Bundesbank kept control of the primary bond market through the consortium of major banks, while the secondary market migrated on the grounds of 'the pre-eminence of the London market in the domain of corporate finance and money management' (*Financial Times*, 28 November 1984).

The Bundesbank's preferred option was to have the DM's rate set on world financial markets, as was the case in 1973–77. The Bundesbank set foreign exchange policy, not the government, and it was under no obligation to intervene in foreign exchange markets. Neighbouring small countries hitched their currencies to the DM, as a means of exerting a price discipline on their economies. Inflation-riven countries such as Italy, Britain, France and the smaller European Mediterranean countries were excluded from the DM zone. But the whole arrangement depended on a relatively stable dollar–DM exchange rate. This was ended in 1977 by President Carter who chose domestic growth over dollar stability, leading to a strong upward pressure on the DM. The Bundesbank sold DM to keep the rate down, prompting its rapid growth as an international reserve currency.

Depreciation of the dollar, and upward pressure on the DM in the winter of 1977–78, convinced Chancellor Schmidt of the urgency of extending the DM zone to incorporate the French franc (Ludlow 1982). Tying the DM to a weaker currency would shield German exporters on world markets. President Giscard d'Estaing gave Prime Minister Barre a mandate to import to France the virtues of 'the German model'. The European Monetary System (EMS), conceived as a Franco-German initiative in April 1978, was launched in March 1979. Two key issues emerged during the negotiations: first, Germany was concerned not to bear the burden of adjustment; second, France wanted to widen the coalition of members beyond the DM zone, requiring inducements to bring the weaker currencies into the scheme.

The question of adjustment hinged on the intervention mechanism to maintain exchange rate stability. France won recognition for the European Currency Unit (ECU), whose value was equal to a weighted average of all currencies. The ECU was a central bank unit of account to define the value of each currency and hence their bilateral parities. As the DM weighed most, the Bundesbank would have been most called on to maintain currency relationships to the ECU. Bundesbank Governor Emminger wrote to the German Chancellor, registering Bundesbank reservations about having to intervene to support weaker currency countries, a statement that came back to haunt European monetary relations.[4] The Bundesbank also opposed the ECU (the French called it écu), on the grounds of its being an index of currencies. Had it been allowed to develop, the Bundesbank feared that it would have to buy ECUs, that is weaker currencies, for DMs, and without counterpart. In effect, the EMS rapidly acquired the DM as its central indicator.

The inducements related to the availability of funds to help reduce inequalities among EU member states. Weaker currency countries had serious concerns about being tied in to a DM bloc. Italy and Ireland in particular requested EU funds to help deal with unemployment, regional poverty and low productivity. France and Germany eventually granted Italy a 6 per cent band of fluctuation in the EMS, to make allowance for its chronic financial difficulties. Britain retained its option to join, but showed no willingness to make parity changes for sterling a matter of EU concern. The fiscal transfer mechanism to help finance deficit countries remained modest. The proposed pooling of foreign exchange reserves with a European Monetary Fund (EMF) was postponed in December 1980. The EMF was quietly dropped, in view of Bundesbank opposition to its creation. In February 1981 it went on unilaterally to raise interest rates to unprecedented levels in order to stabilise the DM and stem the outflow of capital to the USA. It thereby became Europe's de facto central bank.

The heyday of a DM zone disguised in the clothes of the Exchange-Rate Mechanism (ERM) came in the years 1981–7 when the Bundesbank supervised regular but small currency realignments. A crucial episode was President Mitterrand's decision in March 1983 to keep the franc in the ERM. He had little choice, given the explosion in French debt charges payable in harder currencies (*Le Monde*, 15 November 1983).[5] Indeed, a prime objective of French financial reforms in the years 1984–88 was to lower the cost of finance for the public purse. Bank reforms were initiated by Delors during his years as Finance Minister (1981–84), but the major reforms were launched that September by the new Finance Minister Bérégovoy, whose prime objective was the constitution of a 'unified capital market, covering short to long-term instruments, and all economic agents'.[6] Paris was to develop as an international financial centre, and French corporate financing moved towards the model of Anglo-American financial market economies (Zerah 1993: 125). In particular, the Trésor fostered highly liquid money, bond, and futures markets, whose major products, all originating with the Trésor, included the Euro DM contract launched in May 1989, and the long-term écu contract floated in October 1990 to develop Paris as the centre for trade in écus. In December 1985, the Banque de France modified monetary policy, and tied the franc's exchange rate more clearly to the DM. 'France,' the Governor declared, 'now accepts the exchange rate constraint' (*Le Monde*, 7 December 1985).

Mitterrand's decision of March 1983 also helped revive the momentum in EU monetary affairs. Finance Minister Delors negotiated with the Bundesbank and Finance Ministry to keep the franc in the ERM and to stabilise the French economy, ending the hopes of reducing the nation's unemployment rates through the gentle expansionary policies of the preceding two years (*L'Année* 1984: 35–6). Delors bludgeoned the German government into a reluctant upwards realignment of the DM, while complaining of the 'arrogance and incomprehension' of German financial circles (*Financial Times*, 31 March 1983). This experience confirmed his conviction that the only answer to stagnation in France lay in expansionary EU economic policies, and the creation of a 'single European social space' (Delors 1984). This was consistent with Keynesian policy whereby high rates of employment could only be attained in sticky labour markets through an expansion of demand. Maintenance of Western Europe's mixed economy welfare states was vital to ensure continued popular support for the EU internal market programme (*Futuribles* 1985: 3–18).

In view of the more market-based policy consensus of the 1980s, an EU growth strategy could only be achieved in the very long run. In the meanwhile, Delors, and France, had to accept Kohl's insistence on liberalisation of capital movements as a precondition to the internal market, for which he was prepared to consider monetary union as a 'goal'. From the French government's perspective, liberalisation of capital movements had the benefit of touching on all aspects of the internal market programme and of monetary policy. But a removal of capital controls by the French government was bound to make the franc more vulnerable to speculation, while Bundesbank reluctance to intervene on foreign exchange markets in support of weaker currencies, indicated that France would have to align economic policy even closer than it already was on German priorities.

This message was borne home brutally to the new conservative government of Prime Minister Chirac in January 1987 when a weakening of the dollar prompted an eleventh and acrimonious parity realignment in the ERM. Convinced that the fundamentals of the French economy were now sound, the government launched the 'hard franc' policy the same month. Rather than have the Bundesbank accumulate dollars as the counterpart to German external surpluses, the French Finance Ministry sought to have the Bundesbank hold écus, and use them to subscribe to French Treasury bonds (Fabra, *Le Monde*, 27 September 1987), as the Bundesbank had done since the 1960s with regard to US Treasury bonds. The use of the écu as central bank unit of account would also avoid the convergence demands that the Germans had appended to the single currency discussions of the early 1970s. It would permit a relaxation of macroeconomic policies, and a rapid easing of pressures on the European labour markets. This was the intent behind the creation in January 1988 of the Economic and Financial Policy Council, within the bounds of the 1963 Franco-German Treaty. Finance Minister Balladur expressed the French position clearly in his memorandum of February 1988 to the EU Finance Ministers, proposing a 'common currency', and an ECB. The ERM, he wrote, effectively exempted 'any countries whose policies were too restrictive from the necessary adjustment' (Gros and Thygesen 1992: 312).[7]

France challenges the DM

Kohl recognised that French dissatisfaction with the ERM would have to be accommodated (Balkhausen 1992: 71), and shared Genscher's view that EU integration had to be accentuated as Europe's security context changed. The Finance Ministry was unsure of the French proposal, but the most serious reservations were expressed by the Bundesbank. It feared isolation in the proposed bilateral Economic and Finance Council, where finance ministries would have the upper hand in view of the subordinate position of the Banque de France. The German Cabinet hammered out a common position, presented in a February 1988 resolution. 'The longer term goal is economic and monetary union in Europe, in which an independent ECB, committed to maintaining price stability, will be able to lend effective support to a common economic and monetary policy' (*Financial Times*, 23 June 1988). Foreign Minister Genscher summarised the German government's position: free capital movement, priority accorded to price stability, political independence of the ECB, no inflationary financing of government deficits, and a federal structure, in the manner of the institutions of the Federal Republic or the USA (Genscher 1989: 13–20). In effect, the German government revived a version of the Werner Report, minus the idea of a centralised EU economic policy body.

Genscher determined to make a success of the German EU presidency of early 1988 (Hort 1988: 421–8; Puaux 1989: 159–77). On 13 June the Finance Ministers decided to liberalise capital movements, as the prerequisite to a more efficient allocation of European savings (*Economie Européenne* 1988: 9–10). At the European Council of Hanover on 27 June, the EU political leaders agreed to incorporate the central bankers into talks on monetary matters. The German government preferences were for an independent central bank, economic convergence of participating states on low inflation before and after the conversion to a single currency, and no weakening of the Bundesbank during the transition phase. The French government in effect proposed a 'common currency', through a revival of the original design of the EMS. This would entail the progressive construction of a 'European Reserve Fund', with the task of administering the stability of EU currencies towards third parties, and in support of the ERM. This Fund would have foreign exchange reserves placed at its disposal by the central banks. In the longer term, it would prepare the way for completion of the monetary union (Aeschimann and Riché 1996: 88).

As president of the committee, Delors presented the report in spring 1989. It represented a victory for the German position, not least in that the report made clear that the 'transition' to a single currency represented a marathon with a receding winning post.[8] The ECB was to be independent; there were to be binding rules on government spending; the report incorporated the earlier Werner Report's proposal of a three stage transition; and the narrow ERM band was presented as providing a 'glidepath' to monetary union. The bland text, replete with barely concealed differences, was vaguer with regard to timing. Stage one in July 1990 entailed liberalisation of capital movements. Stage two, to start at an unspecified date, was to witness new institutions (with unspecified powers), precise but not binding rules relating to the size of budget deficits, and a reduction in margins of currency fluctuation. The third stage, also starting at an unspecified date, would lead to 'irrevocably fixed' parities, the replacement of national currencies by a single currency, and would only be embarked upon once all the instruments of the internal market were in place (an efficient competition policy, regulation of takeover bids and corporate control, a set of common fiscal policy goals and close monetary policy co-ordination).

Mitterrand's immediate concern was to tie Kohl down on the timetable. The Chancellor did not share the Elysée's sense of urgency. At the June 1989 European Council meeting in Madrid, it was agreed that the Delors report was to provide the basis for future discussions. The first stage was to start on 1 July 1990, entailing liberalisation of capital movements. These took effect on schedule, followed by German monetary union. EU institutions were to make 'complete and adequate' preparation for an intergovernmental conference that would establish the timetable and substance for the later stages. France then took over the rotating EU presidency for the second half of 1989. 'I am a determined supporter of a political Europe and seek to bring about economic and monetary union, an obligatory passageway,' Mitterrand declared (*Le Nouvel Observateur*, 27 July 1989). A catalogue of proposals for treaty changes was duly drawn up. By contrast, Kohl moved fast on German unity without consulting Paris, and then went along with Mitterrand's urging in order to secure French support for German unity. At the EU Strasbourg summit of 8–9 December, the EU heads of state and government reiterated support for the German people to 'find unity through free self-determination', and Bonn concurred in Paris' request that a new intergovernmental conference begin prior to the German elections in 1990, with a view to incorporating monetary union into the Treaties (*Le Monde*, 10–11 December 1989).[9]

In order to retain coherence during negotiations, the German government adopted a maximal position. In doing so, it responded to three imperatives. First, the DM was the pre-eminent symbol of Germany's post-war recovery. It signified the Federal Republic's stability, and like the Federal Republic, had taken a deep hold on the German people's affections. Such an asset could only be abandoned in the name of some transcendent value. As the Bundesbank Governor Pöhl candidly stated, the German people were being asked to sacrifice 'a hard currency on the European altar without knowing what we would get in return' (*Die Welt*,

4 September 1990). Definitely, the écu, which Paris and London were so eager to develop, was no substitute (*Financial Times*, 2 March 1991).

The second was rooted in the Bundesbank's determination to preserve its regalian powers to issue DM that underpinned its regulatory prerogatives over the financial system. Its natural constituency was the 'buy and hold' DM bondholder, whose returns had consistently exceeded those from German equities (*Financial Times*, 28 February 1996).[10] The doubling of the German debt in the six years following unity expanded the constituency considerably, and made it all the more important to maintain the DM's credibility as a store of value, yet all the more difficult to achieve as Kohl sidelined the Bundesbank on German unity, and then signed up to its conditional absorption into an ECB at Maastricht. The Bundesbank had no alternative but to reassure its constituency of worried DM savers and investors by redoubling its determination to defend the currency (*Süddeutsche Zeitung*, 1 February 1996).

The third imperative was to protect Germany's social market practices from dilution by the internal market.[11] German proposals filled the content of the EU Social Chapter; but as Germany's economic problems mounted, corporate Germany began to look more favourably on 'Anglo-Saxon' shareholding as an alternative to German methods of corporate governance (*Financial Times*, 27 February 1995). This required major restructuring of the German economy, prompting trade unions to accuse Kohl of abandoning consensus politics (*Financial Times*, 25 April 1996).

German unity was completed on 3 October 1990, followed by Kohl's victory in the December general election. Whatever his aspirations to promoting EU integration with France, Kohl had no option but to support the Bundesbank's hard-line in the forthcoming monetary talks. At the European Council in Rome on 27–28 October 1990, Chancellor and Finance Ministry won acceptance of the Bundesbank's conditions. These had been circulated in an unofficial paper, 'Compromise Proposal for the Second Stage of EMU' among other central banks. They were presented as '*non-negotiable*' (my italics) demands: political union, price stability, completion of the internal market, political independence of the ECB and member banks, and an ECB monopoly on all necessary instruments (*Frankfurter Allgemeine Zeitung*, 26 September 1990). Prior to union, price levels had to converge to a stable and low norm. There was to be no inflationary financing of government deficits, and there were to be binding rules on government spending.

This German position was incompatible with French demands for a 'common currency'. Mitterrand therefore decided to concede as the price to pay for France gaining a voice in an independent ECB.[12] But he continued to maintain, after Kohl had agreed to surrender the DM by January 1999, that the economic governance of a united Europe would have to be predicated on the Council of Ministers, and answerable to the European Parliament. Mitterrand forcefully reiterated the French government's position at the time of the September 1992 referendum on the Maastricht Treaty: 'Those who decide economic policy, of which monetary policy is only one instrument, are the politicians elected by universal suffrage, the heads of state and government who make up the European Council' (*Le Monde*, 5 September 1992). At the Brussels summit of December 1994, the EU governments welcomed the Delors White Paper on growth, competitiveness and employment. President Chirac returned to the theme, indicating thereby that the French concept of 'economic governance' of the EU was not to be circumvented.[13]

Once the German conditions had been accepted, Kohl, in a gesture to Mitterrand, announced January 1994 as the date to start the second stage, prior to the Rome Council of October 1990. But the German government's discourse hinted at that concession with the argument that fulfilment of the conditions was more important than the timetable. As an ECB had to 'succeed at the first attempt', Bundesbank and Finance Ministry sharply opposed French plans for a powerful ECB until the last phase, and they found allies in the UK and the Netherlands to keep monetary sovereignty in national hands until then. During this period, stability oriented policies were to be applied, and tough EU examination procedures established for passage to the third stage, to start in 1999. France insisted against a general opt-out clause for Britain, that would also have been available to Germany. But as the German delegation boasted about the treaty, 'we have de facto exported German monetary order to Europe'.

The protocol on convergence criteria would lie at the heart of the treaty's implementation. The balance sheet was thus stacked heavily in favour of Germany. Both sides used the future as a place to locate their present disagreements: the German delegation had negotiated a marathon obstacle course, with seemingly only a distant prospect of more than a few member states reaching the finishing line on 1 January 1999. But at the last moment Mitterrand won Kohl's commitment to override the battle of the experts as to whether the timetable or the conditions should take precedence. By agreeing to an 'irrevocable' commitment to the timetable, Kohl in effect signed the DM's death warrant.

A glidepath to (dis)union

Kohl's commitment to monetary union, and the Bundesbank's active dislike of the Treaty, proved quite compatible. The Bundesbank's determination to present the Treaty as partial and incomplete enjoyed the support of the Chancellor and Finance Ministry. For the EU to enjoy the full benefits of one money, an ECB meant full political union; it would have to make monetary policy for the EU as a whole, have the monopoly of money creation, and undivided power over exchange rate policy, binding on all members. But the Bundesbank's demands did not stop there: the ECB would have to be located in Frankfurt; the interests of individual financial centres, such as London, would be subordinated to the ECB's paramount goal of price stability, and by Bundesbank methods.

The Bundesbank also deployed its structural power over the DM in financial markets to register its disapproval of Kohl's concession. As soon as Germany began to move to unity, Bonn had indicated a preference for Paris to agree to the DM's upward alignment. But the request was stifled, as that would have entailed devaluation of the franc. Furthermore, Kohl's overriding of Bundesbank advice on the course of German unity impaired the institution's credibility on international financial markets; prompting the DM's guardians to redouble their anti-inflationary vigilance. The Bundesbank allowed interest rates to rise both to keep inflationary pressures down, and to attract foreign capital into German bonds to help finance eastern reconstruction.

EU neighbours were therefore caught in a double bind: high interest rates in a fixed rate system exerted a deflationary pressure on business activity across the continent and increased the debt charges on European governments. On foreign exchange markets, the dollar floated down from spring 1990 on, as the Federal Reserve moved to lower interest rates in response to lower domestic growth and fears of financial fragility. Weaker currency countries in the ERM were therefore squeezed between higher interest rates, and more US competition on product markets. The Bundesbank nonetheless saw fit to raise rates in December 1991, and again in July 1992, to the highest levels since 1931. This left the other European countries no option but to engage in a spate of currency realignments, or give absolute priority to policy convergence based on price stability.

This played havoc with the French corporate sector. World financial markets smelled blood, once Mitterrand decided to hold a referendum on the Maastricht Treaty on 20 September 1992. But Kohl could not afford to see Mitterrand defeated in a crucial referendum by a de facto alliance of the Bundesbank with international speculators. Bonn and Paris concluded a 'sweetheart deal', whereby the Bundesbank intervened with the Banque de France in massive support of the franc.[14]

For France to be a viable partner for Bonn in a Maastricht Europe, there was never any doubt that the apparatus of monetary control practised in Germany would have to be imported wholesale. This was consecrated by the May 1993 law 'on the status of the Banque de France and the activity and control of credit establishments'. The Banque was 'to define and implement monetary policy in the framework of the government's general economic policy'. A Monetary Policy Council was created to supervise the money mass. Appointments of the governor and two deputies were made by the government, but the government was not to give the Banque orders, and its deficits were not to be financed by money creation. The Banque was given control of the banking system. The government, though, was to determine exchange rate policy. Governor Trichet's first public testimony on behalf of the newly independent central bank was to the Bundestag, not the National Assembly (*Financial Times*, 24 March 1994).

The 'sweetheart deal' proved temporary. Mitterrand's very different intepretation of the Treaty provided one excuse for the Bundesbank to break free of its tight relationship with the franc. The second was the 23 September 1992 Franco-German statement, demanded by Kohl, that bound the Bundesbank to expend reserves on the franc. The third factor was the election of a Gaullist-conservative coalition government in spring 1993. Many in the majority had campaigned against the Maastricht Treaty and the 'social Munich' which France was paying in order to appease the Bundesbank. This was the spirit in which Finance Minister Alphandéry announced on radio in June 1993 that the Germans should lower their rates 'That is why I took the initiative … to ask my colleague Theo Waigel, the German Finance Minister and Helmut Schlesinger, the president of the Bundesbank, to come to Paris in the context of the Economic and Financial Council to discuss together the conditions for a concerted lowering of interest rates in France and Germany.'

With Kohl's agreement, Waigel had the meetings cancelled. A month later, Prime Minister Balladur invited Kohl to have the Bundesbank either defend the franc without limit or to lower interest rates. This was also turned down, as was the French proposal for the DM to leave the ERM. Kohl found no fault in Bundesbank and Finance Ministry proposals to widen the ERM band, finally agreed on in the EU Finance Ministers Council of August 1993. Paris acquiesced, on the grounds that wider bands shifted the foreign exchange risk to speculators.

Freed of any immediate political pressure for the Bundesbank to support weak currencies, the German government could now impose its interpretation of the Treaty. Dutch pretentions for Amsterdam as the site for the future ECB were dismissed, on the grounds that the matter turned on Germany's right to choose the future central bank's location (*Financial Times*, 26 October 1994). The reward came for Bonn at the October 1993 EU summit at Brussels, when Kohl persuaded a majority of member states to locate the ECB in Frankfurt. The interim European Monetary Institute (EMI) started work on the Maastricht Treaty's second stage in early 1994, and in the Bundesbank's shadow. 'Hard core' countries were advised against following the pound or lira against the DM. They had to get their fiscal houses in order and ensure the stability of their currencies.

The German government's aspirations to lord it over Europe proved short-lived. It ill befitted a government to lecture others, while funding its huge budget deficit on European savings. Its problems were redoubled when in the winter of 1994–95 the dollar fell in response to the financial fallout from the Kobe earthquake in Japan, and the collapse of the Mexican peso, sending the DM skywards. Then in May 1995, Jacques Chirac was elected to the French presidency, accompanied by renewed rumours that the Elysée was considering bringing Italy and the UK back into a renewed ERM, predicated on the ECU (*Le Monde*, 18 May 1995).

Was a Gaullist France not returning to its 'common currency' project? Both Finance Ministry and Bundesbank made clear that the name écu for the future currency was not acceptable to the German people. Finance Minister Waigel then launched the idea of a 'stability pact', whereby governments running excessive deficits would be fined.[15] The target audience for this proposed tightening of the fiscal screw were anxious German bondholders, who doubted the ability of Italy to control its public spending. Waigel then told a Bundestag committee that there was little chance of Italy's joining the EMU in 1999, and the Bundesbank reinforced the message by stating that it would deliver its own judgement on which members should qualify for the final stage. This was tantamount to saying that EU examination procedures took a back seat to the Bundesbank's verdict to the Bundestag. Kohl delivered a similar message to Chirac in October about the importance for France of implementing the convergence criteria.

While the German government was constantly tightening its interpretation of the Treaty, the French government moved to emphasise the Treaty commitment to the timetable. This centred on the Commission's proposed 'critical mass' strategy which suggested a fast transition to the new currency. From the Commission's perspective, prompt use of the new currency in wholesale markets would ensure immediate credibility for the whole operation.[16] Its position was elaborated in close co-operation with the European Banking Federation; the chairman of the Commission's working group, Cees Maas, was a former senior official at the Dutch Ministry of Finance and a member of the board of the ING bank

By contrast, the Bundesbank favoured the EMI's plans for a prolonged transition, between the 'irreversible' fixing of currencies in 1999, and conversion to retail use of the new currency in 2002 (*Financial Times* and *Le Monde*, 15 November 1995). The longer transition would provide the country's numerous savings banks with time to adapt to the currency. This concern of the Bundesbank for the savings banks and local institutions reflected the consensual nature of decision-making in a federal institution, where the states were amply represented in the Council. But the Bundesbank's opposition to the fast track strategy of France and the Commission was entirely compatible with its clear hostility to Italy's entry in 1999; its fear of losing the DM and its bond market for an untested Euro, with its highly liquid Euro-bond market, which, it feared, would move corporate financing towards short-termism (*Frankfurter Allgemeine Zeitung*, 18 March 1996), and weaken its relations to the German commercial banks.

However, the big battalions of continental financial institutions were not in the Bundesbank's camp. The German commercial banks favoured the 'critical mass' strategy, and feared that Bundesbank policy would damage Frankfurt as a financial business location, in competition with Paris and London (*Süddeutsche Zeitung* and *Financial Times*, 1 September 1995). The French government pursued its goal of turning Paris into a centre for the Euro markets and declared its intent to have the Paris-based banks issue securities in Euros from January 1999 (*Financial Times*, 21 February 1996). This put pressure on the German government to follow suit. Large corporations were likely to use Euros immediately.

At the Madrid European Council of December 1995, the German Finance Ministry secured a unanimous vote in favour of 'Euro' as the name for the new currency. The start of the third stage was quietly postponed until January 1999. In deference to French government concerns to have the decision prior to the general elections that spring, a deal was struck whereby early 1998 was to be the final date for judging which member states would enter monetary union. Britain would then have the presidency, with the freedom to invoke its 'opt-in' protocol. But what would Britain be opting into? Germany secured support for yet another three-stage transition phase after 1999 in order to allow regional banks longer to adapt. But France ensured that governments in the monetary union would be allowed to issue tradable debt in Euros as soon as the exchange rates were fixed in 1999. In deference to Germany, non-tradable debt could continue to be denominated in national currencies. This was tantamount to keeping an option open for the whole project to start not as one money, but as a common currency, thereby preserving the DM.[17] In other words, if Germany secured no satisfaction on fiscal probity, the DM would survive, in competition with the Euro.

As a senior official from the German Finance Ministry lamented at Dublin, 'our French friends are not what they used to be' (*Financial Times*, 14 December 1996). Unlike Mitterrand, Chirac's government was not tempted by a Franco-German 'go-it-alone' scenario. 'Hard core' currencies, presently hinged to the DM, faced overvaluation on world currency markets, and both Germany and France were suffering from unprecedented levels of unemployment. Prime Minister Juppé rejected the idea, and German officials cited constitutional reasons against changing the status of the Bundesbank outside the context of the Maastricht Treaty (*Financial Times*, 13 February 1996).

Rather, French diplomacy was busy crafting an EU coalition to balance Germany. One way was to bring Britain back into the negotiations. Some French banks wanted to join with Frankfurt in restricting UK-based banks' access to the Euro settlement system. But such a policy threatened to undermine the single market in financial services regime, while Paris and London were co-operating to co-ordinate the Euro-time zones with Asian and North American markets. London and Paris had long co-operated in the development of the écu, and their institutions favoured the decision to convert écus to Euros at parity. Not surprisingly, it was the Ecu Banking Association which offered London banks an alternative to the official settlement system, if a British government were to recommend opting in, and lose a referendum, or to opt out and win a referendum (*Financial Times*, 14 December 1996).

Another means for France to craft a coalition to balance Germany was to link a renewed ERM, incorporating the 'outs', to Germany's demands for a cast-iron stability pact.[18] In April 1996, the Finance Ministers agreed to tighten joint supervision of exchange rate policies, whereby 'out' currencies would move within the prevailing 15 per cent bands in a grid hinged on the Euro. Italy's return in June 1996 precipitated a rush by Spain and Portugal to prepare for 1999. This widened the French-led coalition in favour of restraining German demands for near automatic sanctions on fiscal delinquents The compromise at the Dublin European Council in December 1996 meted sanctions to fiscal delinquents experiencing negative growth of less than 0.75 per cent.[19] But the pact was re-dubbed 'stability and growth', indicating that finance ministers retained discretion.

Conclusion

The politics of monetary union have lain at the heart of Franco-German relations, and of EU affairs, since the late 1960s, when the DM began its ascent as the world's second reserve currency. As Germany became Western Europe's prime power, France quietly jettisoned its policy, inherited from de Gaulle, in favour of a Europe of the states and adopted a more integrationist stance with regard to the EU. The French Finance Ministry's preferred solution for the 'common currency' was intended to reconcile stable exchange rates, jointly managed through common reserves, with economic growth under conditions of sticky labour markets. The idea was predicated on a confederal design for the EU, allowing for the preservation of national currencies and regulatory authorities, co-operating also within EU institutions. Mitterrand's decision in 1991 to override his Finance Minister, Bérégovoy, and adopt Germany's proposal for a single currency, requiring a more federal constitution for the EU, may be seen in retrospect to mark a decisive turn in French policy.

By contrast, the German government from the time of the Werner Report on, adopted a maximalist position in favour of a single currency, which experience had shown in the early 1970s was unlikely to be acceptable to France. The German government's preferred solution for a single currency entailed the adoption of anti-inflationary policies by member states, if necessary at the expense of employment. The same maximalist position was presented in the German government's proposal for an ECB in 1988, in the Delors Report, and in the Bundesbank's position paper of October 1990. Indeed, the German government could not have asked for less, in view of German public opinion, DM bondholders' concerns, and the central role played by the Bundesbank in Germany's social market economy. Clearly, though, the French government's switch of position in favour of a single currency confronted the German government with its own rhetoric. Kohl opted to live by its promise and to grant Mitterrand an 'irrevocable' commitment to move to a single currency by 1999. But he also used the Bundesbank's hostility to the timetable to extract concessions from EU partners, most notably with regard to the ECB's location in Frankfurt and the 'stability pact'.

The fundamental differences between German and French objectives remain: both Mitterrand and Chirac indicated that once the currency was introduced, the ECB would be flanked by the finance ministers, who, in the French view, would set the parameters of monetary and exchange rate policy. In other words, there was to be a significant role for national fiscal policies within a single currency area. These would be conducted in a non-inflationary manner, as France has done since the mid-1980s. The German government by contrast emphasises the independence of the ECB, contests recurrent French references to a parallel role for national fiscal policies, and interprets the Treaty as imposing strict fiscal constraints before and after 1999. The German government repeatedly claims monopoly powers for the ECB in monetary and exchange rate policy, as well as in regulation of the Euro capital markets.

These different positions indicate that trust remains a scarce resource: the German government has repeatedly suggested that France and Germany go ahead in a 'hard core' of stability oriented countries. This would mean placing France, with its growth orientation, in a minority of one in a club of smaller states closely tied to Germany. France has repeatedly sought to widen its alliances, to incorporate

Britain and Italy in order to balance Germany. This would mean placing Germany in a stability oriented minority, in a broader coalition dominated by countries with a record of preferring inflationary growth.

Germany's hard-line position on stability weakened from the mid-1990s on. Once German business was converted to the urgent need for the Euro, supporters of the DM had no power base. Their position was fatally undermined in May 1997, when the German Finance Minister, confronted with the prospect of not meeting the 3 per cent GDP deficit target, sought to have the Bundesbank's gold and foreign exchange reserves revalued. The Bundesbank ensured that the revaluation was postponed, but the incident opened Bonn to the charge that it was engaged in accounting gimmickry. It weakened Germany's case for keeping Italy out and enabled Paris to draw a discreet veil over its own creative accounting practices. Meanwhile, Paris determined to convert its French franc bond markets to Euros, whether or not Germany went ahead in 1999 or waited until 2000, as allowed at the Dublin Council. The German government insisted on monopoly powers for the ECB in Frankfurt, as one means to promote Germany's leading financial business location.

France and Germany have dominated the agenda of monetary union, with their conflicts and their partial accords. As a result, they exported the costs of their incompatible policies to each other and to the rest of the EU. They may have failed to win the active consent of their citizens, concerned about the high rates of unemployment in the EU or about the EU as an unaccountable and distant political market. But, equally, opponents of EMU have not been able to overcome public apathy on the subject. The turning point came in the Hamburg state elections in September 1997, when the Social Democrats recorded their worst result since World War II, running on an anti-EMU ticket. The result sapped the confidence of opponents who were pressing for a delay. Monetary union hardly featured as an issue in the German national elections of September 1998, which brought an end to Kohl's 16-year chancellorship.

France and Germany have been able to mediate their differences and advance their distinct goals. Both used the future as a location to place present disagreements, without disturbing the continuing rounds of negotiations in the EU over incremental accords. By deciding on a deadline, Mitterrand and Kohl deprived their governments of their habitual use of the future as a means of evasion. They overcame the stalemate between experts over timetable versus content by opting for an act of faith, that the big leap to monetary union in the EU would be successful. An EU Council meeting under the British presidency in May 1998 decided that eleven countries would participate in the launching of EMU in 1999. Of the fifteen member states, only Greece failed to meet the 3 per cent deficit ratio. Italy and Belgium were included, even though their debt-to-GDP ratios were twice as high as the reference level. Germany also failed to keep its own debt-to-GDP ratio under the 60 per cent ceiling. Against the French government's preferences, the Dutch central banker, Wim Duisenberg, was appointed as the ECB's first governor.

Meanwhile, the introduction of the Euro will bring with it a capital market as big as the US domestic market, stimulating competition between financial centres. After years of dilatory negotiations between the stock exchanges of Frankfurt and Paris, Frankfurt announced an alliance with London in early 1998. Monetary union had been a Franco-German affair. An even greater test awaited Franco-German relations once the Euro was introduced and a capital market created that would accelerate existing trends towards 'Anglo-Saxon' shareholder capitalism.

Notes

1 For an overview of the economic literature on monetary union, see Eichengreen (1993). His conclusion is that the rationale for EMU has to be found in political economy, as economic arguments for and against are inconclusive.

2 On the 'German model', see Une enquête (1979).

3 Interview with Helmut Werner, head of the executive board of Mercedes Benz (*Financial Times*, 26 May 1995).

4 In his letter to the German government in November 1978, Bundesbank Governor Emminger indicated that Bonn and Frankfurt agreed that a 'definitive' regulation for the EMS would require a change to the Rome Treaty, and that a crucial aspect of Germany's stability policy was to place '*a limit on the intervention responsibilities*' of the Bundesbank (Emminger 1986: 361; original emphasis).

5 *Le Monde*, 15 November 1983.

6 Ministère de l'économie, March 1986.

7 See Finance Minister Balladur's memorandum, quoted in English translation in the EC Monetary Committee of 29 April 1988 (Gros and Thygesen 1992: 312).

8 'The Delors Committee,' wrote Helmut Schmidt, 'did not satisfactorily state why it turned down a partial solution, whereby the ECU would serve as a parallel currency alongside national currencies and gradually squeeze them out. This refusal closes a pragmatic way, which the bond markets are already taking' (*Die Zeit*, 7 September 1990).

9 *Le Monde*, 10–11 December 1989. No date was named for the completion of monetary union, reflecting Kohl's reticence and Thatcher's opposition.

10 *Financial Times*, 28 February 1996. From 1960 to the mid-1990s, German bonds returned 3.7 per cent per annum in real terms, compared to equities' 2.3 per cent. In the UK, real return on equities was 8.7 per cent, versus 2.5 per cent on government bonds.

11 See Presse- und Informationsamt der Bundesregierung (1988) and Handelsblatt (1989).

12 By adopting a single currency, 'France, Mitterrand stated, 'will exert more influence in an ECB than it does today over the DM' (Aeschimann and Riché 1996: 91).

13 *Le Monde*, 25 March 1996: 'It will be up to the European Central Bank, which we have wanted to be strong and independent, to guarantee the future solidity of the European currency. But it will be the job of the Council of Ministers, the institution representing the states, to define the orientation of the union's economic policy.'

14 There are many accounts of this 'sweet heart deal' (See *Financial Times*, 19 September 1992; *Financial Times*, 12 December 1992; *Financial Times*, 13 December 1992; Connolly 1995: 150–60; Aeschimann and Riché 1996: 148–53).

15 'Europäische Einheit und Stabilitätspakt für Europa', Finance Minister Waigel's speech to the Bundestag on 7 November, on the occasion of the budgetary debate (Bundesministerium der Finanzen 39/95, 8 November 1995).

16 European Commission, 10 May 1995. Compiled by the Expert Group on the changeover to the single currency, it fed into the Commission's Green Paper, which suggested that the interbank market function immediately in ECUs in 1999 (European Commission, 31 May 1995).

17 On 15 January, a senior Bundesbank official, Otmar Issing, asked 'whether the states will succeed in launching this great project in such a short time in conditions such that the future European monetary policy can start in good condition with *the common currency*' (*Le Monde*, 18 January 1996; my italics).

18 *Le Monde* 18 May 1995; *Financial Times* 18 March 1996; Aeschimann and Riché 1996: 324.

19 Member states could escape sanctions in the event of a natural disaster or if GDP fell by 2 per cent in any one year, while finance ministers would have the discretion to decide in cases where GDP fell by between 0.75 and 2 per cent.

References

Aeschimann, Éric and Pascal Riché (1996) *La Guerre de Sept Ans: Histoire secrète du franc fort 1989–1996*. Paris: Calmann-Levy.

L'Année Politique, Economique et Sociale en France 1983 (1984). Paris: Editions du Moniteur.

Balkhausen, Dieter (1992) *Gutes Geld und schlechte Politik*. Düsseldorf: Capital.

Connolly, Bernard (1995) *The Rotten Heart of Europe: The Dirty War for Europe's Money*. London: Faber and Faber.

Cornish, Paul (1996) 'European Security: the end of architecture and the new NATO', *International Affairs* 72:4, 751–69.

Croft, Stuart (1996) 'European integration, nuclear deterrence and French–British nuclear co-operation', *International Affairs* 72:4, 771–87.

Delors, Jacques (1984) *Pour une Nouvelle Politique Sociale en Europe*, avant-propos. Paris: Economica.

Dominique, David (1989) *La Politique de Défense de la France: Textes et Documents*. Paris: Fondation pour les Etudes de Défense Nationale.

EC Commission (1970) 'Economic and Monetary Union in the Community' (Werner Report), *Bulletin of the European Communities*, Supplement No. 7.

Economie Européenne (1988) 'La création d'un espace financier européen', No. 36, 9–10.

Eichengreen, Barry (1993) 'European Monetary Union', *Journal of Economic Literature* 31, 1321–57.

Emminger, Otmar (1986) *D-Mark, Dollar, Währungskrisen: Erinnerungen eines ehemaligen Bundesbankpräsidenten*. Stuttgart: Deutscher Verlag.

European Commission (1995) *Progress Report on the Preparation of the Changeover to the Single European Currency*, 10 May.

—— (1995) *Une Monnaie pour l'Europe, Livre Vert sur les modalités pratiques d'introduction de la monnaie unique*, 31 May.

Fabra, Paul (1987), 'Le SME: un étalon-deutschemark une zone franc?, *Le Monde*, 27 September.

Financial Times (1983) 'Double delight in Paris, but no thanks', 31 March.

—— (1991) 'Pöhl attacks use of ecu as substitute for D-Mark', 2 March.

—— (1992) 'Kohl paid secret Friday visit to the Bundesbank', 19 September.

—— (1992) 'The monetary tragedy of errors that led to currency chaos', 12 December.

—— (1992) 'The day Germany planted a currency time bomb', 13 December.

—— (1994) 'Odd couple's testing tiffs', 24 March.

—— (1994) 'How Kohl linked EMI choice to Delors succession', 26 October.

—— (1995) 'Cracks around the edges', 27 February.

—— (1995) 'Why Europe needs a single currency', 26 May.

—— (1995) 'German banks call for quick action on eurocurrency name', 1 September.

—— (1995) 'Euro-bank takes cautious line on monetary union', 15 November.

—— (1996) 'France rejects link to D-Mark', 13 February.

—— (1996) 'France wants rein on non-emu states', 21 February.

—— (1996) 'Why bond markets reign supreme for German investors', 28 February.

—— (1996) 'Row as France presses for Italy's return to ERM', 18 March.

—— (1996) 'German work consensus turns to conflict', 25 April.

—— (1996) 'France and Germany struggle to turn their European dreams into reality', 14 December.

—— (1996) 'New Euro clearing system could ease target tensions', 14 December.

Frankfurter Allgemeine Zeitung (1990) 'EG-Länder werden auf Gedeih und Verderb miteinander verbunden', 26 September.

—— (1996) 'Der Euro verändert die Rolle der Bundesbank', 18 March.

Futuribles (1985) 'Les orientations de la Commission des Communautés Européennes', March.

Garton Ash, Timothy (1993) *In Europe's Name: Germany and the Divided Continent.* London: Jonathan Cape.

Genscher, Hans-Dietrich (1989) 'Die Rolle der Bundesrepublik Deutschland bei der Vollendung des Europäischen Währungssystems', *Ergebnisse einer Fachtagung: Strategien und Ergebnisse für die Zukunft Europas.* Gütersloh: Bertelsmann Stiftung.

—— (1995) *Erinnerungen.* Berlin: Siedler Verlag.

German Monopolies Commission 1973–83 (1987) *Summaries of the First Five Biennial Reports.* Baden-Baden: Nomos.

Gros, Daniel and Neils Thygesen (1992) *European Monetary Integration: From the European Monetary System to European Monetary Integration.* London: Longman.

Handelsblatt (1989) 'Europakonferenz: Kohl will Mitbestimmungsmodell offensiv vertreten', 31 August.

Hort, Peter (1988) 'Ein Bilanz der deutschen EG-Präsidentschaft', *Europa-Archiv* 15, 421–8.

Kohl, Helmut (1988a) 'Europas Zukunft – Vollendung des Binnenmarktes 1992' in *Bulletin des Presse- und Informationsamtes der Bundesregierung*, 42, 22 March, 333.

—— (1988b) 'Erklärung des Bundeskanzlers zur Eröffnung des nationalen Europa-Konferenz in Bonn' in *Bulletin des Presse- und Informationsamtes der Bundesregierung*, 172, 9 December, 1525.

Ludlow, Peter (1982) *The Making of the European Monetary System.* London: Butterworths.

Ministère de l'Economie, des Finances et du Budget (1986) *Le Livre Blanc sur la réforme du financement de l'économie*, Paris: Ministère de l'Economie, des Finances et du Budget.

Monde, Le (1983) 'Le poids du service de la dette éxtérieure interdit pour longtemps à la France une politique de relance', 15 November.

—— (1989) 'Les Douze acceptent que le peuple allemand retrouve son identité', 10–11 December.

—— (1995) 'L'autre scénario monétaire', 18 May.

—— (1995) 'Le passage à la monnaie unique', 15 November.

—— (1996) 'La coalition du chancelier Kohl se divise sur la relance de l'économie', 18 January.

—— (1996) 'L'Europe selon Chirac', 25 March.

OECD, *Statistics of Foreign Trade*, Series A.

Presse- und Informationsamt der Bundesregierung (1988), *Bulletin*, No. 40, p. 333, 22 March, Bonn.

Puaux, François (1989) *La politique internationale des années quatre-vingt.* Paris: Presses Universitaires de France.

Süddeutsche Zeitung (1995) 'Plädoyer für schnelle Währungsunion', 1 September.

—— (1996) 'Vier von fünf Deutschen gegen den Euro 1999', 1 February.

Une Enquête du Monde: Vingt Ans de Réussite Allemande (1979). Paris: Economica.

Waigel, Theo (1995) 'Europäische Einheit und Stabilitätspakt für Europa'. Bundesministerium der Finanzen, 29/95, 8 November.

Welt, Die (1990) 'Pöhl pocht auf Unabhängigkeit einer Europäischen Notenbank', 4 September.

Zeit, Die (1990) 'Am Sankt-Nimmerleins-Tag?', 7 September.

Zelikow, Philip and Condoleeza Rice (1995) *Germany Unified and Europe Transformed: A Study in Statecraft.* Cambridge MA: Harvard University Press.

Zerah, Dov (1993) *Le Système Financier Français: Dix Ans de Mutations,* Paris: La Documentation française.

3

FRANCE, GERMANY, THE IGC AND EASTERN ENLARGEMENT

Patrick McCarthy

Introduction

This chapter concerns the way Eastern enlargement has been handled by the Franco-German couple. The emphasis is not placed on the candidacies of Central European countries and their viewpoint is, yet again, neglected. Our aim is to throw light on the Franco-German relationship by analysing how the two countries have dealt with a problem about which they held very different views. We shall argue that they drew closer together, albeit with painful slowness, and that their difficulties and modest success have been reflected in the EU approach to Eastern enlargement as well as to the Intergovernmental Conference which was supposed to make the institutional reforms that were considered a necessary prerequisite to enlargement. At the same time, France and Germany have no monopoly on Eastern enlargement. Other countries, whether large like Italy or small like Portugal, exert some influence, while institutional actors, such as the Commission, are also active.

Since the Franco-German relationship was formed to resolve the traditional conflicts between the two countries and thus avoid the troubles that these differences provoked in Europe, it is worth recalling that the 1930s saw a struggle between France and Germany for influence in Eastern Europe. Aware of the fragility of the new states carved out of the Habsburg Empire, France helped form the Petite-Entente that linked Romania, Yugoslavia and Czechoslovakia. France signed treaties, made loans and used the weapon of its culture. But Germany was militarily and economically too strong. Hubert Beuve-Méry, future editor of *Le Monde*, watched from Prague as the Romanians used a French loan to buy German weapons (with French permission). The francophile Edward Benès believed as long as he humanly could in the Paris–Prague axis and Beuve-Méry denounced the contradiction of forming alliances in the East and sitting on the Maginot Line. Neither could prevent Germany from breaking up the Petite-Entente. Long before Munich, the Third Republic demonstrated that it could not compete with the Reich in Eastern Europe.[1]

In 1989 there was neither a Third Republic nor a Reich, but it may not be too fanciful to imagine that François Mitterrand felt the Fifth Republic would fare no better against the Bundesrepublik. He may also have felt that de Gaulle's *Ostpolitik* had made less impact than Brandt's. The Franco-German relationship was from the outset 'a struggle to co-operate' and the Soviet withdrawal from Eastern Europe was one of the many problems in the relationship, as the French government perceived it.

Like other problems, it had to be tackled and a common Franco-German position found. If no common position existed, then the conflicting views could not be allowed to undermine co-operation as a whole. If a strongly held common position could be advanced via the EU, its chances of being translated into Community policy were good. A weak agreement meant that leadership on the issue would pass to other EU actors and the chances of effective action reduced.

Two other problems predated the fall of the Berlin Wall. Despite its relatively high growth in 1988 and 1989, approximately 4 per cent, France ran a trade deficit with Germany of FF50 billion in 1988 and unemployment remained obstinately high at 9.5 per cent in 1989. Attempts to persuade the Bundesbank to reduce interest rates failed. Second, when France demonstrated sympathy for German opposition to NATO's desire to modernise the Lance Missile, it had strayed from its role as a security power. Yet this role was considered important because it balanced German economic power.

There is neither space nor need to recount Mitterrand's view of German reunification.[2] Suffice to note that Mitterrand was unable to play the role of guarantor and that his meeting with Gorbachev at Kiev did not produce a Franco-Soviet partnership to ensure German good behaviour. Yet Mitterrand was less weak than he appeared because his goal of ensuring good behaviour was shared by the German government itself, which had no desire to repeat the Reich's 'successes' in Eastern Europe and still needed to co-operate with France. After neglecting his EC partners in order to seize the opportunity for reunification, Helmut Kohl returned to Adenauer's principle that the German state must be rooted in Western Europe.

In fact, neither the German nor the French position was so simple. One way to tie Germany down in Europe was monetary integration. However, for the Bundesbank and even for Helmut Kohl, 'being tied down' did not exclude imposing on the EC/EU the German model of a strong currency and a horror of inflation. For Mitterrand 'tying Germany down' meant gaining some influence over Germany monetary policy, that would enable France to expand its economy and reduce unemployment. Here a fresh problem would be created: France and Germany would take quite different views of the Euro.

But one may sum up French policy from March 1990 until the elections of 1993 as a bid to gain concessions from Germany, in return for accepting reunification, which would strengthen France's position in its dialogue with Germany, in the EC as a whole and via the EC in the world. Such a blend of agreement and competition constituted the essence of Franco-German co-operation.

1990–93: Rapid enlargement versus indefinite postponement

How did Eastern enlargement fit into these visions? To Germany it was the obvious solution to the problems caused by the break-up of the Communist system that had provided order of a kind, however unpleasant. Without EU enlargement, Germany might be left on its own to cope with re-emerging nationalism and economic disarray. With enlargement, the entire EU would help, but no other country could seriously compete with Germany for influence in Eastern Europe. By 1994 German trade with the region represented as much as 14 per cent of its total trade and in 1997 Germany was the leading trading partner of Poland, Hungary and the Czech Republic.[3] Yet a Germany simultaneously tied down in the EU could hardly be accused of following a *Sonderweg*, an autonomous foreign policy, or of recreating a German zone of influence in central Europe, a new Mitteleuropa.

Predictably, France has been unable to compete with Germany in Eastern markets and in 1997 it did not figure among the first three trading partners of any of the above-mentioned countries. To take only one more example, when Chirac visited Warsaw in 1996, 20 per cent of Polish imports came from Germany and only 5 per cent from France.[4] Total Polish–German trade amounted to DM25 billion. German businessmen used old contacts, drew on and helped expand the Poles' knowledge of the German language and, while obsessed with not appearing arrogant, demonstrated a knowledge of the Polish economy that French business-men could not match.

Germany has continued to pursue the goal of Eastern enlargement, although an increasing awareness of the problems posed to the EU, and hence to Germany, by taking in anywhere from four to nine new Eastern countries, as well as the effort of absorbing the DDR, has caused the Kohl government to move more slowly. In 1997 it was doubtful whether even Poland, Hungary and the Czech Republic will obtain limited membership by 2003. There were many reasons for this but flagging German will, which reflects an overloading of the political system and of economic resources, was certainly one.

A watershed in the evolution of its policy was the German presidency of the EU Council of Ministers in the second half of 1994. Hopes of a rapid enlargement vanished at the very moment when it was most eagerly sought by the government. But the government had too much to do. France linked movement on the East with movement on the South and the EU was embroiled in tasks that ranged from the European Free Trade Association (EFTA) enlargement to the domestic economic difficulties of most member countries. Yet if the 1994 Essen summit set no timetable for Eastern enlargement, it did make the process irreversible.

Within Germany not all political actors held the same view. From the outset, the Kohl government wanted to ensure economic and political stability on its eastern border. Employers saw the possibility of investing in countries with low labour costs, while the trade unions sought to prevent the development of cheap-wage countries and the Bundesbank was preoccupied with monetary union.

France has gone through three periods of policy, the first of which was the Mitterrand solution that might be defined as indefinite postponement. Mitterrand gave priority to tying Germany down and tilting the balance of power in the existing EU towards France. The result was the Maastricht Treaty with its plan for monetary union and its proposal for a Common Foreign and Security Policy (CFSP). In the name of deepening political unity, small concessions were made to Germany through the extension of Qualified Majority Voting (QMV) and extra power to the European Parliament (EP). Of course monetary union represented a gamble that the French rather than the German version would win out and that the conditions of entry imposed by the Bundesbank would not prove unduly arduous. The second part of the gamble has been lost, which has damaged national economies, weakened public support for the EU and thus made Eastern enlargement more difficult.

In 1990, Mitterrand's plan for Eastern Europe was a Grand Confederation that recalled de Gaulle's vision of a Europe from the Atlantic to the Urals. It was to serve four purposes: it would exclude the US; it would include the USSR, regarded as an essential partner in any European security settlement; it would offer a framework to the Eastern countries; and it would be too loose a grouping to interfere with the process of tying Germany down in the West. It was the perfect instrument of postponement, except that it irritated the countries in question. Vaclav Havel declared that the Confederation must not slow down entry to the EU but Mitterrand stated that the Eastern Europeans must wait 'for decades'.[5]

Both France and Germany made distinctions among the former Communist countries. A full discussion of this theme would require a separate chapter but the main areas of French and German agreement and disagreement may be listed. The two agreed that the less democratic should receive less help.

Poland was a special case to Germany because of the Nazi *Blitzkrieg* (*Süddeutsche Zeitung*, 26 April 1995)[6] and to France because Kohl's tardiness in recognising the Oder-Neisse boundary had provided Mitterrand with his sole convincing argument against rapid reunification. Moreover, Poland was the only excommunist country, with the exception of the USSR, that possessed strong armed forces. A special relationship grew up among the three countries. In August 1991 the French, Polish and German foreign ministers met to discuss developments in Yugoslavia and the three countries formed the 'Weimar triangle'.

France supported Romania with which it had longstanding cultural ties, whereas one always feels that, when German leaders discuss the Baltic states, they dream of reviving the Hanseatic League. Similarly, Germany was bound to be the leading partner for Czechoslovakia. Although the process by which Skoda chose Volkswagen over Renault for its joint venture was long, the result was unsurprising.

During the Mitterrand period the events of Yugoslavia helped to divide France from Germany on Eastern European issues. To simplify, Germany was pro-Slovenia and pro-Croatia, whereas France was initially pro-Serbia or at least feared that the first two would fall under German influence as soon as they became independent. However, France was willing to participate in an EU intervention force, whereas Germany felt its constitution prevented it from joining up. The reluctance of other EU members, especially Britain, which feared becoming embroiled in a second Northern Ireland, condemned the EU to inaction. Despite Mitterrand's theatrical trip to Sarajevo after the EU summit of 1992, there was no EU military intervention in Bosnia.

The Yugoslav war demonstrated to France and Germany the absence of a joint military force capable of intervening in trouble spots and able to serve as the nucleus of an EU force. Steps towards these goals were the creation of the Franco-German army corps in October 1991 and the sections of the Maastricht Treaty that dealt with the CFSP and with the Western European Union (WEU). However, the corps was and is of dubious military value, while the Maastricht wording left the WEU poised between the EU and NATO. While the Yugoslav wars may in the very long run spur the Franco-German couple and/or the EU to improve their defence forces, they have so far demonstrated the need for American leadership and for NATO. They have also shown that in the area of EU defence Britain is needed.

The civil war removed Yugoslavia as a candidate to enter the EU and replaced it by Slovenia, with which preliminary agreements were reached by 1993. Then, as if to demonstrate again that France and Germany cannot dominate the EU, the Berlusconi government, backed by the ex-Fascist National Alliance, blocked talks about associate membership until Slovenia recognised the rights of Italian owners who had left the country under Communism to recover their property. Not until Berlusconi fell in December 1994 could the issue be approached in a more equable manner.

Meanwhile the narrow victory of the yes vote in the 1992 French referendum on Maastricht announced the beginning of a difficult period for Franco-German co-operation and for the EU. After a brief moment, when reunification boosted French exports to Germany and reduced the French trade deficit from FF59 billion in 1989 to FF42 billion in 1990, high German interest rates were held responsible, rightly or wrongly, for rising French unemployment. Germany was absorbed in rebuilding former East Germany, a task which proved more difficult than anticipated. In September 1992 Britain and Italy were forced out of the EMS. Throughout the EU subsidiarity became the magic word.

The Eastern countries suffered from the EU's weakness. In the years after 1989 they looked to Western Europe for aid but more eagerly for trade. Disillusionment was rapid and in 1993 the Hungarian foreign minister accused the EU of 'treachery'.[7] The goods that the Eastern countries wished to sell were in highly sensitive areas: agriculture, which would have meant reshaping the Common Agricultural Policy (CAP), textiles which were a key export for South European countries, and steel, where the EU was trying to cut its own production.

'Europe agreements' had been signed with Poland, Hungary and what became the Czech Republic and Slovakia in March 1992. Romania and Bulgaria followed suit but the move towards free trade between the EU and its eastern neighbours was marred by the EU's defence of its own sunset industries. Portugal, very dependent on textiles, showed how well one small country could defend its national interests. Splits that existed already in the EU were widened: France pointed out that the admission of the Central Europeans would double the cost of the CAP, while Britain barely hid her aims of using enlargement to scrap the CAP and to prevent further moves towards political unity. Small wonder that Vaclav Klaus declared himself a 'Europessimist'.[8]

What are the causes of this feeble Western European response? To affirm that the EU can only move ahead boldly when France and Germany are in agreement is correct but simplistic. France and Germany are bound to have differing views and interests and the real question is why they were unable to overcome them. One answer is that on this issue the differences were unusually great, and involving other countries would shortly grow into a North–South division. Moreover, since this was a new issue, France and Germany had not had much practice at working out a common position.

A second set of causes would start with the limits of Franco-German power in the EU and point to the blocking role played by Italy, Portugal and, in its own way, Britain. The conclusion might be that in its present form the EU is barely capable of developing and promoting active policies. A third set of causes might begin with the assertion that most, albeit not all, EU initiatives occur during periods of high economic growth. Without accepting such a general proposition, we would like to suggest that the energy and the economic hardship that have gone into monetary union have drained member countries. This has weakened the EU in other areas.

Of course the picture would be changed drastically, if one made the judgement that the EU's record in assisting the Central Europeans was moderately good. After all, the ex-Communist countries were starting from very far back and yet transition agreements were worked out by the end of 1994. One should give the credit for this progress partly to Germany for its energy and for bringing France along, and partly to other actors like the Commission. While not omitting the positive actions of the EU, our viewpoint is that more could have been done so the key question remains why it was not done.

Mitterrand's policy of indefinite postponement had become, outside the islands of the Commission and Germany, the unofficial EU policy. Its success coincided with his party's crushing defeat in the 1993 parliamentary elections. The Socialists plunged from 37 per cent of the vote to 20 per cent. They too were victims of the EU's inability to relaunch its economies.

1993–94: From French parliamentary elections to German presidency

During this period, which covers most of 1993 and all of 1994, there was a keener interest in Eastern enlargement, even if it resulted in less action than was hoped. The first reason was that the EU institutions, working for political reasons at a snail's pace, finally got the Maastricht Treaty ratified after a second referendum in Denmark and persistent foot-dragging by the British Conservatives. This left a window for other issues before the Treaty was to be re-examined. In reality, enlargement meant first the EFTA countries which were mostly affluent and could help finance the Mediterranean members of the EU. This turned out to present difficulties of its own and much time was spent discussing Arctic agriculture. The enlargement was not completed until 1995 and even then Norway voted against ratifying the agreement.

Eastern enlargement also moved forward when in the Copenhagen summit of June 1993 the Council of Ministers declared that the associated members 'shall become members ... but must satisfy political and economic conditions'. Moreover no date was set.[9] Yet there were other developments: the six associate members formed councils that were to work with the Commission on satisfying the conditions, which included maintaining stable democratic institutions and operating a market economy.

Meanwhile negotiations over Europe Agreements were begun in February 1994 with the Baltic states. The same procedures were to be followed: free trade, associate status and full membership. This breakthrough followed a statement by Kohl in October 1993 which put the Baltic states ahead of Romania and Bulgaria in the membership queue. Kohl's remarks were part of a renewed diplomatic campaign by Germany to settle the Eastern question. One reason was that, in a brief revival of the Cold War, pressures of different kinds were exerted by Russia and the USA. In Russia the flare-up of nationalism offered a potential threat to the Central Europeans and the USA responded by impressing on the EU the need to act. Another reason was the German parliamentary election of October 1994, which made Kohl resolve not to run on a European platform that consisted solely of giving up the mark.

A third reason, although a complex one, was the change of government in France. It can hardly have pleased Kohl, who had differences with the French right between 1986 and 1988 and who had not hidden his preference for Mitterrand in the 1988 presidential elections. Yet the Gaullists, the major right-wing party, had mixed views on Germany, the EU and Eastern enlargement, as well as on NATO and the USA. On the last two they were critical of Mitterrand for simply resisting every American initiative. Since the world was no longer bipolar, NATO could not maintain its simple, centralised structure but would form subgroups. Power would be more diffuse and US hegemony would be weakened. It was time for France to return to the military wing of NATO, provided the USA agreed to share power.[10]

In turn this led the Gaullists to take a fresh look at NATO and WEU enlargement. Provided it did not take place solely under American aegis, the expansion of the security apparatus to countries like Poland and Romania would mesh with France's plans to promote the CFSP and the WEU and to return to the military wing of NATO. France would enhance its counterbalancing security role. From this some Gaullists drew a more general conclusion: France had no reason to fear Eastern enlargement, which would loosen the often asphyxiating tie with Germany and which corresponded to de Gaulle's vision of a broad Europe of the Fatherlands liberated from the bipolar universe.

Not all Gaullists held all these views. Philippe Séguin liked the last part and continued to entertain grave doubts about monetary union and the Europe of Maastricht. Chirac, who began his presidential campaign in autumn 1994, was biding his time. The wing of the party that was most orthodoxly Europeanist, led by Prime Minister Edouard Balladur, was closest to Mitterrand's position. Above all, Balladur wanted to tie Germany down with monetary union and on his visit to Warsaw in July 1994 he went some way towards repeating Mitterrand's proposition to Havel. Certainly, Poland should join the EU 'one day' but no 'precise calendar' could be fixed.[11]

In the meantime the security concerns of the Eastern countries should be met. Balladur proposed a Stability Pact to monitor border disputes and equal rights for ethnic minorities. This sounded rather like Mitterrand's Grand Confederation except that, on this point, true to the new Gaullist thought, Balladur did not exclude the USA and Canada.[12] An inaugural conference was held in May 1994. To deal more specifically with an unstable Russia, Balladur planned to offer the Eastern nations 'associate membership' in the WEU. After opposition from existing associate members like Turkey, the Eastern nations were given 'associate partnership'. They continued to seek membership in NATO and were supported, with different nuances, by France and Germany.

One might sum up this second phase by stating that the French elections and continued German pressure had changed France's view of Eastern enlargement from indefinite postponement to a 'yes, but when'. Continuity with the first period was provided by the Minister for Europe, Alain Lamassoure, an associate of Giscard d'Estaing. Shortly after his appointment he advised the Central and Eastern countries to form a free trade area among themselves. They were unenthusiastic and pointed out that, in order to attract investment, they must export to hard-currency countries. Foreign Minister Alain Juppé, who had received German help during the agricultural dispute of the Uruguay Round, was more ready to break with Mitterrand's line.

So this was a case where a domestic political change in one of the two countries altered the Franco-German relationship. Yet the differences were not all of a kind. In the area that concerns us, the Gaullists were in general more favourable to the German view of Eastern enlargement. But in other areas they, or some of them, were more difficult partners for Germany. Two Gaullist voters out of three had voted no in the Maastricht referendum, while Séguin was the champion of an alternative economic strategy, *l'autre politique*.

Meanwhile, Eastern enlargement was overshadowed not only by the negotiations concerning the European Free Trade Association (EFTA) states' negotiations to enter the EU, but also by two other issues. The first was EU institutions. Drawn up for a community of six, they were strained by the increase to twelve and would be overwhelmed by expansion to twenty or twenty-five. Yet it was not easy to agree on changes. Spain wanted the blocking vote against QMV kept at twenty-three. If, as suggested, it were raised to twenty-seven, the olive-oil alliance (Italy, Spain, Portugal and Greece) would fall below it. Spain found an ally in Britain which simply resisted any and every attempt at more efficient integration. France, which had, under German pressure, agreed to an expansion of QMV, still held to an EU that was, in Lamassoure's words, a 'community of nations' rather than a federation or a confederation.[13] In return for obtaining an expanded QMV, the German government, which was pressured by the Bundesbank to create some sort of European government to which the Euro could be entrusted, also postponed federalism until the distant future. So France and Germany had a common position but it was not a creative breakthrough. The two were no longer providing leadership for an EU that was floundering.

The second and more controversial debate of 1994 was triggered by Karl Lamers and Wolfgang Schäuble of the German Christian Democratic Party who called for a hard core of countries that would press ahead with integration, leaving the others to follow at their own speed.[14] Although this was not a new idea and although there existed groups of countries, such as Benelux, that were more closely tied to one another than to the rest of the community, Lamers and Schäuble created a storm of protest. It was all the greater because they were widely regarded as expressing a view that Kohl would have liked to express but could not. Italy, already outside the EMS, feared permanent relegation to the second division. To Southern countries, a hard core consisting of Germany, Benelux, France and per-haps Denmark would enshrine the domination of the North in the EU. In fact, by stirring up the already restive South, Lamers and Schäuble made northern hegemony less likely.

The key question was France's reaction. If one assumes that its major goal was to obtain monetary union, then the Lamers–Schäuble plan offered a short cut. But France sought not monetary union in itself but a measure of control over its own and Germany's monetary policy. To be locked up in a box with Germany and the Netherlands was to risk having no influence over the future European Central Bank and falling under German domination. The alternative route to monetary union was longer, but France might arrive there with South European allies which shared its irritation with the Bundesbank's obsessively anti-inflationary policy.

The resolution to resist German hegemony was common to Mitterrand, Chirac and Balladur, not to mention Séguin. Public opinion, alarmed by the monetary crisis of mid-1993, when the EMS band was widened to 30 per cent, and troubled by high unemployment, which defied Balladur as it had defied his predecessors, Bérégovoy and Cresson, was cool towards further internationalism. It would have been hard to explain to the country how French interests were served by entering a German-dominated core. So France reverted to its traditional habit of seeking allies to reinforce its position in the competition/dialogue with Germany. This is the policy which culminated in November 1996 in French and Spanish support for the lira's re-entry into the EMS and Italy's participation in monetary union.

In 1994 French policy was summed up by Balladur's 'concentric circles', which also allowed for overlapping circles. The concentric structure would begin with an EU which would gradually be extended to include the Central Europeans. The evolution of French policy was clear when Balladur stated in November 1994 that 'the broadening of the EU is inevitable' and cited the associated members whom France had 'no moral right, no political reason and no economic interest' in excluding. Although this was consistent with his July affirmations, the emphasis was no longer on the waiting but on the joining. The 'when' of the 'yes, but when' had drawn closer. The outer circle would be roughly the nations of the Stability Pact, which appeared ever more like a French renaming of the Organisation for Security and Co-operation in Europe (OSCE).

The real answer to Schäuble and Lamers was the notion of circles within the EU circle: 'I am deliberately saying circles and not one circle'.[15] France and Germany might indeed form a core of countries that would initiate monetary union but simultaneously France and Britain might form a core that would press ahead with CFSP. Other candidates for the CFSP circle were Spain and Italy. The flaws in this approach are obvious. Franco-British military co-operation works well as long as it remains a technical matter handled by experts. The moment it becomes political the contradiction between the Gaullist and Atlanticist viewpoints causes co-operation to collapse. Balladur might hope that the new Gaullist view of the USA would prevent this. Yet the problem of Britain's general lack of enthusiasm for the EU would remain.

Still France was seeking to respond actively to the Lamers–Schäuble proposal and was no longer adopting a stance that could be defined as conservative or favouring a small EU. Now France responded to the renewed German pressure with a suggested trade-off. At the Franco-German summit of 26 November, Germany wanted to offer early membership to the Visegrad four while France defended the claims of Romania and Bulgaria. But the new element was the case made by France for an opening to the Mediterranean. The compelling reason was the need to find a solution for Algeria before its virtual civil war spilled over into France. But more stable countries like Morocco needed encouragement. The EU was to set up a Euro-Med Economic Area. This was anything but an exclusively French initiative. A conference on the Mediterranean would be held at Barcelona during the Spanish presidency in the second half of 1995, while Italy had a long-standing interest in the area.[16] Euro-Med represents an example of France's 'Southern strategy'. The entry of this new actor was to increase enormously the cost of Eastern enlargement since a smaller but very considerable sum of money was, concomitantly, to go to the South. In effect, between 1995 and 1999 ECU 6.7 billion was to march east and 4.7 billion south.

The German presidency ended without a grand triumph but with reasonable progress. To symbolise it, the heads of six Central European countries, the Visegrad four plus Romania and Bulgaria, were invited to Essen at the end of the EU summit. They were allowed ninety minutes of discussion, lunch and a photo opportunity. They were also warned by Kohl not to expect rapid membership.

Can one conclude that Germany refrained from pressing for Eastern enlargement because of the need to maintain good relations with its prime ally? This is partly true but far too simple. First, France succeeded in rallying a group of EU countries to the view that there were other priorities. Germany had by now realised that it could not afford to fund the Central Europeans and the Mediterranean as well as pouring aid into former East Germany and meeting the Maastricht criteria that it had itself laid down. In the reluctant decision to slow up the pace of Eastern enlargement, German economic self-interest was as important as the struggle to co-operate with France. But the Essen summit marked a stride towards Eastern enlargement. The governments of associate member countries would be invited to future summits and so many assurances had been given that Eastern enlargement had become inevitable.

1995–96: President Chirac, IGC and obsession with monetary union

Chirac's election as French President in 1995 had contradictory effects on the overlapping problems we have been examining. Chirac succeeded in overtaking Balladur on the first decisive round by stressing that his top priority was domestic unemployment and that the French state was not rendered powerless to help its citizens by its commitments to Germany, the EU and monetary union. Never troubled by contradictions, Chirac switched policies after he was elected and gave priority to meeting the Maastricht criteria and hence to cutting the deficit. There would have been protests in France anyway but, by arousing expectations he could not meet, Chirac worsened them and made Prime Minister Alain Juppé's position all but impossible. Chirac also increased public discontent with 'Europe'. Still he pushed ahead with the more dynamic foreign policy that his advisors like Pierre Lellouche had been advocating since 1993.

This included the construction of a large Europe that found a space for the poorer Easterners, expanding military operations in Bosnia to help the Muslims, seeking a greater role for France in the CFSP and in NATO, asserting French power in Africa and in the Middle East and resuming tests on France's independent deterrent. In his speech before the Institut des Hautes Etudes de Défense Nationale (IHEDN) Juppé called on the EU countries to make a greater effort to defend themselves.[17] In the Gaullist tradition Chirac gave priority to foreign and security policy. Germany, however, grew less activist as its economic difficulties mounted and the domestic debate about monetary union sharpened.

In 1995 came the opening to the South. Plans were made to launch the Euro-Med Economic Space: by the year 2010 the EU would arrive at free trade with Algeria, Tunisia and Morocco, but not Libya, as well as with a group of Middle East countries (Egypt, Lebanon, Jordan, Syria), which made its participation dependent on progress in its talks with Israel, and between Israel and Palestine, Cyprus and Malta, which were then hoping to become EU members, and Turkey, which the EU had sadly neglected. The twelve countries were encouraged to develop free trade among themselves and to improve their political ties.[18] The value of the Euro-Med project is obvious, although one should not expect dramatic short-term results. If the project reflects the different Franco-German views of the world, on this point the two were able to reconcile these differences.

The IGC was a more complex matter. The review process was initiated at the Corfu summit of mid-1994 and a Reflection Group was set up to fix the agenda. At this point the IGC ceased to be a bureaucratic requirement and came to life. It had a shadowy existence because there was no consensus on why the IGC was being held or what it was supposed to achieve. One topic that could not be avoided was institutional reform, a prerequisite both for Eastern integration and for monetary union. But what kind of reform was required? Kohl needed to show there was political unity but he did not, like France, want the political authorities to share in monetary decisions. If the EU expanded to twenty or twenty-five nations, then a Commission where each country had at least one member and a Council of Ministers that took so little account of population could hardly continue.

Yet institutional reform continued to prove elusive. Britain saw federalists under every stone, while the small countries cherished their right to a commissioner. The Franco-German couple did not galvanise the IGC as the Mitterrand–Kohl statement on defence had galvanised the 1990 IGC. No other actor could offer leadership. The weary phrase 'democratic deficit' was bandied around but there could be no dramatic change in procedures, such as a substantial increase in the powers of the European Parliament. Scepticism about the EU was directed less at its lack of democracy than at its inefficiency.

The German foreign minister, Klaus Kinkel, had made the by now usual appeal on behalf of the Eastern countries, couched in language that German leaders favour. Kinkel introduced a post-war theme when he argued that Western Europe's self-renewal, undertaken in the 1940s, should be carried over into the East. This would mark the end of the post-war era since Germany, Austria, Poland, the Czech Republic and Hungary would cease to live in a political order that had, so Kinkel maintained, been invented by Hitler and Stalin. Once again, Eastern enlargement was depicted as a deeply personal issue for Germans.[19]

So the period when Germany had played such a destructive role in Eastern Europe would come to an end. For the same reason Kinkel spoke, albeit in general terms, about the need for NATO expansion and for an agreement with Russia. The German debate about the nation's past and future, a debate that ran parallel to the discussions in other Western European countries, was continued in the run up to the IGC by historian Michael Stürmer. The movement towards a Europe of the Fatherlands would reopen the national question in Germany. Germany had not yet decided, Stürmer argued, whether it wished to be a nation or not and whether it wished to take over the leadership of the EU or not.[20] Implicit in this article was the theme, raised by Lamers and Schäuble, that, if the EU did not reorganise itself and deal with the problems of Eastern Europe, Germany might deal with them on its own, which would reawaken traditional fears.[21] Another warning against isolation and arrogance came from Helmut Schmidt who saw traces of both in the Bundesbank's determination to obtain a strong Euro.[22]

These fears were alive in France where the Chirac government sought to assuage them by accepting the challenge in the East. In September 1996 Chirac visited Warsaw to set a schedule for Poland's admission to the EU and to NATO. He called Poland France's 'Eastern sister' and mentioned the cultural bonds between the two countries.[23] Chirac's goal was to stop seeing Eastern expansion as an inevitable defeat for France. Similarly, a strengthened CFSP would give France European backing for a world role that would help dispel the pessimistic mood that pervaded the country.

These national monologues, each containing its own vision of 'Europe', shaped the agenda of the IGC but diminished the chances of its success. Further obstacles came from the national monologues of other countries: Britain was determined to retain what it perceived as its independence, while Italy wanted above all to re-enter the leading group of EU countries. As always there were several Europes: most countries had their own vision which they wanted to impose on the competing visions. (The Central European countries also have their national monologues, which we are once more neglecting.) Moreover, each nation was distracted by other concerns. The IGC began life under the Italian presidency when Italy was holding elections and it continued under the Irish presidency when Ireland sought above all to maintain good relations with Britain in the hope of reaching a solution for the North.

Such concerns could not be admitted but they were present as silences in the IGC debate. Officially separate but in fact a meta-narrative was the preparation for monetary union, the top priority for most countries. Nor had the terms 'core' and 'concentric circles' been forgotten. Of particular relevance to the CFSP were NATO's debates over its own Eastern enlargement and over the enhanced role of the Europeans. New issues were pressing: the so-called third pillar of internal security: immigration, police co-operation and drugs. The Central Europeans could not be blamed for thinking that they were being stranded in this labyrinth of words. Jacques Santer, who became head of the Commission in 1995, was eager to promote enlargement but he lacked Delors's prestige.

So expectations of the IGC were not high. In late 1994 *Der Spiegel* still felt that 'ever since Maastricht there has been no vision of what Europe might be'.[24] Enthusiasm for European unity was at a low ebb: only 41 per cent of the electorate bothered to vote in the Swedish elections to the European Parliament. Only 28 per cent of Spaniards described themselves as possessing a strong European identity, while in traditionally faithful Germany the figure was down to 42 per cent. This led Laurent Fabius to call the IGC 'the last chance to save the EU'.[25]

In late 1996 it appeared that the pessimists were right. The Irish presidency had produced a draft of the Maastricht-2 Treaty that offered several wordings to reflect several, unreconciled opinions.[26] Meanwhile the Council of Ministers' meeting of 13–14 December was, predictably, dominated by the question of whether countries entering the monetary union group should commit themselves to continued austerity.

Eastern enlargement had reached the paradoxical stage where Kohl and Chirac competed to insist that negotiations must begin soon, in 1998, and that membership would arrive quickly, in 2000, but great problems remain. The CAP, the reconciliation of South and East and more efficient institutions are merely a few. It seemed likely that the Eastern countries should prepare themselves for yet more waiting.[27]

Conclusion

Eastern enlargement proves that the Franco-German partnership remains a struggle to co-operate between two countries with different, often conflicting world views. Their very differences force them to hammer out agreements, if their historic method of solving their disputes is not to be repeated. The task of turning such agreements into steps towards European unity has also fallen to them. Yet at present they can do no more than reach compromises that permit but slow down Eastern enlargement and minimise institutional reform. Power in the EU could pass into other hands but, while initiatives are taken by institutional actors and third countries, there are no rivals capable of major or sustained efforts of leadership.

In December 1997, there seemed little reason to change either the story told above or the gloomy but not catastrophic judgement on the present state of the Franco-German relationship. There has been, however, another chapter in the still unfinished tale of Eastern expansion and fresh tensions have emerged in the 'struggle to co-operate'.

The tensions have been created, as so often before, by domestic political and economic changes. Chirac's decision to gamble on parliamentary elections brought to power the Parti Socialiste (PS), whose leader, Lionel Jospin, became prime minister on a platform of reconciling France's commitment to Europe (and to Germany) with a greater effort to reduce unemployment and repair the damage done to French society. It was reminiscent of Chirac's 1995 presidential campaign and, although Jospin has benefited from a certain improvement in the economy, he has not been significantly more successful in helping the jobless.

This has led Jospin to seek European and German co-operation in the form of an EU initiative to combat unemployment. He has also questioned the stability plan, designed to punish countries that stray from the path of austerity once they have entered the monetary union, and he has expressed a distaste for further cuts in social spending in order to meet the Maastricht criteria. Kohl's reaction has been predictable: a right-wing distrust of 'Keynesianism' and a determination to maintain the German version of monetary union.

But his stand forms part of what could be construed as a major German shift of policy towards Europe. At the Amsterdam summit of June 1997 Kohl resisted a proposal to increase the use of QMV in the Council of Ministers, demonstrating an opposition to greater European unity. Explanations for this resistance range from the thesis that a united Germany has, without conducting the debate advocated by Stürmer, arrived at the conclusion that it no longer needs a united Europe, to the more prosaic view that an economically strained Germany wished to cease being the 'paymaster' of the EU. An additional reason may be found in the opposition of the Länder to political centralisation.[28] This development in Germany is counterpoint to an increase in French enthusiasm for European unity, as demonstrated by the support of Jospin and Chirac (who has not been successful in defending the president's reserved domain of foreign policy) for the expansion of QMV.

Such a perverse reversal of position does not in our view suffice to explain the French and German policies. Kohl is guided by his need to stand for re-election in a Germany where popular reaction against giving up the Deutsche Mark is understandably strong. Whether it brings a lasting change in the German attitude towards Europe in general and France in particular depends on how monetary union turns out. At present Germany is overstrained: too weak to impose on the EU the shop-worn 'German model' (*Modell Deutschland*), but also too weak to dispense with France and Europe.

In French policy there is more continuity than might appear. The proposal for a reduction of the veto, that quintessentially Gaullist practice, is the framework for greater co-operation with, and influence over, Germany in two key areas. The first is monetary policy, where France seeks to strengthen political control over the euro at the expense of the European Central Bank. This is a more important issue than the nationality of the Bank's governor and the Jospin–Chirac tandem is following the strategy devised by Mitterrand to combat the German obsession with inflation. The second area is defence policy where France wants closer ties between the EU and the WEU.[29] In turn this reflects French disappointment with American reluctance to cede power in NATO, which has relaunched the de Gaulle–Mitterrand policy of creating a European defence entity founded on Franco-German military co-operation. Now, as before, Germany's desire not to offend the touchy USA is an obstacle to such co-operation. Now, as before, French policy is designed to use Europe and Germany in order to increase the power of the French state.

The old conflicts inherent in the relationship between France and Germany take new forms but neither country has convincing alternatives. There could not be a German–British axis until Blair changed his policy on monetary union. Despite the very real successes of the Prodi government, Italy still cannot and does not hope to lead Europe. Meanwhile the EU has moved forward with exasperating slowness. The Amsterdam agreement does not realise the IGC's goal of reforming EU institutions prior to the entry of new member states. Eastern enlargement, however, has acquired a momentum of its own and is going ahead, albeit with an equally exasperating slowness.

Five of the applicants, the three discussed above as well as Slovenia, whose cause was pressed by Germany, and Estonia (also backed by the Scandinavians), were declared by the Commission to be sufficiently far along the road towards democracy, the market economy and the *acquis* of the EU to begin the process that will culminate in full membership. The pace of their initiation will be influenced most by their own actions, although the EU and hence the Franco-German couple will spur or rein in the movement towards membership. The Commission will be the chief interlocutor of the aspirant members, leaving the French and the Germans to concentrate on the many unresolved problems of monetary union.

Notes

1 For Beuve-Méry's lucid vision see Greilsamer (1990).
2 See McCarthy, 'France looks at Germany, or how to become German (and European) while remaining French' (in McCarthy 1993a: 51–72).
3 *Financial Times*, 24 May 1995 and *Economist*, 15 March 1997, 30.
4 *Le Figaro*, 10 September 1996.
5 *Libération*, 18 June 1991
6 Kinkel, *Süddeutsche Zeitung*, 26 April 1995.
7 *Handelsblatt*, 15 April 1993.
8 *Financial Times*, 12 May 1993
9 *Financial Times*, 23 June 1993
10 See McCarthy (1993b).
11 *Le Monde*, 4 July 1994. Elsewhere Balladur distinguished between political and economic membership and argued that the former could be rapid (see Sutton 1994: 153–6). Sutton sees a greater difference between Mitterrand and Balladur.
12 *The Economist*, 19 June 1993, 35.
13 *Le Monde*, 31 May 1994.
14 *L'Expansion*, 9 January 1994, 68–71.
15 Edouard Balladur, *Le Monde*, 30 November 1994.
16 See Agnelli (1995).
17 *Le Figaro*, 11 September 1996.
18 *Financial Times*, 17 May 1995.
19 'Rede des Bundesministers des Auswärtigen, Klaus Kinkel', Das Auswärtige Amt, Mitteilung für die Presse, No. 1090/194.
20 *Financial Times*, 19 September 1995.
21 Lamers (1995: 68–71).
22 *La Republica*, 19 December 1996.
23 *Le Monde*, 13 September 1996.
24 *Der Spiegel*, 48/1994, 147.
25 *Le Monde*, 12 September 1996.
26 *The Economist*, 7 December 1996, 38.
27 I wish to thank Guido West, who has worked as my research assistant on this paper and who also allowed me to draw on his excellent thesis. I also wish to thank Karen Smith, who has been generous with her knowledge of Central Europe, Roger Morgan, who commented on my paper, and Douglas Webber, who suggested improvements for the final draft.
28 For an evaluation of the various reasons see *The Economist*, 15 November 1997, 27; *Le Monde*, 19 June 1997.
29 I wish to thank John L. Harper for providing me with information on EU developments in 1997.

References

Agnelli, Susanna (1995) *The Mediterranean and the Future of Europe*. Bologna: John Hopkins University, occasional papers.

Auswärtiges Amt, Mitteilung für die Presse No. 1090/194, 'Rede des Bundesministers des Auswärtigen, Klaus Kinkel'.

Greilsamer, Laurent (1990) *Hubert Beuve-Méry*. Paris: Fayard.

Lamers, Karl (1995) *L'Expansion* 9 January, 68–71.

McCarthy, Patrick (ed.) (1993a) *France-Germany 1983–1993: The Struggle to Co-operate*. New York: St Martin's Press.

—— (1993b) *The 1993 French Elections*. Washington: FPI Policy Briefs.

Sutton, Michael (1994) 'France and the EU's enlargement eastwards', *The World Today*, August– September, 153–6.

West, Guido (1996) *Der deutsch-französische Bilateralismus in der europäischen Integrations- entwicklung der neunziger Jahre*. Unpublished thesis, Free University of Berlin.

4

MASTERING DIFFERENCES

The Franco-German alliance and the liberalisation of European electricity markets

Susanne K. Schmidt

Introduction

European energy policy has been one of the least successful enterprises of the initiatives under the Single Market Programme. Only in mid-1996 could a compromise on a directive be reached, opening European electricity monopolies incrementally. For the final agreement on the electricity directive, a previous Franco-German understanding was paramount, just as the differences between Franco-German interests caused much of the long and protracted negotiations.

On the one side stood France with its centrally planned, monopolised, public electricity system, a reliance on nuclear power and long-term planning. With low electricity prices there was little need for reform of a system that was generally hailed as a successful example of a French *grand projet*. European attempts at policy change were regarded as an attack on the *service public*. As the largest exporter of electricity in Europe, many member states were dependent on French electricity exports. France could therefore hardly be isolated in the Council, where the governments also honoured the French difficulty to adapt to Europe, although formally recourse to Qualified Majority Voting was possible. On the other side stood Germany, with its decentralised system under mixed ownership, producing electricity at prices well above the European average, and being therefore in need of reform. Given these circumstances, the liberalisation of electricity seems particularly interesting from the point of view of the Franco-German relationship.

In the following I will first present the details of the two national electricity systems. On this basis, the history of the attempts to draw up a European policy will be told, with special consideration of the Franco-German role. We will see that this is indeed a special relationship, but not necessarily because of similar policy preferences. Being nevertheless united in valuing their alliance highly, it may amount to a significant asset, facilitating European integration despite significant differences. Similarly, the Commission has played a crucial role by seeking recourse in the Treaty's rules.

Entrenched national differences: French and German
electricity systems

Electricité de France (EdF) was founded in 1946 by a nationalisation law which expropriated the previously private power companies. It is the largest electricity company in the world. After the war, it was believed that only a public company, enjoying broad monopoly rights, could reconstruct and build up the French electricity system and make the necessary investments, especially in the country-side. Notably some municipal distribution companies remained outside of the monopoly, representing 5 per cent of consumption today. Regarding generation, some exemptions were granted to particularly small power stations or those used for self-generation. Over time, power generated by producers other than EdF has even decreased from 20 per cent in 1970, 15 per cent in 1980, to 6 per cent in 1994 (Poppe and Cauret 1997: 206). EdF's monopoly comprises '91 per cent of the installed power capacity, 94 per cent of electricity production, 95 per cent of the high-voltage (HV) transmission grid, and 95 per cent of electricity distribution' (ibid.: 205). EdF is regulated by the Directorate of Gas, Electricity and Coal in the Ministry of Industry. Since 1982, 'contract plans' have been negotiated every four years to define objectives.

After the oil crisis of the 1970s had demonstrated a dangerous dependence on foreign energy sources, France mounted a significant nuclear programme. In 1995 nuclear power plants provided 75 per cent of electricity production, and hydro power 18 per cent (Poppe and Cauret 1997: 205). Thanks to this programme, France could heighten its overall energy independence from 22 per cent in 1973 to 51 per cent in 1995. France accrued significant over-capacities in the 1980s, and electricity exports now amount to 18 per cent of domestic consumption (ibid.: 210). The nuclear power programme has hardly been challenged in France, unlike the EdF. The efficiency of the electricity system is well recognised, and the features of the *service public* remain uncontested. Among these is the principle of price equalisation, so that electricity tariffs are the same, whether the user is in Paris, the countryside, or even overseas territories. The French price level is much lower than the German one as the comparison of electricity prices shows (Figure 4.1).

The German electricity system is still largely determined by the pre-war Energy Management Act of 1935. The German system is a decentralised one. The dominant actors are the nine companies operating the national high-voltage grid, which generate 78 per cent of electricity. These companies differ widely in size, with the largest one supplying ten times more electricity than the smallest (Mez 1997: 234). The grid companies distribute 33 per cent of electricity to final, mainly industrial, customers, and the most part to the other two levels of the German electricity supply system: on the one hand there are eighty regional supply companies, which produce only 10 per cent but supply 35 per cent of all electricity; on the other, there are about 900 municipal utilities which generate about 12 per cent of electricity themselves and contract the rest either from the regional or the grid companies. Their share of total supplies is 32 per cent (VDEW 1997).

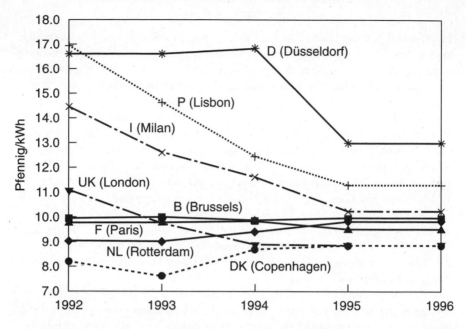

Figure 4.1 European electricity prices 1992–96 (10 MW/ 5000 h/a)

Source: VIK

The German electricity system is largely regulated through two different types of contracts. First, demarcation agreements exist between the utilities, guaranteeing each its own regional monopoly where no other utility will interfere. This cartel structure is exempted by the German Cartel Law. Second, the municipalities sign long-term concession agreements with a utility, for which they get concession fees, paid by the utility for the right of way. These fees are an important source of income for the municipalities, which any reform of the German system would have to safeguard.

German electricity generation in 1996 comprised 35.6 per cent nuclear, 28.6 per cent lignite, and 27.5 per cent hard coal. With this large share of fossil fuels and an environmentally conscious public, environmental regulation plays a large role for the German electricity supply industry (ESI). As a result, next to the responsible Federal Ministry for Economics, the Ministry for the Environment is an important actor in German electricity policy. In addition, there was a massive subsidisation of German coal which until 1995 was financed by the *Kohlepfennig* (coal penny), a levy imposed on all electricity customers (in 1993 it amounted to 7.5 per cent of electricity bills).

Attempting to integrate: European electricity policy

The significant differences between the French and the German electricity systems needed to be overcome for a common European policy. In view of French satisfaction with the domestic system and German eagerness to enact domestic reforms in an EU context, it is surprising that an agreement could be reached at all.

First steps

In the context of long and persistent French opposition to European electricity liberalisation, it is ironic that it was in fact France which initially dared to push European policies in this highly nationally regulated market. In February 1988 France filed an official complaint with the European Commission, alleging that German state aid to coal was distorting competition and blocking French exports to Germany. The fact that it is extremely rare for a government to call openly on the Commission to examine another member state points to the significance which France attached to this matter. Normally it falls on the Commission to initiate investigations into possible infringements of European Treaty law, since member states hesitate to make allegations against each other. This move came when the Commission was just starting to tackle the energy market. Despite the fact that two of the three founding treaties relate to energy, proposals for common policies had not fared well against the member states' interests to pursue national objectives in energy policy. In mid-1988, however, the Commission published a detailed policy document *The Single Market for Energy* (COM [88] 238 fin, 2 May 1988) in which it listed the persisting barriers to a single energy market and made some initial policy proposals. The fact that oil prices came down in 1986, lowering concerns for the security of supplies, was not unimportant for such a common policy plan.

In its document, the Commission estimated the costs of non-Europe at 0.5–1 per cent of the Community GDP in this sector, or ECU20–30 billion per year. Particular emphasis was laid on the need incrementally to liberalise the network based energies, i.e. electricity and gas. Mineral oil, in contrast, was already much closer to being a single market, and coal was mentioned mainly with regard to state aid. The need to apply the Treaty rules to the energy sector received much attention in the document, relating to market freedoms as well as to competition.

The Commission's plans were received critically by the governments. They had endorsed the plan for a policy document in a previous Council resolution, but the Commission had gone much further than they expected. In order to judge the initial reception of the Commission's proposals it is quite revealing to note that the Commission consciously avoided the Green Paper format used for telecommunications. An open invitation to discuss the future evolution of a sector would have exposed the opposition of the involved actors. Particularly contentious was the plan to realise 'common carriage'. Though it was in no way precisely defined, this concept implied the opening up of the existing electricity and gas networks in order to further trade and competition.

In Germany particularly, this suggestion met with strong criticism. In view of the semi-private ownership of the electricity companies, such a forced opening of networks was associated with an attempted socialisation of private assets. The electricity supply system, it was feared, would be subject to similar attempts to create an administered market as took place in agriculture (Baur 1990: 82). Not surprisingly, the European electricity suppliers united against the Commission's plans, with the initial exception of EdF. Instead of attempting to open up systems exhibiting the character of a natural monopoly, the aims of the Commission could be more easily realised by strengthening the existing co-operation of the European high-tension grid operators in the Union pour la Co-ordination de la Production et du Transport d'Electricité (UCPTE) and furthering harmonisation. Diverging regulatory obligations and financial obligations were the cause of the price differentials to be found across the Community. However, the large electricity users, such as the chemical industry, welcomed the Commission's move.

Under these circumstances it was not unimportant that the early Commission plans coincided with a determined French move to improve the export conditions for its surplus electricity. Similar to the Netherlands and the UK which profited from exports of gas and oil, France should be able to exploit its comparative advantage in the production of electricity, it was argued. At the time France had twelve nuclear power plants under construction while being already able to export electricity worth DM2billion (FAZ, 20 May 1989). Though the main target, Germany was not alone in being touched by French activism. The French government also lodged a complaint with the Commission's Competition Directorate General IV to examine an abuse of a dominant position by the Spanish electricity operator, which had demanded the right to deliver a part of the electricity to be exported by EdF to Portugal (Ritter 1994: 140). The Commission examined both complaints.

The first concrete directives which the Commission proposed were rather modest. One directive aimed to increase the transparency surrounding the prices paid by high-volume users in member states. It was accepted by the Council in mid-1990 under Article 213 of the Treaty, requiring only a simple majority. Another proposal to improve mutual information about planned investments in the energy sector was not approved. Also adopted were two directives on the transit of electricity and gas supplies through the networks of third parties at the end of 1990 and in mid-1991. These directives were modelled on the problem encountered with Spain in the electricity trade between France and Portugal, which had been settled in the meantime. The directives laid down detailed procedures with transparent criteria to facilitate network access under the condition that one inner Community border was being crossed.

At this time France was still a supporter of the Commission's proposals, and the transit directives in fact corresponded quite well to the French ideas about a European electricity market. In it, the role of the utility operating the electricity system would not be questioned, only its interaction with its European counterparts was to be regulated and improved.[1] The transit directives are also interesting because they already showed the particular problems which the German actors faced with the energy market, centring on the question of reciprocity. Because of the decentralised German system, the transit directives meant that EdF could acquire the right of transit through the network of the Badenwerk to supply the Energieversorgung Schwaben, two of the southern grid companies. Similarly, the Badenwerk could transit EdF's network in order to export electricity to Spain, but this would not be economically feasible over such a distance.[2] In the case of the transit directive for gas the disadvantages of the German decentralised system were even clearer: here, twenty-nine of the forty-two enterprises bound through the directive were German.

It was not long before France lost its common market zeal and noted the mistake it had made: in the summer of 1989 a period of drought meant that EdF temporarily had to close down seventeen nuclear power plants, negotiate supply stops and reductions with foreign customers, and even import electricity itself (*Wirtschaftswoche*, 10 November 1989). Already at the end of 1988 when discussing the Commission's policy document in the Council, the German Minister Bangemann had made clear that parallel to reducing German state aid to coal, other distortions to competition would have to be tackled, such as existing monopolies for the production of electricity (*Agence Europe*, 9 November 1988). The disadvantages of relying on the EC Treaty thus became increasingly clear. In addition, the Franco-German confrontation about energy questions had been settled through bilateral talks and the Kohl–Mitterand summit in November 1989 which approved a nine-page Protocol on Franco-German energy policy (Padgett 1992: 67f).[3]

But the Commission could not easily be stopped. In order to assess further possibilities for the opening of networks, it had established advisory committees with representatives of the member states on the one hand, and representatives of the ESI as well as users on the other. These committees met monthly from 1990 until the beginning of 1991, and shortly afterwards reports were published (European Commission 1991). By now the heated discussion on 'common carriage' was transformed into one on 'third party access' (TPA). TPA was to give a broad right of network use to actors, also within member states. The implications of such a liberalisation for the three parts of the electricity system – production, transmission and distribution of electricity – were contentiously discussed in the advisory committees. For the participating Commission officials these discussions were an excellent opportunity for getting to know the different arguments of the debate on the liberalisation of electricity, while not altering their determination to follow this aim.[4]

A major problem at this time was the lack of experience with competition in electricity supply. The UK was only just implementing its own reform in 1990, and gradually became the main supporter of the Commission as a result. Consequently, the European ESI was split. In parallel to the Committee report, the 'continental members' of the newly founded association Eurelectric issued a document with their position on TPA (Eurelectric 1991). The UK ESI was joined by its Irish counterpart in supporting the Commission. However, in this regard the very different circumstances of the UK and Ireland have to be noted. Hardly being connected to the West European high-tension grid of the UCPTE, both member states had not been touched at all by the previous transit directive. And as far as TPA was concerned, at least direct exports from other member states would not matter. The only small connection between the UK grid and the UCPTE was already being used for French exports into the UK.

Despite their opposition, the continental members of Eurelectric also tried to be constructive in their comments, avoiding the impression of an absolute blockage of the Commission's plans. To understand why the ESI were aiming at co-operation, it is useful to expand on some rules of the EC Treaty. In it, the Commission could find several potentially useful means for breaking up the existing monopolies, and these were eventually highly relevant for bringing about the single market for electricity.

Existing constraints: the treaty provisions

The uniqueness of the European Community is mainly due to its extraordinary legal system (Weiler 1991). Over the years the European Court of Justice has confirmed the direct effect of most Treaty articles. Coupled with the established supremacy of EC law, it implies that the Treaty's rules can also be applied to sectors for which more precise Council directives or regulations are still missing. Therefore, for the electricity monopolies too, change did not depend exclusively on Council decision-making. The Treaty articles also had to be regarded, and of these the freedom to market goods and the right of establishment were particularly important, next to the competition rules.

The precise implications of the Treaty law were very contentiously discussed, and they are in fact still not fully settled. Potentially the freedom to trade goods could apply to electricity, as well as the need to adapt state trading monopolies (Article 37), and the requirement to lift export restrictions (Article 34) (Ehlermann 1988). For France and other member states with integrated state monopolies these rules could require alterations. In addition, the competition rules included the prohibition of cartels (Article 85) and of an abuse of a dominant position (Article 86). Perhaps such an abuse could be found, were an electricity monopoly to deny network access to a third party. A cartel, in contrast, could possibly be seen in the UCPTE as well as in decentralised systems, like the German one, should the operators be found explicitly not to supply each other's customers. As the application of European competition law is not strictly tied to cases involving trans-border transaction, it could even apply to the inner German situation.

Last, Article 90 restricted the granting of special rights in as far as these privileges were not necessary to fulfil services of a general economic interest. This exemption of Article 90.2, which also covered the other Treaty and competition rules, was argued by some to be clearly applicable to the supply of electricity. However, this was the only relevant exception to competition law and the Court had interpreted it very narrowly. In as far as electricity monopolies were not exempted, there was moreover the possibility that Article 90.3 could be used, allowing the Commission to lift existing special rights by issuing decisions or even directives, which in this case did not have to be approved by either Council or Parliament (Schmidt 1998).

The Commission drew on these and other articles, like those for controlling state aid, a few times with regard to electricity systems. Next to the examination of the German coal subsidies and of the Spanish inhibition of French exports, both instigated by France, the British Electricity Act of 1989 was inspected. It included a provision for a fossil fuel levy imposed on consumers in order to compensate the newly privatised distribution companies for their requirement to contract higher priced nuclear power. In order that this should not be an illegal state aid, the Commission required that this compensation be paid on all nuclear energy, including imported French nuclear power (IP/90/267). Consequently, the French imports into Britain were subsidised by an additional 10 per cent by British consumers.

Another examination responded to a complaint placed by Dutch local electricity distributors. They were hindered in importing electricity since the operator of the Dutch grid had the sole right to import electricity, which was supported by a system of exclusive private contracts among the actors of the electricity supply system. As the Commission only investigated part of the complaint in this *IJsselcentrale* case, which was later tied up with other Court rulings (Hancher 1995: 307–9), the case is too complicated to concern us here. But it shows very clearly how those profiting from liberalisation could turn to the Commission, not waiting for Council decisions.

Changing gear: trying to circumvent the Council

Viewing these powers, and the very contentious discussions in the advisory committees, the Commission changed gear. In March 1991 it initiated infringement procedures against the import and export monopolies for electricity and gas in ten member states. Involved were nine member states for electricity (Denmark, France, Greece, Ireland, Italy, the Netherlands, Portugal, Spain and the UK) and three for gas (Belgium, Denmark and France). It was not coincidental that this move happened shortly after an important success of the Commission with its telecommunications terminal directive at the Court of Justice. In a speech to the British Employers' Association (*Agence Europe*, 6 April 1991), Competition Commissioner Brittan drew clear parallels between the two policies:

> The benign precedent in telecommunications shows the way forward in a way which minimises the conflict … In the energy field we now have to consider the merits of a similar approach. There is much to be said for a dual track policy. Competition policy can be used to liberalise markets

in a very effective way. Where accompanying measures are needed to facilitate liberalisation, for instance by harmonising standards, the necessary proposals can be put forward to the Council of Ministers. In the area of energy, the most important objective must surely be to open up networks to those who wish to use them, even if they do not own them.

It should be indicated, however, that the Commission was not acting without taking precautions. Thus, it would have been possible to direct immediately binding decisions based on Article 90.3 against the member states, or to question next to the import and export also the transport monopolies.[5] Of its different possibilities, the Commission was therefore choosing the most incremental one.

Shortly thereafter, a much more radical step was considered. In the summer of 1991 DG IV drafted directives based on Article 90.3 to liberalise electricity and gas. They would have abolished the existing monopolies for the production, transport and the import and export of electricity. These drafts were never officially issued but they became known, and the concerned actors reacted ferociously. These were wide-ranging changes in a sector of central importance. At the most, they found the support of the UK and Portugal (which endorsed liberalisation but was still partially exempted in the interim after joining the Community). Member state governments put heavy pressure on 'their' commissioners and cabinets, the ESI lobbied, and finally the European Parliament protested, which was also being bypassed via Article 90.3. In the college of Commissioners, Brittan could only obtain the support of Energy Commissioner Cardoso e Cunha.[6] Given the opposition of the other Commissioners it was decided to introduce the project as a Council directive.

After this move, the threat of a Commission directive was constantly present in the ensuing negotiations. But the fact that the Commission had already withdrawn such a proposal once made the threat less credible. After the successful use of the instrument for telecommunications, electricity policy highlighted the necessary broad support of the governments for the Commission to proceed in this way (Schmidt 1998). It seems that Brittan had seriously underrated the dependence of the Commission on support. But it may also be that Brittan had been mistaken on the position of Delors in view of the early French backing of liberalisation. Had Delors taken sides with Brittan, the chances for a Commission directive would have been much better.

However weighty this failure, it did have one positive side effect for the Commission. Having withdrawn from its plans, at least it pursued the infringement procedures and sent letters to nine governments (Portugal was no longer concerned) starting the formal proceedings. This was another controversial move, but the Commission could not easily resign again. Since the matter had roused much attention, and with a recent example of succumbing to pressure, it was highly necessary to push these procedures in order not to lose credibility as an independent agent (Majone 1996).

Protracted negotiations

The Commission introduced the new proposal (COM [91] 548 fin, 21 February 1992) to the Council and the Parliament in late 1991. It was meant as a second step towards liberalisation, following the existing transit directive, while a third and final step was still planned (Argyris 1993). The opening of networks through a concept of regulated third party access (TPA) remained the most criticised element of the proposal. Both Germany and France were among the large majority opposing the proposal. Though the German government and the responsible Ministry of Economics became increasingly favourable towards liberalisation, the proposal implied too much regulation and could not have been integrated into the German Cartel Law. Germany opposed a sector-specific regulation of competition in energy markets. Moreover, parts of the proposal would have necessitated the establishment of a national grid company and partial expropriation of the enterprises currently operating the grid. France had different, but at least as far-reaching, problems with the project. The long-term planning necessary for the nuclear power programme could not be pursued under liberalisation, and there was little interest in changing the domestic system.

In view of the contentious reception, the Council asked the Commission to present an altered proposal, for which the Commission awaited the statement of the European Parliament. The latter had been significantly lobbied by the ESI, and forwarded about a hundred alterations to the directive in October 1993. At the end of this year, the Commission published its revised directives (COM [93] 643 fin, 7 December 1993) for electricity and gas. The regulated TPA was now modified to a negotiated TPA, in addition to the licensing of new production and transmission capacities a tendering procedure was allowed, and vertically integrated companies would no longer need separated management but only separated accounts.

All this time the infringement proceedings were looming in the background. The second phase of the procedure had been completed, however slowly, at the beginning of 1993, so the next step would be to call upon the ECJ. This was not without effect. In June 1993 Competition Commissioner Van Miert conceded to the French Industry Minister Longuet in stalling the proceedings so that the necessary national developments could be prepared. The government under Balladur subsequently created a commission, which analysed possible options for the French system and reported at the end of 1993. It is interesting briefly to refer to the parliamentary debate about the *Rapport Mandil*, named after the General Director for Energy in the Industry Ministry heading the commission. This debate clearly shows the influence of the supranational negotiations on the definition of French interests, an interaction that intergovernmentalist explanations (Moravcsik 1993) fail to capture, as is often criticised (Sandholtz 1996).

In the debate, the Minister emphasised that it was no option for France simply to oppose the European policy proposals because it wanted to retain its own system: 'The most dangerous attitude for our country would consist in deliberately refusing to take into consideration our partners' preoccupations' (p. 2). The merits of the French system were repeatedly underscored: 'Why jeopardise something that works well?' (p. 13). The most visible result of the report was the 'single buyer' proposal that France submitted to the Council in mid-1994 as an alternative to TPA. This proposition left the monopoly of EdF basically intact, but gave third parties the right to buy cheaper electricity from alternative sources and to sell it to the network operator (for instance EdF) as the single buyer. Users would profit from these transactions and not directly from liberalised electricity.

The Commission had strong reservations about this idea, as had Britain, Germany and the Netherlands which were tending towards the modified TPA approach. Nevertheless, it was quickly accepted that a two-tiered policy had to be followed. The differences between the national systems were too great to be subsumed under a single approach. As seems to be generally the case in the Council when a government struggles with an issue of high national political salience, it was clear that one country should not be isolated, despite the formal option of resorting to qualified majority voting. Moreover, several member states depended on France as the largest electricity exporter in the Union. Notwithstanding this general recognition, it took the Council the determined attempts of four presidencies (German, French, Spanish and Italian) finally to reach a compromise in June 1996. Until the end the agreement was uncertain as several countries backing the modified TPA proposal (UK, Germany, Portugal, Sweden, Finland, the Netherlands) wanted further liberalisation while France was reluctant to concede more alterations to the single buyer proposal, which was also backed by Belgium, Spain, Italy, Greece, Ireland and later Portugal. In the deliberations, issues of reciprocal market opening, especially between France and Germany, were paramount.

France and Germany and the European negotiations

Franco-German efforts were essential for a compromise finally to emerge. It is quite normal that the two countries, often joined by Britain, co-ordinate their positions on European energy policy before meetings of the Council. The responsible directors in the ministries meet for a meal once per semester. The Franco-German summits are an additional venue to overcome differences. In this particular dossier, the special relationship could be put to good use. Because both countries represented very different electricity systems, the German ESI feared to suffer most from a European accord that included the single buyer model. Being burdened with demanding regulatory standards, resulting in high electricity prices, the German ESI feared that the market opening would lead to an inundation of French electricity into Germany, while the German actors would most likely be hindered from becoming active in France, for instance by building power plants. The fact that France had forwarded the single buyer proposal was interpreted by the German ESI as a defection of EdF from the coalition among the European suppliers opposing liberalisation.[7] The existence of the proposal made an accord much more likely, and while EdF would keep its monopoly largely intact, it could additionally profit from the market opening around it.

Like the French position, the attitude of the German actors had changed during the years of negotiations. The Economics Ministry, first of all, became a convinced liberalisation supporter. In view of high German electricity prices, domestic reform was believed to be vital, but at the same time it would be difficult to open the German market unilaterally, without a European reform. A first proposal for a national reform by the Economics Ministry had failed to receive cabinet support (Eising 1997). For the Ministry, therefore, a European agreement was necessary, and the constraints of European negotiations strengthened the Ministry's position vis-à-vis the powerful electricity industry. The German ESI had long resisted liberalisation, favouring instead an improved European harmonisation of policies. The more liberalisation seemed inevitable, the grid companies especially started to support the modified TPA approach. Gradually, they realised that they could possibly profit from a lifting of the cartel restrictions. For them, it was especially relevant to restrict the rights of the municipal companies, which were arguing for the adoption of the single buyer approach. Given that the large companies became involved in the liberalised telecommunications markets, it was additionally difficult to request fair competition in one field while clinging to own monopolies.

In the negotiations France was under pressure through the infringement proceedings which were handed to the Court in June 1994. Germany with its decentralised system had not been affected, although de facto similar monopolies existed. It fell upon the German Cartel Office, which may apply European competition law, to highlight incompatibilities with European law. In early 1993, the Office declared the existing concession contract between Kleve, a town bordering the Netherlands, and the Rheinisch-Westfälisches Elektrizitätswerk (RWE) an illegal cartel under European competition law. Third parties were hindered from importing electricity from the Netherlands. No complaint stood behind this action. RWE was quick to apply for an exemption at the Commission, where the case was, however, not decided until the concession ended in 1994 (Markert 1995).[8] Shortly afterwards, the Cartel Office took up another concession contract between RWE and Nordhorn, again on the Dutch border. This time, the Commission is not involved and the responsible German Court posed a preliminary reference to the European Court of Justice (ECJ) in 1997.

These cases and others put the German actors under some pressure but this could not be compared to the situation in France. The long-term nuclear programme, the integrity of EdF, and the equalisation of tariffs were at stake. For the latter, an inclusion of the independent supply companies as eligible users of liberalised electricity had to be prevented. Much depended on the interpretation of the ECJ. During 1994 the Court issued two judgments of relevance to electricity policy, the Corbeau and the Almelo cases, which seemed to indicate that the Court now accorded much more scope to public service obligations, departing from its previously very liberal position (Hancher 1994, 1995). Should this be the case, not too many concessions should be made in the Council.

Simultaneously, there was yet another avenue to protect the French electricity system. A Treaty revision was coming up in 1996, and with it a chance to exclude the French service public from its purview. The Centre européen des entreprises à participation publique (CEEP) launched a public service debate with the aim to define a Public Service Charter for water, gas, electricity, transport, posts and telecommunications (EIPA 1997). This initiative found particular support from French, Belgian and Italian actors, who could secure the interest of Jacques Delors, the European Parliament, the Economic and Social Committee, and different associations, most of all unions.

In this context the negotiations on the directive took place. The judgment of the Court in the infringement proceedings was originally awaited in 1996; the parallel Treaty negotiations showed that France was only joined by Belgium in demanding a public service provision. Therefore it was a question of whether the Court or the Council would set the parameters of the future shape of the European electricity market, and for the latter an accord between France and Germany was necessary. This had become clear since the time of the German presidency in late 1994.

Both countries represented different ends of the EU's heterogeneous national electricity systems, so that a compromise would be difficult to reach but stood a good chance of being acceptable to the other governments. France needed an agreement so that it could co-determine future European constraints, while Germany was trying to overcome domestic ones. The high priority of domestic reform in view of high electricity prices and mounting signs of economic crisis was also alleged to weaken the position of the Federal Economics Ministry at the European bargaining table. The German Economics Ministry found itself in the difficult situation that it had an increasingly disparate ESI at its side, and had moreover to find support in the Cabinet for its own position. France, in contrast, had a successful system it wanted to keep, and with an integrated public monopoly next to the government it was easy to draw up a national position.

After the astute management of the French presidency and the establishment of the single buyer as an equivalent option against demands of considerable refinement in mid-1995, German utilities lobbied the Federal Parliament not to accept an unfavourable European deal. In view of its liberalisation interests, the Economics Ministry was seen to sell out German interests. Accordingly, the CDU/CSU parliamentary party argued during the final negotiations not to accept a deal which fell behind European competition law.

Hopes for an agreement rested on the Franco-German summit in December 1995. But the general strike against the cuts in social security in France prohibited an agreement. Therefore, it fell upon the Italian presidency and further Franco-German negotiations to reach an accord. An agreement had been reached to accept only a directive which both governments supported. This political understanding helped the search for a compromise of the responsible administrators in the German federal ministry of economics and the French industry ministry. The contacts between the responsible division heads had already intensified during the time of the presidencies of the two governments. Now frequent telephone calls and meetings in Paris and Bonn took place. In particular, the Franco-German summit in Dijon in early June 1996 allowed the breakthrough. The French position was always co-ordinated in the Secrétariat général du comité interministériel pour les questions de co-opération économique européenne (SGCI), and the industry ministry faced few demands from other sides. Despite their more difficult situation given the very heterogeneous interests involved in German electricity politics and a less stringent national co-ordination of positions, the German administrators also managed to be accountable partners.

The common position that was finally agreed in the Council in June 1996 rested on the previous Franco-German compromise. Particular solutions could be found for the various sensitivities. Based on the two models of negotiated TPA and the single buyer, the market will be incrementally opened for large volume users, starting in 1999. After six years, 32 per cent of the market will be opened. Because of different national consumption patterns, governments will designate eligible users until the agreed market share is achieved with only very large users qualifying automatically. A specific *service public* clause will allow France to exclude its independent distributors, and thus to maintain the equalisation of tariffs. In the interest of the German ESI a reciprocity clause was included that supply contracts can be outruled to categories of customers that are not eligible users in the supplying country. As France is likely to exclude its distributors, the German municipalities will probably not be able to buy from EdF.

Conclusion

The electricity case is interesting in several respects. One of the most difficult single market dossiers, the significant heterogeneity of member state electricity systems was finally overcome by a directive offering variable solutions, instead of requiring uniformity. Thus, a flexible approach was found, which is more generally called for to improve the decision-making capacity of the EU in the face of increasing heterogeneity (Scharpf 1997). However, it has to be cautioned, this example may not persist as it is not clear whether the Court of Justice would consent to the reciprocity clause that was included, given that it violates comprehensive market freedoms.

For the compromise to emerge, the Franco-German alliance was paramount. Despite different interests, and a very unco-operative French start, it was agreed to find a common solution. The difficult French position was generally accepted among the member states. Notwithstanding the formal qualified majority principle, this shows how it is not legitimate to isolate a country on an issue of high national salience, at least as long as it is clear that the responsible government tries to find a solution, and does not only aim to veto.

In times of controversies and high distributional concerns, the role of the governments, notably the presidencies, seems generally heightened vis-à-vis the Commission. The governments were the actors searching actively for a com-promise, and the Commission accepted their compromise. Several presidencies altered the Commission's proposal. Its role as an agenda setter, often hailed in the literature (Garrett and Tsebelis 1996), was hereby considerably lessened. Also with regard to another notable Commission competence, its right to issue directives based on Article 90.3, the electricity case is instructive. While on the basis of the experience in telecommunications it often seems that the governments are helpless in view of this Commission competence (Sandholtz 1998), the electricity case shows their ability to prevent such a measure (Schmidt 1998).

This does not mean, however, that the EU is an intergovernmental enterprise. Rather, the electricity case shows how the supranational legal framework, and the Commission's right to enforce it by calling upon the ECJ, provides incentives for change. As such, France had no reason to alter its electricity system in view of widely recognised efficiency and broad public support. But membership of the EU made it necessary. In sum, some liberalisation was achieved as the Commission had supported, but the new European policy is one offering multiple options, as was notably forwarded by the French government.

The future shape of the European electricity market now depends on the transposition of the directive. In October 1997 the ECJ gave its ruling on the import and export monopolies, not backing the Commission's liberalisation zeal. This accords greater leeway to the member states to determine their electricity supply systems. Moreover, in view of the flexible approach found in the directive, it is interesting to note that this might lead to new convergence.[9] Thus, in a surprising turn, EdF now appears to favour the negotiated TPA for the transposition, while the German municipalities will be accorded the status of a single buyer.

Acknowledgements

I would like to thank the officials I interviewed, and the Maison Suger in Paris for welcoming me.

Notes

1 Interview at the French Ministry of Industry, 21 April 1995.
2 Interview at the German Electricity Suppliers' Association (VDEW), 1 June 1995.
3 According to Padgett, the compromise included a larger share of French electricity exports into Germany, which however could not be revealed statistically (interview German Federal Economics Ministry, 2 December 1994).
4 Interview with Commission official, 10 November 1994.
5 Interview with former Commission official, 16 June 1995.
6 Interview with Commission official, 24 October 1994.
7 Interview at RWE, 5 April 1995.
8 For the Commission this was a very difficult case, given that the distribution monopoly being questioned was not to be abolished under the planned directive. Thus, had the Commission denied the exemption, the liberalisation in Germany would have been disproportionately advanced; had the Commission exempted the arrangement, this would have stopped the liberalisation process prematurely.
9 Interviews at EdF, 5 November 1997, and at the industry ministry, 14 November 1997.

References

Argyris, Nicholas (1993) 'Regulatory reform in the electricity sector: an analysis of the Commission's internal market proposals', *Oxford Review of Economic Policy* 9:1, 31–43.

Baur, Jürgen F. (1990) 'Normative Grundlagen für die europäische Politik im Energiebereich', in Jürgen F. Baur (ed.), *Leitungsgebundene Energie und der Gemeinsame Markt.* Baden-Baden: Nomos, 59–83.

Commission of the European Communities (1991) *Directorate-General for Energy: Reports of the Consultative Committees on Third Party Access to Electricity Networks.* Brussels: Commission of the European Communities.

Ehlermann, Claus-Dieter (1988) 'Die rechtlichen Instrumentarien zur Verwirklichung eines Gemeinsamen Marktes nach dem EWG-Vertrag', in Rudolf Lukes (ed.), *Ein EWG-Binnenmarkt für Elektrizität: Realität oder Utopie?* Köln: Carl Heymanns Verlag, 28–42.

EIPA (1997) *Managing Universal Service Obligations in Public Utilities in the European Union.* Maastricht: European Institute of Public Administration.

Eising, Rainer (1997) 'Sektorielle Institutionenpolitik und sektorieller Institutionenwandel', in Thomas König, Elmar Rieger and Hermann Schmitt (eds), *Europäische Institutionenpolitik.* Frankfurt, New York: Campus, 239–63.

Eurelectric (1991) 'Wettbewerb in der Elektrizitätswirtschaft. Stellungnahme des Europäischen Komitees Eurelectric zur Frage der Öffnung der Versorgungsnetze', *Elektrizitätswirtschaft* 90:12, 627–39.

Garrett, Geoffrey and George Tsebelis (1996) 'An institutional critique of intergovernmentalism', *International Organization* 50:2, 269–90.

Hancher, Leigh (1994) 'Case C-320/91 P, Procureur du Roi v. Paul Corbeau', *Common Market Law Review* 31, 105–22.

—— (1995) 'Case C-393/92, Gemeente Almelo and Others v. Energiebedrijf IJsselmij NV', *Common Market Law Review* 32:1, 305–25.

Majone, Giandomenico (1996) 'The European Commission as regulator', in Giandomenico Majone (ed.), *Regulating Europe.* London: Routledge, 61–79.

Markert, Kurt (1995) 'Neueste Entwicklungen im Energie-Kartellrecht', *Recht der Energiewirtschaft* 56:2, 60–4.

Mez, Luz (1997) 'The German electricity reform attempts: reforming co-optive networks', in Atle Midttun (ed.), *European Electricity Systems in Transition.* Oxford: Elsevier, 231–52.

Moravcsik, Andrew (1993) 'Preferences and power in the European Community: a liberal intergovernmentalist approach', *Journal of Common Market Studies* 31:4, 473–524.

Padgett, Stephen (1992) 'The single european energy market: the politics of realization', *Journal of Common Market Studies* 30, 53–76.

Poppe, Marcelo and Lionel Cauret (1997) 'The French electricity regime', in Atle Midttun (ed.), *European Electricity Systems in Transition.* Oxford: Elsevier, 199–229.

Rapport Mandil, Compte rendu analytique officiel de la séance de l'Assemblée Nationale du 25 novembre 1993, 'débat d'orientation sur l'organisation électrique et gazière dans le contexte européen' (82ème séance de la première session ordinaire de 1993–94).

Ritter, Kurt Lennart (1994) 'EC Antitrust Law and Energy', in Barry E. Hawk (ed.), *Antitrust in a Global Economy: 20th Annual Proceedings of the Fordham Corporate Law Institute.* Irving-on-Hudson NY: Transnational Juris Publications, 127–57.

Sandholtz, Wayne (1998) 'The emergence of a supranational telecommunications regime', in Wayne Sandholtz and Alec Stone Sweet (eds), *European Integration and Supranational Governance.* Oxford: Oxford University Press, 134–63.

—— (1996) 'Membership matters: limits of the functional approach to European institutions', *Journal of Common Market Studies* 34:3, 403–29.

Scharpf, Fritz W. (1997) 'Balancing positive and negative integration: the regulatory options for Europe'. Max Planck Institute for the Study of Societies, Working Paper 97/8.

Schmidt, Susanne K. (1998) 'Commission activism: subsuming telecommunications and electricity under European competition law', *Journal of European Public Policy* 5:1 (March 1998), 169–84.

VDEW (1997) *Strommarkt Deutschland 1996*. Frankfurt: VDEW.

Weiler, Joseph (1991) 'The transformation of Europe', *The Yale Law Journal* 100, 2402–83.

5

FROM HIGH TO LOW POLITICS IN FRANCO-GERMAN RELATIONS

The case of telecommunications

Volker Schneider and Thierry Vedel

Introduction

The unique history of interaction over the last forty years and the multitude of bilateral institutions have given the Franco-German relationship a special character in the emerging multilateral setting of European integration, sometimes referred to as the 'core' or 'engine' of a united Europe. Although this 'axiomatic character' of Franco-German relations in the domain of high politics (e.g. foreign and security policy) has been a popular topic in political research, there is only a few studies on areas of low or sectoral politics.

The advantage of these sectoral studies is to concentrate not only on the intergovernmental level of power politics in which states are often treated as unitary actors, but also to take into account that interstate relations in modern politics have multiple levels where intergovernmental relationships are paralleled by transnational links between private and public actors. Such studies seem more appropriate in revealing the 'micro physics' of Franco-German political interaction within the EU policy network in which intergovernmental, transnational, bilateral and multilateral relations are just different levels of the same political reality.

In this chapter we will study such multi-level interactions in the telecommunications industry where we will try to discover similarities and differences in policy patterns between both countries, and their European dimensions in this sector. We start with the observation that France and Germany have developed highly similar policies in the telecommunications domain during the last decade which we will outline in the following sections before we deal with EU telecommunications policy and the effect of Franco-German relations on it. In order to emphasise the interaction between bilateral and the multilateral levels in the EU, this section then will be followed by an analysis of Franco-German co-operation in a series of joint ventures on which EU decision-making has had an important effect.[1]

French and German telecommunications policy in an emerging European political system

Franco-German bilateral political interactions in the telecommunications area are a rather new phenomenon. Prior to the 1970s and 1980s, telecommunications in most countries was an area of no relevance to intergovernmental relations. Telecommunications systems were run as state monopolies which at the same time were protected from international competition (Genschel and Werle 1993). Co-operation and interaction with other countries was restricted to mere technical dimensions, to co-ordinate and administer the interconnection of national tele-communications systems. Related international matters were dealt with by 'technical' international organisations such as CEPT and ITU.

It is only since the 1970s, when this sector gained increasing weight in commer-cial and industrial policies, that telecommunications have generated international political issues. Since the 1980s then, when the sector became liberalised and deregulated in a growing number of countries, its particular issues and policies became more important in a number of international organisations, thereby gaining a more prominent place on the agenda of the European Community and other regional and international negotiation fora.[2] As Germany and France not only provided for the two largest European telecommunications markets, but also for the two nationally most powerful telecommunications industries in Europe, the structural conditions of both national sectors and their related policy programmes are important not only for the understanding of Franco-German economic diplomacy but also of EU policy in this sector.

In a historical perspective, the institutional evolution of French and German telecommunications systems display some striking similarities but also some important differences. Both telecommunications systems were run as state mono-polies for more than a century and, at the same time, they were almost completely closed to international commerce. At the technical level, however, both networks evolved quite differently, implying divergent consequences for industrial development and national policy with respect not only to policy goals but also to rhythms of organisational and institutional change. These similarities and differences and their consequences for Franco-German relations in bilateral and multilateral settings will be dealt with in the following section.

German telecommunications and policy patterns

The German telecommunications sector became, apart from technical inter-national co-ordination, a matter of foreign policy only in the late 1970s, when the waves of liberalisation and deregulation originating in the US were reaching Europe.[3] When the technological revolution in microelectronics also affected the telecommunications sector in the late 1970s, the German telecommunications industry came under increasing pressure from foreign and domestic computer firms to open up its protected markets for new telematic services. This triggered a series of domestic reform activities.

In 1980, inspired by American liberalisation measures, the German anti-trust commission began to scrutinise the procurement policy of the German Bundespost and the telecommunications equipment market. In its report, the commission questioned the cartel arrangements and demanded a number of liberalisation measures in the terminal market and also a certain degree of service competition within the public telecommunications network. At the time, however, this reform initiative was not yet sufficiently supported among the relevant telecommunications policy actors.

A few years later the situational context was more supportive. In 1982 a new federal government under Chancellor Helmut Kohl, a coalition of the Christian Democrats and the Liberals, came into office and started to revitalise the reform process. As the new Post and Telecommunications Minister Schwarz-Schilling had formerly been a strong critic of the PTT monopoly, one could expect the German government would adopt a positive stance toward this sectoral reform. Still, it took another three years for this to materialise. In 1985 the federal government established a specialised advisory commission to be charged with the setting up of reform proposals. The commission took two years to formulate a set of reform proposals which subsequently became draft law. This was adopted in 1989 by the German parliament. Major changes were the transformation of the post, banking and telecommunications divisions of the former Bundespost into separate public corporations, the liberalisation of the terminal market, and a number of market openings in the domain of telematic services. The telephone service, however, remained a monopoly.

These initial openings demanded changes in other areas since liberalisation and deregulation created 'auto-dynamics'. The freeing of markets without improving the efficiency and flexibility of the former monopolistic postal and telecommunications operators (PTOs) rather tended toward an unstable situation. Thus a logical 'next step' was the transformation of the former public administration into a private corporation part of which was to be sold on the stock exchange. In Germany this was also supported by the reunification which burdened the Bundespost with giant reconstruction investments in the East, creating enormous financial problems for the new public company which were to be solved by giving it private legal status and a partial stock market sale.[4] To this end a privatisation bill was introduced to the Bundestag in February 1994, adopted in July, and came into force at the end of the year. Since 1995 the three Bundespost companies (Telekom, Postdienst and Postbank) have become private corporations and the first tranche of Deutsche Telekom shares was sold in November 1996.

Finally, in 1996 the most recent reform move led to a Telecommunications Act aimed at eliminating the remaining monopoly barriers in the traditional telephone sector. A further important measure was the delegation of regulatory tasks to an independent regulatory authority. This was at the same time a measure to conform with the major EU telecommunications policy goal of achieving complete liberalisation in telecommunications in 1998.

French telecommunications and policy patterns

In France, the liberalisation of telecommunications has been on the political agenda since 1986, following the appointment of Jacques Chirac as Prime Minister.[5] The cable TV market was opened to private operators as early as September 1986, and, in 1987, a private mobile operator was licensed and the terminals market was liberalised. However, a first attempt at passing a law to introduce a tiny dose of competition in the provision of telecommunications services failed during the summer of 1987 because of union opposition. For the same reason, and also because of the next general election, changes in the statutes of France Télécom were postponed.

When the Socialists came to power in 1988, a public debate on the future of post and telecommunications was launched. This process resulted in significant changes. First, France Télécom was transformed from a public administration into a public corporation and became fully separate from the postal branch. Second, a law was passed which partially and gradually liberalised two segments of the telecommunications market: mobile services and value-added services. But the telecommunications infrastructure remained a France Télécom monopoly although private networks were allowed as long as they were not open to third parties.

Between 1988 and 1994, French governments tried to reconcile the conflicting aims of building the single market and avoiding internal political conflict. As a result, France implemented a kind of soft liberalisation of its telecommunications market. While the French government officially voiced a strong opposition to the Commission push toward liberalisation, at the same time it gradually implemented significant changes in its own telecommunications system.

Since 1994, France has speeded up the liberalisation of its telecommunications, sometimes ahead of European deadlines. This shift followed a report prepared by Bruno Lasserre, head of the Regulatory Directorate at the Post and Telecommunications (PTT) Ministry. Lasserre argued – and convinced the government – that France Télécom's monopoly could not resist technological progress and the liberalisation of mobile and satellite communications. He advocated an early demonopolisation of French telecommunications in order gradually to prepare the public operator for a tougher environment and to foster the emergence of strong new (French) actors (Lasserre 1994).

In January 1996, the PTT Minister, François Fillon, introduced a bill which was adopted by the French parliament in June 1996.[6] On 1 January 1998 all telecommunications services were opened to competition. Licences are awarded by the PTT Ministry. Universal service – comprising the nationwide provision of telephone service at affordable rates, information service, and telephone books, etc. – is provided by the public operator France Télécom and any other operator willing. Competitors share the costs of universal service through payment to a special fund as well as paying local network access and interconnection fees. Finally, an independent regulatory agency monitors operators' activities, administers the universal service fund and solves conflicts among operators.

Even the privatisation of France Télécom was now on the political agenda. This move had been postponed several times in the past. During the summer of 1994 a report on the future of France Télécom submitted to the French government by the former chairman of France Télécom, Marcel Roulet, called for the sell-off of a minority share of the public operator while maintaining the employees' civil servant status. This strategic reform was not endorsed by Prime Minister Edouard Balladur, who decided to drop the privatisation of France Télécom, arguing that it should follow the completion of the liberalisation of the market rather than precede it. However, after the election of Chirac as President in May 1995, France Télécom's privatisation was no longer taboo. Following the law of 26 July 1996, France Télécom was transformed into a national corporation and 20 per cent of its assets sold on the stock exchange market in spring 1997.[7]

France has now joined the general trend toward telecommunications liberalisation. The only domain in which it continues to exhibit its exception is the one of universal service. On this issue, the French government advocates a 'service public à la française', which in the Jacobine tradition emphasises the autonomous and central role of a public power to a greater extent than public service concepts in Germany, where also various forms of private self-regulation are legitimate forms of providing public goods. In this respect the French conception of universal service provision differs sensibly with the definition of universal service by the European Commission. However, on the other hand, one can wonder if the actual notion of 'service public à la française' still corresponds to the old ideal which the French government will strongly defend at the European level or has just developed into some kind of political slogan for internal use.

Our process description has shown that in France and Germany the telecommunications sectors have changed radically, and it is striking to note that there was a strong parallelism in these changes over the last ten to fifteen years. While some earlier analyses (e.g. Morgan and Webber 1986; Grande and Schneider 1991) were expecting notable divergences in policy outcomes based on varying national political structures and actor constellations, on a longer perspective, however, both structural reform processes (liberalisation of the various segments of the markets, privatisation of the public telecommunications operators) have not only taken place at about the same time but also clearly show a highly similar result. In the following sections we will show that these similarities cannot be explained either by a hierarchical implementation of 'superior' common policy goals determined by Franco-German 'high politics' or the EU, by horizontal diffusion, mutual influence or even by policy concertation between both countries alone, but are explicable only by using a dynamic perspective in which national policy making and EU developments closely interact.

Europeanisation of telecommunications policy

Closely related to the national reform processes, the liberalisation and deregulation of telecommunications also became an important policy topic in the European

Community.[8] Three stages can be distinguished in the emergence of a European telecommunications policy with the Commission gradually emerging as a corporate actor fighting for radical liberalisation and deregulation in this sector.

Commission as corporate actor in telecommunications policy

Until 1977, there was no EC action in the telecommunications domain. State members shared the opinion that the Treaty of Rome did not give any authority to the Commission in this field. When the Commission attempted to take action, for instance by promoting the harmonisation of public procurement of PTT administrations in October 1968, it met with Council opposition. The real forum for European co-ordination was the Conférence européenne des administrations des postes et telecommunications (CEPT), set up in 1959, which issued non-mandatory recommendations for the harmonisation of national technical systems.

Toward the end of the 1970s, the Commission became more active in telecommunications. However, it entered the sector indirectly, through information technology issues. Taking advantage of the debate on the coming of an information age, the Commission issued a report in 1979 which insisted on the role of networks in economic competitiveness and on the necessity for co-operation in the development of new networks and services. This bypass strategy allowed the Commission to appear as a legitimate actor in the telecommunications sector while not attacking directly the power of the PTT administrations.

As a result, a task force for information technologies and telecommunications was created within the Commission in 1983 and later incorporated in the DG XIII which became the DG for telecommunications, information industries and innovation in 1986. Subsequently, various programmes, such as ESPRIT and RACE, were launched by the Commission with the objective of developing a pan-European telecommunications infrastructure. These programmes enlarged the network of actors involved in the European telecommunications policy. So far, the Commission strategy was designed through the SOG-T, an expert group comprising representatives of national PTT administrations. Through R&D programmes such as ESPRIT and RACE the Commission found new allies among large industrial firms and increased its power (Sandholtz and Zysman 1989; Grande 1996).

A new stage began in 1984 when the Commission prepared a Green Paper on telecommunications. This process took place at the time of the divestiture of AT&T in the USA and the beginnings of the telecommunications liberalisation in the UK. The Commission dramatised these changes to broaden its scope of action. To the harmonisation of networks and the promotion of new services, the Commission added a new objective – the introduction of competition within national markets. To implement this, the Commission made use of Article 90.3 which gives it an unconventional power directly to issue laws dealing with public service monopolies without going through the normal decision making process in the Council of Ministers (Chamoux 1993: 175–7; Schmidt 1997).

This move, initiated in 1988 with the directive on terminals, was a frontal attack on national PTT administrations, but also a further sign of an increasingly autonomous Commission, provoking fierce criticism from most of the European member states, including the UK. Being not only against the form but also very much against the content, France used this to try to impede EC liberalisation plans by suing the Commission at the European Court of Justice (ECJ) for overstepping its powers. A few months later Italy, Belgium, Greece and Germany supported the suit. Other, more liberal member states such as the UK, despite their anger at the Commission's style, refrained from this action because they generally liked the aims of the Commission directive. Germany opposed this move because of procedural reasons. In 1991, however, the Commission's action was upheld by the ECJ, a significant event emphasising the court's central role in the Europeanisation of policy making which has also been noted in other policy areas (Burley and Mattli 1993; Alter and Meunier-Aitsahalia 1994).

Trend toward liberalisation

Despite a partial convergence of interests, during the late 1980s Germany and France were fighting in rather different 'teams'. An electoral switch to a socialist government turned France into a group leader of member states largely opposing a too extensive liberalisation in telecommunications, whereas Germany was allied rather with more liberal countries like the UK and the Netherlands. Both camps reached a compromise agreement in late 1988 which safeguarded the public monopolies of the network infrastructure and the traditional telecommunications services like telephony and telex, but provided for a complete liberalisation of new services.

However, this was not the last word. As we will show, the European dynamics that started with international liberalisation (above all in the USA) and emerging global alliances between the world's largest operators were feeding back into telecommunications policy making at the national and European level. A key event was the agreement also to introduce full competition in traditional telephony. In May 1993 the European Council of Ministers agreed that its national telephone operators should be obliged to allow competition in conventional telephony from 1998, with longer transitional periods for four poorer member states.[9]

This further step in liberalisation had already been proposed by the Commission in June 1992, but at this time, as the Maastricht Treaty referendum campaign was taking place in France, it was politically inopportune to deal with this issue and the Germans did not want to weaken the Bundespost/Telekom which were strongly involved financially in the reconstruction process in Eastern Germany. Increasing support from lobbies (firms and associations) at the national and European level then encouraged the Commission to put the full liberalisation programme on the Council agenda the following year. That this pathbreaking step was then supported by member states indicates that most of them saw more advantages in this development than otherwise.

One of those benefits was clearly the opportunity for international co-operation, now considered essential. A headline of the German newspaper *Die Zeit* expressed the general feeling: 'The monopolies are falling in Europe, and now the power struggle between the telecom giants is beginning' (15 October 1993). A first strategic move in this 'telecoms war' was to look for strong global partners and international alliances.

Franco-German co-operation in telecommunications has to be seen in this context. It is a process in which the perception of competition via liberalisation changed from a threat to an opportunity. As soon as the major telecommunications operators realised that global competition in telecommunications was inevitable, they anticipated the adaptation needed and supported the Commission and their governments in further liberalisation steps. This complex development cannot be explained by a fixed preference order, but suggests that EU policy in this area has to be seen in a dynamic multi-actor perspective in which national private and public actors as well as supranational European institutions such as the European Court of Justice and the European Commission played a significant role. (See Table 5.1).

Table 5.1 Summary of French, German and EU Telecommunications policy

EC/EU level	France	Germany
		1977 First agenda building related to conflicts about fax terminals and telematic services.
1983 Commission outlines strategies for a common telecommunications policy. Establishment of expert group SOGT.		1981 Report of German monopoly commission with reform proposals.
1984 Council recommendation on harmonisation in the field of telecommunications.		1985–87 Development of reform proposals by expert commission (Witte Commission).
1986 Council directive on mutual recognition of terminal equipment.	1986–87 First attempt to liberalise French telecommunications (draft law by Longuet, withdrawn due to union opposition).	
1987 Green Paper on Common Market for Telecommunications Services and Equipment.		
1989 Council decision gradually to liberalise telecommunication with the exception of telephony and public infrastructures (7 December).	1989 Public debate on post and telecommunications	1989 Law separating telecommunications and postal services, transforming Bundespost into a public corporation and introducing partial liberalisation in telecommunications.
1990 Commission Directive on telecommunications	1990 Law transforming France Télécom into a	

Table 5.1 Summary of French, German and EU Telecommunications policy (continued)

EC/EU level	France	Germany
services liberalising all services with the exception of telephony, mobiles and satellites communications. Council directive on Open Network Provision requiring the separation of operating and regulating functions. **1993** Council Decision to open all telecommunications services to competition as of 1 January 1998 (16 June).	public corporation. Law introducing partial liberalisation of telecommunications.	
1994 Council resolution on universal service principles (7 February). Commission directive extending competition to satellites communication (13 October). Council decision to liberalise telecommunications infrastructures as of 1 January 1998 (17 November). **1995** Commission directive liberalising the use of alternative infrastructures as of 1 July 1996 (18 October).		**1994** Transformation of the public enterprise DBTelekom into the private legal form Deutsche Telekom AG (DTAG).
1996 Commission directive extending competition to mobiles (16 January). Commission directive to implement full liberalisation of the telecommunications market (13 March).	**1996** Law on the regulation of telecommunications establishing full competition in the telecommunications market. Law transforming France Télécom into a commercial company. **1997** Partial privatisation of France Télécom.	**1996** Complete liberalisation of the telecommunications sector through the Telecommunications Law. Sale of Deutsche Telekom's first tranche of shares at the end of the year.

Co-operation at grass-roots level: from discordia to Global One

The implications of these developments for international relations in this sector are obvious. The protected environment in which the traditional PTOs had grown up was under increasing threat from world market competition. This, in turn, encouraged the former PTTs to move beyond their national boundaries. In this respect, however, France Télécom was clearly more dynamic than its German counterpart. While this could be explained by a general 'neo-mercantilist' background in telecommunications policy in France, another plausible explanation is that the special mode of French telecommunications modernisation (i.e. through attracting expensive international capital, in order to finance the massive telephone investments during the late 1970s and early 1980s) created stronger pressures toward efficiency and commercialisation than the more continuous network growth in Germany.

Already in the 1980s the French PTT established autonomous subsidiaries such as Intelmatique to market its products and services internationally. One of its 'best offers' was its Videotex system, Minitel.[10] Another showpiece was its data transmission network Transpac. As soon as the relevant markets became liberalised in Europe, France Télécom started to sell these systems in neighbouring countries. In the mid-1980s it tried to market Minitel services and terminals in Germany, and in 1991 France Télécom even challenged British Telecom (BT), when it launched Transpac Network Services in the UK to operate private telecommunications networks for large companies. According to the *Financial Times* (15 October 1992), this was the first time that a national telecommunications operator from one European country had tried to compete on the fixed networks of another.

From conflict to co-operation

Between Germany and France, the first major relationships in this area were related to the internationalisation of Videotex. In 1984 there was an agreement between France and Germany to open mutual access to their respective systems Minitel and Bildschirmtext. This contract principally permitted France to offer information services via the German telephone network and also implied the permission to connect Minitel terminals to the German telephone network. The same, in principle, should have been possible for the Bundespost in France except that the French system was developing much faster then the ailing German Bildschirmtext. From 1986 on, the German Bundespost thus became very reluctant to stick to the 1984 agreement, a decision mainly justified on technical grounds.

The Minitel problem created a heated dispute between the two telecommunications authorities, leading to an escalation in which France even filed a formal complaint to the EC Commission accusing the Bundespost of abusing its monopoly position. In order to find a solution, the French PTT minister Longuet began talks with his German counterpart Schwarz-Schilling in September 1987. The ministers agreed to establish a bilateral working group. Through this dialogue not only was a compromise in the Videotex case found, it was also the starting point of a 'positive co-operation' approach. France Télécom and the Bundespost decided to join forces in competing against American and Japanese computer and telecommunications groups in the supply of advanced telecommunications services.

The following year the two companies launched a jointly controlled commercial company for value-added telecommunications services in data communications. The legal format of this co-operation was a financial holding named EUCOM with a capital base of DM80 million. The company was jointly directed by an official of the Bundespost, and an official of COGECOM, a subsidiary of France

Télécom. For the *Financial Times* (5 May 1988) this represented 'the first such venture by two state-owned public telecommunications authorities and reflects their efforts to adapt to the increasingly deregulated and competitive European telecommunications environment'. A related project was the plan to jointly operate a fibre optic link between Karlsruhe in Germany and Mulhouse in France.

The rationale behind this new bilateral co-operation was explained by France Télécom's chairman, Marcel Roulet, in an interview with the French newspaper *Le Figaro* in May 1989. Emphasising that the real competitors to France would not be the Germans but the Americans, Roulet said that the only way for France Télécom to cope with the new world context was to play the 'European card'. A first step in this direction would be the intensification of co-operation with Germany:

> It is much easier for two players to start constructing Europe than for 12 to do it. In an area as complex as telecommunications, you have to pursue the most pragmatic, concrete and voluntaristic path. The bilateral approach is thus a good way of participating concretely in the develop-ment of a European [telecommunications] area. From this point of view, our co-operation with the Bundespost, our privileged partner for a number of years now, is exemplary. We have gradually extended this approach.

From discordia to Eunetcom

The early co-operation projects between France Télécom and the Bundespost did not remain singular but created their own dynamics and laid the foundations for more extensive co-operation in the early 1990s, although this was not without difficulties and conflicts.

A key condition for the extension of Franco-German relations was the aggressive global expansion of telecommunications operators such as BT. In late 1991 this company, which had already been privatised in the early 1980s, announced that it would enter a new era in telecommunications by starting to provide global voice, data and video links for the biggest multinational corporations (*Financial Times*, 20 September 1991). BT also tried to convince Deutsche Telekom and Japan's Nippon Telegraph & Telephone Company (NTT) to join a global venture named Syncordia. The Germans, however, were rather hesitant, having had offers from two other global players. The managers of Deutsche Telekom had three main doubts about the Syncordia project: first, they were afraid of angering France Télécom with which they had had a privileged relationship since 1988; second, there was some unhappiness that they were offered only a 26 per cent stake; third, it was uncertain whether Syncordia could prove successful in the USA without yet having a big American partner.

While BT was trying to get the Bundespost on board, France Télécom was not sluggish. The *Financial Times* (14 October 1991), for instance, quotes Marcel Roulet as saying that Europe's telecommunications companies should organise themselves so that BT's prediction that it would become the only truly global carrier in Europe would not come true. Likewise, MCI and AT&T tried to impede British plans.

In February 1992 it suddenly looked as though France Télécom would also join the Syncordia club. Following persistent lobbying through political and commercial channels (i.e. France Télécom urged the Bundespost not to join unless it were also admitted), it succeeded in being accepted in this global club. A compromise was reached under which the German company would sell a share of the stake it bought from BT to the French company, whereas BT itself would only be dealing directly with Deutsche Telekom rather that with France Télécom.

Shortly after, however, Deutsche Telekom and France Télécom changed their plans and withdrew from Syncordia, announcing their intention to set up their own alliance, Eunetcom. The new venture would be equally owned by the two PTOs and was to be in place within three months. Marcel Roulet described it as an important contribution to defeating BT's ambitions to be 'the only European operator that counts on the world scene at the end of the decade'. But Roulet also declared that the alliance would be open to other partners, including BT, though the original partners would always be central.

The details of the joint venture had still to be determined and the problem of finding a clear common strategy delayed the settlement considerably. A break-through was only achieved in 1993 when new events at the European level (above all the decision to introduce full competition into telephony) and some global events (BT's entering into a 20 per cent participation in the American MCI) created new pressures, so that in September 1993 an agreement was signed.

At the same time, however, obstacles also emerged on the regulatory front. The European Commission's competition authorities showed concern about the anti-competitive effects of the now much closer links between the French and German PTOs. In the press there were reports that the competition directorate might require both governments to open their telephone markets to competition before 1998. The *Financial Times* (6 December 1993) noted that, apart from banning any alliance, the European Commission would have two options: it could ask for an acceleration of liberalisation or extend competition to infrastructure, so that competitors could build their own networks.

From Atlas and Phoenix to Global One

A few weeks later it was announced that the Franco-German alliance had tried to enlarge Eunetcom, at this time a company with about 300 employees, to form yet another joint venture, named Atlas. It was intended to merge core activities in international voice services and data communications, and a future exchange of equity stakes was also seen as a possibility. Against reproaches from other European telecommunications operators (notably BT, anxious that the alliance could isolate it), the French and Germans were arguing that the co-operation would conform with the strategy to establish pan-European networks as outlined in the Maastricht Treaty.

The concrete plans for Atlas were notified to the Commission in December 1994 . A few weeks later BT filed a formal complaint to the Commission (based on Articles 85 and 86 of the EU treaty), maintaining that the deal would give the two operators a dominant position in the market. Similar criticism also came from the EU Competition Commissioner Karel Van Miert. To illustrate this point, the Commission released figures showing that the European market for data transmission was worth ECU3 billion in 1993, of which France accounted for 25 per cent and Germany 18 per cent.

Other observers were interpreting the conflict through the antagonism between competition policy and industrial policy goals in the EU, since other 'pro-competition' actors such as the German Kartellamt were criticising Atlas as an obstacle to European deregulation. Industrial Policy Commissioner Bangemann, in contrast, viewed the alliance much more positively. Atlas would be one of those strategic alliances allowing Europe to take on the American and Japanese challenge. Others explained the vigorous resistance by the highly effective lobbying of BT within the relevant EU institutions.[11] In order to reach a decision, the Commission asked France Télécom and Deutsche Telekom to submit more information about their plans while encouraging other interested parties to comment on the case.

Around the same time plans materialised for Sprint, the third largest US long-distance telecoms carrier, to be incorporated into the FT-DT alliance. For this global dimension the code name Phoenix was used and the aim was similar to that of BT – to provide services with single standards and conditions for clients operating in many countries. In contrast to Atlas, Phoenix was not only contingent on authorisation by the European Commission, but also by American authorities, the Department of Justice and the Federal Communications Commission (FCC). The chances of permission being granted seemed good, since AT&T had regained a significant market share from competitors such as MCI and Sprint, which the government did not wish to weaken further. However, AT&T tried to delay the authorisation, obviously using the licensing process as a lever to break up still existing monopoly arrangements in Germany and France. Similar pressure also came from the FCC, which tried to link the permission for Phoenix to the acceleration of liberalisation in both countries. The venture was finally authorised by the FCC on 13 July 1995.

Faced with this kind of resistance, France Télécom began to worry that the Germans could lose interest as their market size and geographical situation (close to Eastern markets) may have suggested other interesting strategic options. However, in May 1995 the Germans confirmed they would stick to the alliance. Both partners tried to overcome the Commission's fears by submitting further details on Atlas and Phoenix in September 1995, and they promised to support the liberalisation of alternative networks by their governments before 1 January 1998.

A few weeks later the EU telecommunications ministers met to negotiate these topics. Supporting the acceleration of liberalisation in principle, the German Minister Boetsch indicated that powerful opposition could possibly cause delays in the parliamentary procedure. His French colleague Longuet had just declared that France would be ready to authorise alternative networks from 1 July 1996. The Commission in turn stressed that it would block the Franco-German joint ventures as long as the network monopoly remained in Germany. Permission for Phoenix, however, posed no problem. Further talks between the heads of the PTOs, the telecommunications ministers of both countries and the European Commission finally lead to a compromise in which Atlas could be authorised. Its major conditions were that from 1 July 1996 private operators and public utility companies would be allowed to set up their own telecommunications networks, and the two national data services Datex-P/T-Data and Transpac (covering about 80 per cent of the turnover of the new firm) could be integrated only in 1998.

In mid-December 1995 the remaining American obstacle was lifted. Shortly after a visit by the French Telecommunications Minister to Washington, the Atlas alliance received clearance from the US Justice Department. As in the EU context, authorisation was subject to a long list of conditions ensuring further liberalisation of the French and German telecommunications markets. The most important were that Sprint should be treated as a dominant carrier with specific reporting and authorisation duties with respect to tariffs and network expansion; it could not receive special advantages from the monopolist Deutsche Telekom and France Télécom; and during the next two years France Télécom would have to lower its tariffs in trans-Atlantic traffic to the level existing between the USA, and Germany and the UK.

Similar conditions were set half a year later by the European Commission giving the long-awaited final formal clearance for the 'supercarrier' alliance between France Télécom and Deutsche Telekom. The conditions were that France Télécom should sell Info AG, its data network services subsidiary competing in the German market with T-Data; France Télécom and Deutsche Telekom should allow non-discriminatory access to their networks to competing low-level data service operators; France Télécom and Deutsche Telekom should treat all third party competitors wanting to use their facilities in a non-discriminatory way; no cross-subsidies between the groups would be allowed, and Atlas and Global One should have separate accounting systems from France Télécom and Deutsche Telekom; finally, Atlas and Global One should conclude separate contracts with France Télécom and Deutsche Telekom to act as their distributors in France and Germany.

It was also stipulated that the alliance would be evaluated in 2001, when the Concert alliance between BT and MCI of the USA would also be reviewed, and the main services of the alliance would be authorised only once France and Germany had granted the first telecommunications licences to operators of alternative infrastructures.

It is clear that this arrangement was some kind of compromise between rather liberal competition policy goals at the EU level and a more neo-mercantilist perspective targeted at the global level in which the concentration of economic forces toward the improvement of global competitiveness and deregulation had to be combined. This conflicting dimension between the regional and the global is clearly reflected in the institutional separation between Atlas, which operated at the EU level, and Global One operating in the global arena. The future will show if such a solution really is workable.

When the administrative barriers to the alliance were taken way, the world's third global telecommunications alliance was launched on 1 February 1996 under the name Global One. Deutsche Telekom and France Télécom finally paid a total of $4.2 billion for a 20 per cent stake in Sprint, slightly more than expected. At the moment this company has about 2,500 employees working in 1,200 places in more than fifty countries. At the organisational level Global One consists of two subsidiary companies, in which the founding companies each contribute 33 per cent (Global One Rest of the World), and Sprint with 50 per cent and Deutsche Telekom and France Télécom 25 per cent each (Global One US).

Conclusion

Our analysis has shown that telecommunications policy provides an interesting case for the dynamics of Franco-German relations at a level of sectoral policy and politics. The historical description of telecommunications in France and Germany shows some strong parallels in the institutional transformations over the last ten or fifteen years. Up to the end of the 1980s, these similar changes resulted rather from the fact that both countries were subject to a similar vector of external pressures: the push of the European Commission toward liberalisation, the changes taking place in the UK and USA, technological progress in telecommunications undermining the status quo, and, as a first step, both countries reacted to these pressures independently of each other, since the configuration of political forces with respect to the liberalisation of telecommunications was different in the two countries. Generally speaking, in 1987 the German government was more in favour of competition than the French; the top managers of France Télécom more in favour of changes than the Deutsche Bundespost; and the big telecommunications users in Germany more in favour of liberalisation than the French (Vedel 1988; Schneider and Werle 1991; Grande and Schneider 1994).

However, a first instance of horizontal co-ordination took place in December 1989 when the French and German governments found a compromise in the European council which, in effect, slowed down the rhythm of telecommunications liberalisation driven by the Commission and supported by the UK. This defensive actor constellation only changed in the mid-1990s when both the French and German governments realised that the liberalisation of telecommunications could no longer be opposed, especially before the background of the newly created alliance Eunetcom between France Télécom and Deutsche Telekom in 1993.

As we have seen, the motivation for this alliance was rather complex. It would be too simple to reduce it to either a top-down process imposed on both companies from higher political levels (e.g. in the interest of 'Franco-German friendship'), or to simple strategic planning at company level. The decision to enter into this alliance was made by two autonomous public companies, whose choices were influenced, however, by governmental actors in the policy network. Once the alliance between Deutsche Telekom and France Télécom was formed, the context was changed again, and the French and German governments felt obliged to support their companies against the counter-attacks of the Commission and BT. In the end they agreed to a full liberalisation of telecommunications infrastructures in their respective countries on condition that the Commission gave the go-ahead for the Atlas and Global One alliances.

Overall, the development patterns of French–German relations in telecommunications seem to correspond neither to the pure intergovernmental model nor to the functionalist integration at grass-roots level. More appropriate would seem to be a policy network model in which simultaneously autonomous supranational, different intergovernmental and subnational actors participate in the policy process. Within this overall network, however, the centrality of governmental actors should not be neglected, since most EU decisions are agreements at the intergovernmental level, and most of these decisions presuppose some Franco-German understanding. Even when EU decisions are taken by qualified majority procedures they are never governed by the logic of 'minimal winning coalitions' but must rather be based on broad agreement at least among the major European countries. In this sense the settlement of the Atlas dispute was highly contingent on the supportive role that the two governments played in negotiations with Brussels.

Notes

1 The sources we have used are the EC Information Society Trend publications (1994–96) <http:// www.ispo.cec.be/ ispo/press.html>; related press publications in *Le Monde*, *Le Figaro*, *Financial Times*, *Frankfurter Allgemeine Zeitung* and *Handelsblatt*; expert interviews with C. Leboucher (French PTT Ministry), M. Hirsch and A. Vallee (France Télécom), and K.-D. Ordemann und P. Quander from the German PTT Ministry.
2 For an overview of deregulation, liberalisation and privatisation in advanced industrial countries see Grande (1994).
3 For diverse historical descriptions and interpretations of the German telecommunications reform process see Webber (1986); Grande (1989), Werle (1990), Schneider and Werle (1991), Humphreys (1992), Schmidt (1996).
4 In 1991, it was expected that Telekom's equity capital would amount to less than 24 per cent of its total capital in the coming years. This was far below a legally defined target minimum of 33 per cent (of total capital and reserves).
5 For the French reform process in telecommunications see Vedel (1988; 1991), Humphreys (1990), Chamoux (1993) and Cohen (1992).
6 Loi n° 96–659 du 26 juillet 1996 de réglementation des télécommunications.
7 Loi n° 96–660 du 26 juillet 1996 relative à l'entreprise nationale France Télécom.
8 For the history of EC telecommunications policy see Schneider and Werle (1990); Cohen (1992), Schneider *et al.* (1994), Simon (1994).
9 Council Resolution of 22 July 1993 on the review of the situation in the telecommunications sector and the need for further development in that market (93/C 213/01). The member states with less developed networks (Spain, Ireland, Greece and Portugal) are granted an additional transition period of up to five years, to achieve the necessary structural adjustments, in particular with respect to tariffs.

10 For a comparison of the French Videotex system with the British Prestel and the German Bildschirmtext, see Mayntz and Schneider (1988) and Thomas *et al.* (1992).

11 A general impression is that British Telecom has the strongest position in Community lobbying, influencing the Commission through a myriad of consultancy organisations. The British generally have a better position because they liberalised earlier. Oftel consultants have more experience and write many documents and consultative papers. It also seems that there is some kind of 'perverse effect' in this lobbying market due to the fact that BT laid off a lot of people, creating a large pool of expertise at low cost (these consultants just need to get incremental revenues), and the Commission is able to buy this expertise for half of the market price.

References

Alter, K.J. and S. Meunier-Aitsahalia (1994) 'Judicial politics in the European Community', *Comparative Political Studies* 26, 535–61.

Burley, A.-M. and Mattli, W. (1993) 'Europe Before the Court: A Political Theory of Legal Integration', *International Organization* 47, 41–76.

Chamoux, J.-P., (1993) *Télécoms: La fin des privilèges.* Paris: PUF.

Cohen, E. (1992) *Le Colbertisme 'high tech': Économie des télécoms et du grand projet.* Paris: Hachette.

Genschel, P and Werle, R. (1993) 'From national hierarchies to international standardization: modal changes in the governance of telecommunications', *Journal of Public Policy* 12, 203–26.

Grande, E. (1989) *Von Monopol zum Wettbewerb? Die neokonservative Reform der Telekommunikation in Grossbritannien und der Bundesrepublik Deutschland.* Wiesbaden: Deutscher Universitätsverlag.

—— (1994) 'The new role of the state in telecommunications: an international comparison', *West European Politics* 17, 138–57.

—— (1996) 'The state and interest groups in a framework of multilevel decision-making: the case of the European Union', *Journal of European Public Policy* 3:3, 318–38.

Grande, E. and Schneider, V. (1991) 'Reformstrategien und staatliche Handlungskapazitäten: Eine vergleichende Analyse institutionellen Wandels in der Telekommunikation in Westeuropa', *Politische Vierteljahresschrift* 32, 452–78.

—— (1994) 'Interests and organisations: contingencies of collective action analysed in the case of user organisations in telecommunications', unpublished manuscript.

Humphreys, P. (1990) 'The political economy of telecommunications in France: a case study of "Telematics"', in K. Dyson and P. Humphreys (eds), *The Political Economy of Communications. International and European Dimensions.* London: Routledge, 198–228.

—— (1992) 'The politics of regulatory reform in German telecommunications', in K. Dyson (ed.), *The Politics of German Regulation.* Aldershot: Dartmouth, 105–36

Lasserre, B. (1994) 'Quelle réglementation pour les télécommunications françaises?'. Report prepared for the Minister of Industry, Telecommunications and Trade. Paris.

Lequesne, C. (1996) 'La commission européenne entre autonomie et dépendance', *Revue Française des Sciences Politiques* 46, 389–408.

Mayntz, R. and V. Schneider (1988) 'The dynamics of system development in a comparative perspective: interactive videotex in Germany, France and Britain', in R. Mayntz and T.P. Hughes (eds), *The Development of Large Technical Systems.* Frankfurt a.M.: Campus, 263–98.

Morgan, K. and D. Webber (1986) 'Divergent paths: political strategies for telecommunications in Britain, France and West Germany', in K. Dyson and P. Humphreys (eds), *The Politics of the Communications Revolution in Western Europe*. London: Frank Cass, 56–79.

Sandholtz, W. and J. Zysman (1989) 'Recasting the European bargain', *World Politics* 42, 95–128.

Schmidt, S.K. (1996) 'Privatizing the federal postal and telecommunications services', in A. Benz and K.H. Goetz (eds), *A New German Public Sector? Reform, Adaptation and Stability.* Aldershot: Dartmouth.

—— (1997) 'Sterile debates and dubious generalisations: European integration theory tested by telecommunications and electricity', *Journal of Public Policy* 16:3, 233–71.

Schneider, V and R. Werle (1990) 'International regime or corporate actor? The European Community in telecommunications policy', in K. Dyson and P. Humphreys (eds), *The Political Economy of Communications: International and European Dimensions.* London: Routledge, 77–106.

—— (1991) 'Policy networks in the German telecommunications domain', in B. Marin and R. Mayntz (eds), *Policy Networks: Empirical Evidence and Theoretical Considerations.* Frankfurt a.M.: Campus, 97–136.

Schneider, V., G. Dang Nguyen and R. Werle (1994) 'Corporate actor networks in European policy-making: harmonizing telecommunications policy', *Journal of Common Market Studies* 32, 473–98.

Simon, J.P. (1994) 'Vers une réglementation européene unifiée? Généalogie de la réglementation des télécommunications (1973–1992)', *Réseaux* 66, 119–36.

Thomas, G., T. Vedel, and V. Schneider (1992) 'The United Kingdom, France and Germany: setting the stage', in H. Bowman and M. Christofferson (eds), *Relaunching Videotex.* Dordrecht: Kluwer, 15–30.

Vedel, T. (1988) 'La déréglementation des télécommunications en France: Politique et jeu politique', in Institut Français des Sciences Administratives (ed.) *Les Déréglementations: Etude comparative.* Paris: Economica, 281–312.

—— (1991) 'La réforme de P et T.', in *Universalia 1991: La politique, les connaissances, la culture en 1990.* Paris: Encyclopaedia Universalis, 273–6.

—— (1997) 'Les politiques des autoroutes de l'information en Europe: convergence et écologies des jeux', *Revue politiques et management public* (forthcoming).

Webber, D. (1986) 'Die ausbleibende Wende bei der Deutschen Bundespost: Zur Regulierung des Telekommunikationswesens in der Bundesrepublik Deutschland', *Politische Vierteljahresschrift* 27, 397–414.

Werle, R. (1990) *Telekommunikation in der Bundesrepublik Deutschland: Expansion, Differenzierung, Transformation.* Frankfurt a.M.: Campus.

6

INTEGRATION WITH A SPLUTTERING ENGINE

The Franco-German relationship in European research and technology policy

Burkard Eberlein and Edgar Grande

Introduction

The age of techno-nationalism in Europe is over. On the verge of the twenty-first century, urgent social problems such as the improvement of industrial competitiveness, the elimination and prevention of ecological damage, structural long-term unemployment and the economic exclusion of entire groups of people cannot be solved solely at a national level. Thus, international co-operation has become an indispensable part of technology policy which in most European countries today is embedded in a variable geometry of international agreements and organisations – France and Germany are no exception to this.

The history of European scientific and technological co-operation is characterised by a rich variety of modes and organisations (cf. Krige and Guzzetti 1995). The European Union is not the only European institution relevant in this context. Meanwhile, however, it has gained an outstanding role. With the Single European Act and the Treaty on European Union (Maastricht Treaty), the European Union received extensive political powers in the field of research and technology policy. The EU is not only charged with 'strengthening the scientific and technological bases of Community industry and encouraging it to become more competitive at an international level', (Article 130f (1), EC Treaty), it is also authorised under this newly formulated article '[to] promote all the research activities deemed necessary by virtue of other Chapters in this Treaty'. On this basis, the Council has so far passed four Framework Programmes for Research and Technological Development, the latest in April 1994, in which a total of ECU12.3 billion (now ECU13.1 billion) is made available for the support of science and technology between 1994 and 1998.

Role of the EU in technology policy

It is true that the EU's research budget is still small in comparison to the research budgets of its big member states. In 1992 ECU50 billion were spent by the (then) twelve member states on publicly financed research; in comparison only ECU1.8 billion were spent by the EU, that is approximately 3.5 per cent (European Commission 1994). Of the entire public R&D expenditures in the Federal Republic of Germany from 1987 to 1991, the EU funded only about 0.4 per cent (Reger and Kuhlmann 1995). However, two points have to be given special consideration when assessing the role of the EU in technology policy, since such crude comparisons can lead to a gross underestimation of its real significance.

First, it is important to consider that despite the large number of programmes it supports, the EU clearly sets thematic focal points in technology policy, including key technologies vital to the industrial future of the Union and its member states such as microelectronics, communications technology, new materials, bio-technology, genetic engineering and other areas. In these fields financial support by the European Union is also quantitatively relevant. The largest and most important focal area is certainly information and communications technology (I&C technology). With programmes such as ESPRIT and RACE as well as various programmes for the development of applications in I&C technology, the Union has been trying, since the mid-1980s, systematically to improve the competitiveness of the European information technology industry (Grande and Häusler 1994; Esser *et al.* 1997). These programmes – which, under other names and new focal points, continued in the Fourth Framework Programme – have had more than ECU5 billion in funding. Thus, the shares of funding provided by the member states and by the Union for I&C technology have, within a few years, shifted significantly toward the EU. Meanwhile, a company like Siemens, to name one example, receives approximately half its public funding, albeit only a small fraction of its research budget, from European Union programmes.

The significance of the European Union in technology policy is not limited to research funding, however. The EU is now active in a multitude of areas which are of consequence for the political regulation of technological development and industrial competitiveness. When it comes to issues such as establishing guidelines for environmental protection or the regulation of genetic engineering, the liberalisation of the telecommunications market or data protection, agreeing on technological norms and standards or the approval of corporate mergers, the EU is a crucial actor, or perhaps even the most important one. And in this context, it should not be forgotten that by strictly monitoring the public R&D funding in the member states, the Union has, for quite some time now, noticeably restricted the national governments' capacity to act in the area of technology policy.

The empirical evidence is clear and obvious: whenever the social organisation of technology and the competitiveness of industries in Europe are at stake, the European Union now plays a central role. As a consequence of European integration, a new architecture of stateness has been evolving and, hence, the economic and institutional framework of technology policy-making and the constellations of social interests involved have changed fundamentally (Grande 1993).

The emergence of a common research and technology policy in the 1980s was all but obvious. On the contrary, R&D policy has for a long time been one of those fields in which most attempts at a closer supranational integration failed or remained insignificant. It is true that European co-operation in the nuclear sector had been one of the earliest examples of supranational integration with the European Atomic Energy Community (EURATOM) already founded in 1957. However, after the crisis of EURATOM in the mid-1960s, its initial objective – the development of nuclear power reactors on a Community basis – was abandoned, and then it rather seemed as if the European countries would co-operate only outside the Community framework, if at all. In the aviation sector, bilateral agreements such as the Anglo-French Concorde and the Franco-German Airbus have been the predominant mode of co-operation, and in the space sector co-operation took place in the framework of international organisations such as the European Launcher Development Organization (ELRO) and the European Space Research Organization (ESRO), both founded in 1962, and merged into the European Space Agency (ESA) in 1975. Attempts at European co-operation in data processing (Eurodata, Unidata) and microelectronics, initiated in the 1960s and 1970s, failed completely (cf. Sharp and Shearman 1987: 24–41).

The poor record of Community activities in technology policy until the early 1980s is even more surprising since it was almost undisputed that supranational programmes would be essential for Europe's industrial future. For example, Jean-Jacques Servan-Schreiber in his widely cited book *Le Défi Américain* (1967), concluded that: 'We stand with our backs to the wall – the return to the nation-state is no longer possible; either we develop a European industrial policy, or the American industry will continue to determine the future of the Common Market' (Servan-Schreiber 1968: 168).[1] At the same time, he had to realise that the then existing co-operative ventures among European countries and companies were only a 'caricature' of the response Servan-Schreiber assumed to be necessary and, even worse, that the way towards closer European (i.e. supranational) co-operation seemed to be 'blocked'. The failure of joint nuclear research under the framework of EURATOM in the mid-1960s was a telling example in this respect.[2]

As we all know, the way towards closer supranational co-operation in technology policy remained blocked for years, although Servan-Schreiber's message was well received by the governments of the EC member states. Even more, in their summit at The Hague in December 1969, the heads of the six member states declared 'their readiness to continue more intensively the activities of the community with a desire to co-ordinating and promoting industrial R&D in the principal sectors concerned, *in particular by means of common programmes*' (quoted in Aked and Gummet 1976: 276; emphasis added). These general commitments remained lip-service, however. They did not lead to common programmes, prepared and implemented by the EC. The member states finally agreed to co-operate in R&D policy without giving more legal competences and more financial resources to the EC.[3] In the 1970s, the results of these half-hearted attempts to co-operate were programmes such as COST (*Coopération Scientifique et Technologique*), approved in 1971, and the Commission's first Action Programme on Science and Technology, endorsed in 1973, which both remained insignificant.

Summing up, the process of European integration in technology policy was characterised by a striking discrepancy between general commitments to closer European co-operation on the one hand and the prevalence of national policies and intergovernmental agreements on the other. France and Germany both fitted well into this general pattern. Hence, our first crucial problem is to explain the persistence of national technology policies and the preferences for other forms of co-operation in this policy field.

Why co-operate? patterns of conflict in European technology policy

The key to a better understanding of why there are serious problems of co-operation in European technology policy is the pattern of conflicts among the member states. In the field of technology policy, such an approach is of particular importance, because this policy area is characterised by a very complex, multi-dimensional structure of conflicts. In detail, we can distinguish at least three different dimensions of conflict: strategic, material, and ideological (Grande 1995). Of course, these dimensions interact in policy-making so that it is sometimes difficult to separate and identify the 'real' issues at stake. For our purposes, however, it is useful to treat them separately.

Strategically, in technology policy as in most other policy areas there are several alternative routes which national policy-makers can choose to pursue their goals. The scope of strategic options includes: unco-operative national policies, various forms of intergovernmental co-operation with other European or non-European governments, and, finally, joint EC programmes. The supranational integration of authority and the pooling of resources is only one option and, as we have seen, for most of the time not the preferred one. These options are distinct in various respects: their territorial scope, their decision-making rules, their distributional consequences etc. Most important, the sovereignty of the states involved is affected to a varying extent. This aspect is crucial whenever technology projects are closely linked to national defence and military interests. In these cases, national strategies clearly have been dominant, only complemented by intergovernmental co-operation in very specific cases.

With the advancement of European integration, these strategic conflicts have been transformed at least partly into institutional conflicts at the European, i.e. EU level. The member states did not fully give up their interests in preserving national sovereignty. Rather, these interests are now expressed in institutional conflicts between Council, Commission and Parliament. In the case of technology policy, for most of the time the Commission and the EP have been the driving forces, whereas the Council used to apply the brakes.

In addition, the EU's technology policy has been burdened with intense and complicated material conflicts. To a considerable extent, these conflicts have been the result of the member states' different stages of economic and industrial development and their different R&D capacities. There are a number of indicators which show these discrepancies (cf. Eurostat 1994; OECD 1994). Most striking are the differences between the national R&D expenditures in Europe. In Germany, the member state with the highest R&D spending, these expenditures are a hundred times higher than those of Greece, the member state with the lowest budget of R&D spending. In 1992, France and Germany alone accounted for almost 60 per cent of R&D expenditures in the EU. A comparison of member states' R&D intensity, i.e. their share of GDP devoted to R&D, confirms this general impression. Before the EU's enlargement in 1995, there were only four countries with a high R&D intensity, i.e. devoting more than 2 per cent of GDP to R&D, France and Germany among them of course. On the other hand, there were four countries spending less than 1 per cent of their GDP on R&D.

Different national structures of R&D expenditures and varying roles of the state in the national research systems further add to this diversity. Defence research is an important aspect. Whereas it is insignificant in most member states, it accounts for more than one-third of national R&D expenditures in France and almost half of the public R&D budget in the UK. Similar differences can be observed in the area of industrial R&D. The role of industry in the national R&D systems varies considerably. In Germany, about 70 per cent of national R&D is performed by industry, compared to roughly 25 per cent in Greece and Portugal, to take the opposite extreme.

All these differences in national R&D capacities and national research systems help to explain the striking divergence of national R&D strategies, policies and programmes. Whereas some member states, the small ones in particular but also including Germany, used to employ a 'diffusion-oriented' approach in technology policy, others, especially France, adopted a 'mission-oriented approach' (cf. Ergas 1987).

These disparities between national R&D capacities and the different national R&D policies have been the source of intense distributional conflicts on the level of European technology policy and a serious obstacle to further European integration in this policy field. In general, the smaller and less-endowed member states have been in favour of more European programmes on the premise, however, that funds would primarily be used to promote the development of their R&D capacities. For the very same reason, the big member states, France and Germany among them, have been reluctant to give more legal competences and additional resources to the Commission. In their view, such a transfer would prevent them from catching up with the USA and Japan rather than strengthen European industrial competitiveness.

Finally, European R&D policy always had to cope with fundamental ideological conflicts. In our context the conflict about the appropriate role of the state in economic and industrial policy has been of particular salience. In theory, we can distinguish various paradigms of economic policy-making and these can be related to different 'models of growth', among them a 'state-led' model of growth and a 'market- or company-led' model, and France and Germany are usually taken as the ideal cases for the respective models (cf. Zysman 1983).

The consequence of this complex, multidimensional pattern of conflicts among member states has been diffused and changing coalitions in European decision-making. On top of, and sometimes cross-cutting the distributional divide between poor and rich countries, policy outcomes have also been shaped by the impact of the two other conflict dimensions, namely the institutional tension between supra-national integration (Commission), national sovereignty (Council of Ministers) and parliamentary control (European Parliament) on the one hand, and the ideo-logical tensions between interventionism and market liberalism on the other.

The combined effect of these divides can be observed in the multiple conflicts preceding and surrounding the negotiations of the Framework Programmes. For example, 'poor' Spain and 'anti-interventionist' Britain joined forces in the run-up to the Third Framework Programme, but for very different reasons. Whereas the British opposed any expansion of (supposedly) 'interventionist' EC progr-ammes for ideological reasons, Spain supported a heavy expansion of these programmes in principle, but it did not accept the proposals presented because of their expected distributional consequences. Since qualified majority voting, though formally possible in the instance of specific programmes, has de facto been supplanted by the search for a consensual solution, negotiation processes have been cumbersome and their outcomes hard to predict.

Concerning French and German interest representation, we can identify both correspondence and substantial divergence of interests between the two countries in technology policy. As far as the distributional dimension is concerned, French and German interests converge at least with respect to the smaller, less developed member states. However, both countries tend to diverge on the ideological axis. For a long time, the 'continuing tensions between French interventionism and German commitment to the free market' (Sharp and Shearman 1987: 39) have been an obstacle to the emergence of a European approach in technology policy. Furthermore, both dimensions of conflict overlap, for example, regarding the role of small and medium-sized companies in R&D policy.

It is true that there was some convergence between the French and the German positions in the strategic dimension, but this did not imply that the partners would necessarily choose the way of supranational collaboration. Instead, they used to opt for national solutions or they agreed on patterns of co-operation outside the EC ambit. The foundation of EUREKA in 1985, an incident in which the Franco-German engine was most powerful in European technology policy, is a striking example, as we will see below.

Summing up, compared to other policy fields, because of the complex, multidimensional pattern of conflicts, it was almost impossible to establish a stable Franco-German axis in technology policy. There has been no such a thing as a stable Franco-German coalition or 'engine' and, even worse, in those cases in which Franco-German interests converged, the Franco-German axis was an obstacle to further supranational integration rather than its engine.

Co-operation outside the community framework: intergovernmental minimalism in European technology policy

Despite all the obstacles to co-operation, due to the sheer weight of their national R&D potentials, France and Germany hold dominant positions on the European research and technology stage. Against this background, the Commission was well advised carefully to consider and possibly 'incorporate' French and German reservations and preferences when developing policy proposals in the early 1980s. National policy powers and interests were on top, and consequently, the Commission (rather than France and Germany vis-à-vis the Commission) crucially depended on privileged access to, or a 'special relationship' with, national governments.

As a matter of fact, given the complex, multidimensional structure of conflicts in European technology policy portrayed above, one is tempted to raise the question of how substantial supranational policies ever had a chance of emerging in the first place since any 'pooling of national sovereignty' on the European level was subject to the consensus of the large member states, and notably of France and Germany.

This very institutional constellation of national preponderance was part of the reason why European technological collaboration up to the mid-1970s had a rather poor track record. 'Industrial patriotism' (Hayward 1986) and national champion-centred strategies prevailed. Successful co-operation was most likely to occur if it put minimal restraints on national sovereignty or the competitive position of national industries. 'Franco-German links played a key role in several collaborative ventures, though rivalries between them were important in some others' (Sharp and Shearman 1987: 39). While the Franco-German axis was helpful, for example, in aviation and space technology, rivalries and competition were most prominent in fields like computers, supplemented by ideological tensions between French interventionism and the German commitment to free market economics (Sharp and Holmes 1989; Cawson et al. 1990). Hence, our next crucial problem is to explain the emergence and expansion of supranational policies. What was different in the 1980s and what roles did France and Germany play?

Many observers stress the fact that important economic and technological changes radically transformed European perceptions about technological competitiveness and the need for collaborative efforts on the European level (cf. Sharp and Shearman 1987; Sandholtz 1992; Peterson 1993). The dramatic decline of European industries in strategic sectors like microelectronics and telecommunications, US predominance in increasingly global markets, and the rise of Japan as a technological power combined to trigger a new 'technology gap' debate creating a favourable climate for a 'common European response'. Obviously, the Commission was happy to push the alarmist tone of urgency, which accorded fresh legitimacy to supranational policy proposals (European Commission 1979, 1981, 1982). However, the 'technology gap scare' and, for that matter, the 'défi américain', though this time it reached new dimensions with the SDI programme, were not fundamentally novel phenomena. More important, even the strong and most widespread belief that European industry stood to benefit from collaborative agreements was, as successive failures in the 1960s and 1970s had shown, no guarantee for such a solution to win decisive political support, both among member states and the big companies concerned. We shall now turn to these two sets of actors and their interaction with the 'third man', i.e. the European Commission, as the agent of supranationalisation, in our search for a solution to the puzzle of European integration 'despite a spluttering engine'.

France and Germany in particular had several reasons to oppose a supranational response to technological 'Eurosclerosis'. To be sure, French and German interests in research and technology policy did not always converge, and if they did their common positions were not always driven by common interests. But faced with Commission initiatives for EC-level R&D activities in the early 1980s, French and German interests combined to act, at least initially, as a brake on the ambitious 'Europeanisation' of research and technology pushed by the Commission.

For one thing, in both countries large national programmes to boost domestic capacities in information technology were underway when the Commission submitted proposals for European-level policies designed to improve European competitiveness in the same sectors. This was of particular salience in the French case (cf. Cohen and Bauer 1985; Cawson *et al.* 1990). The incoming Socialist government made the development of research and technology one of its top priorities and launched ambitious public programmes for national techno-industrial renewal, pretty much along the traditional lines of national champion strategy. A prominent example was the 'Programme d'action filière électronique', which, over a period of five years (1982–86), was supposed to provide the national electronics industry with FF140 billion of investment, including FF60 billion in direct state support (Sandholtz 1992: 148–9).

However, with the spectacular U-turn from Keynesian expansionism to liberal austerity in March 1983, thereby announcing a progressive decline of state dirigisme, France quickly had to abandon the costly 'walk-alone' strategy of 'colbertism high tech' (Cohen 1992) and become one of the most vocal supporters of European collaboration. As early as September 1983 the French government suggested the idea of a 'European industrial space' to other member states. This did not mean, though, that France was willing simply to surrender national prerogatives to the Commission. Instead, it hoped to give this co-operation a distinctly French flavour, i.e. to forge patterns of co-operation which were close to French policy needs and concepts and which would, more generally, allow France to pursue national interests at the European level, that is with the help of potent European partners like Germany.

The German counterpart, however, could not be expected to give European technological collaboration an wholly enthusiastic welcome. First, the German government had also launched large-scale national programmes in microelectronics and telecommunications. For example, in the course of the 1980s the German Federal Research and Technology Ministry alone spent more than DM2.3 billion on microelectronics, out of which DM0.7 billion were alloted to applications constituting a new policy focus (Grande 1994: 121). Second, specific adminis_ trative interests came into play, notably ministerial reservations about the benefits of European collaboration. The BMFT was not in principle opposed to trans-national co-operation provided it offered a clear 'surplus', was limited in scope and allowed for substantial national control. The Dutch–German 'Mega-Project', for example, linking Siemens and Philips in the development of advanced semiconductors, received BMFT funding worth DM310 million. But the BMFT was opposed to large-scale, industry-related programmes under ambitious Community leadership involving a significant loss in national control. In this context, the BMFT complained that the Commission, a novice in integrated R&D and innovation policies, would copy and reproduce (old) German-style funding programmes with little additional value and a high risk of duplication.

Moreover, the Federal Ministries of Economics and of Finance shared the British aversion to large spending programmes and the linking of R&D to broader political goals associated with European 'industrial policy', notably steps towards further integration discussed at that time. In a similar vein, they were hostile to the emergence of a powerful supranational bureaucracy, the only point where there was convergence with French reservations. However, France could count on the pro-European stance of the German Foreign Office and, to a certain extent, on the high symbolic value the Franco-German partnership enjoyed in the German political class and in public opinion.

This was particularly evident in the genesis of the EUREKA project, which, more importantly, is highly instructive as to the consequences of the national positions described above for patterns of (non) co-operation: both France and Germany, driven by the 'technology gap debate', perceived the need to take action across national boundaries, but they clearly preferred a least binding type of co-operation, involving minimal constraints on national control and policy powers.

In the mid-1980s, the American invitation to European allies to participate in the large-scale SDI initiative reshaped the strategic context of national R&D policies in terms of technological collaboration. There were two options – the first, to 'go international' and join the American programme, worth $26 billion, over five years. Britain was in favour, Germany was inclined to join, while France was a stark opponent, if only for defence reasons; the second to 'go supranational'. However, for reasons stated above, all three rather opposed the impending expansion of EC-level R&D activities orchestrated by the Commission. Moreover, for the very reason of national opposition to sovereignty transfers, Community programmes could not be expected to be a viable alternative or counterweight to the SDI.

In this context, France, which feared Germany might join Britain in 'going transatlantic', rushed forward and opened up a third option or avenue of co-operation, namely the European intergovernmental one. France pushed for a vaguely defined and loose framework of technological co-operation explicitly outside the ambit of the EC and with the potential to be a match for SDI. This initiative could build on earlier French proposals formulated as early as 1983 when France had realised that the time for national solos in R&D policy was over. German endorsement for EUREKA was indispensable, and skilfully to engage the German foreign office helped the French to secure German support (Peterson 1993: 64; Grande 1994: 226–51).

More fundamentally, the EUREKA framework was a success because it satisfied converging French and German interests, and this is why the 'Franco-German engine', in this particular instance only, worked quite well. First, EUREKA provided national governments with a ready-at-hand response (EUREKA was hammered out in a very short period of time) to the imminent pressure to take action in favour of European competitiveness. (By that time, anti-interventionist Germany and Britain, too, were convinced that there was need for European action.) Second, it neither required the abandonment of national control, nor did it involve redistribution of financial resources across national borders. Thus, it corresponded to a 'least-binding type of co-operation' and the potential for conflict was low. Third, and related to the latter point, it allowed France and Germany to circumvent or at least slow down the outright 'Europeanisation' of research and technology put forward by the Commission. This national 'win set' gave large member states a strong enough incentive to agree to transnational technological co-operation.

Co-operation within the Community framework: neo-functionalist logic of European technology policy

However, over and above EUREKA, as we know today, the 1980s also witnessed a substantial expansion of Community policies in research and technology, most notably with the flagship programme ESPRIT equally designed to improve European competitiveness in information technology. Since France and Germany had been hesitant to go beyond rather minimalist types of co-operation, we need to ask who instead carried the functional dynamic triggered and nurtured by the technology gap debate beyond loose intergovernmental collaborations to the heights of supranationalisation?

The obvious candidate for the role as an engine of European integration was the Commission, which, by the way, first tried but did not manage, to bring EUREKA under Community control. The Commission alone, however, was not powerful enough to press for supranationalisation, and the only institutional ally in the Community framework, the European Parliament, was too weak a support. But how then did the Commission manage to outweigh large member states' resistance to supranational policies, considering that, on top, with EUREKA a convenient strategic alternative to the constraints of Community policies was emerging at the same time?

For one thing, of course, EUREKA was only born after and, most importantly, partly because Community policies, perceived as a threat to national powers by large member states, had already been initiated. To answer our question, we need to turn to the second group of actors with decisive weight in the policy process, namely the big European firms in information and communications technology. Any public policy effort to boost European competitiveness in globalising markets crucially depended on the willingness of these large economic players to participate in collaborative, transnational ventures and European programmes. The poor record of European technological collaboration of the 1960s and early 1970s was partly due to the fact that economic competition between national champions ruled out co-operative agreements with industrial counterparts in Europe, or that these companies preferred alliances with American and, later, Japanese companies.

However, this picture changed quite dramatically in the course of the 1970s. Rapid technological innovation, the escalating costs of R&D and the globalisation of markets accompanied by intensified competition pushed Europe's IT industries to seek interfirm alliances across national borders (Sharp and Shearman 1987; Mytelka and Delapierre 1988; Sandholtz 1992). While national governments continued to reason in terms of national champions and domains, national enterprises started heavily to engage in transnational alliance building and co-operative agreements.

This switch from national competition to transnational co-operation made European companies receptive to the tune of Commission-led technological co-operation. The Commission, under the leadership of Industry Commissioner Davignon, skilfully capitalised on the crisis-induced, co-operative stance of European companies and made them its allies in the crusade for Community-based research and technology policies vis-à-vis member states and the Council of Ministers. As early as 1979 Davignon began 'advocacy-coalition building' (Sabatier 1988) by taking the initiative to invite the twelve biggest European companies in information technology to form a 'Round Table' supposed to discuss and develop Community-based policies in support of European industries.

Initially, scepticism reigned, but eventually the 'Big Twelve' agreed to participate in exchange for a 'bottom-up', industry-led programme (ESPRIT) largely tailored to their needs. It is most interesting to note that half of the companies involved were French or German: Bull, CGE (Alcatel) and Thomson on the one side, and AEG, Nixdorf and Siemens on the other. Another three were domiciled in the UK (GEC, Plessey and STC-ICL), while two were based in Italy (Olivetti and STET) and one in the Netherlands (Philips). Thus, while French and German governments were acting as the brakes, their 'national champions' were among the driving forces of supranational integration.

The political process leading up to the final approval of ESPRIT by the Council of Ministers was long and cumbersome. Member state opposition, expressing national reservations about the upgrading of Commission-led Community policies, was the main obstacle. Here again, both France and Germany acted as troublemakers, rather than as an 'engines' for advances in European integration. France wanted to see total expenditure limited to ECU400 million, while Germany was joined by Britain in repeatedly delaying approval altogether, supposedly until an overall reform of EC finances was agreed. When ESPRIT finally won government endorsement, it only did so with many strings attached, like the imposition of strict financial ceilings and the restriction to pre-competitive research. However, some of these conditions were relaxed later, when ESPRIT became a political success story and the Commission was granted more funds than initially agreed upon.

All along, industry endorsement and support vis-à-vis national governments gave decisive political momentum to the Commission initiative (Grande 1994: 259). In early 1983, for example, the 'Big Twelve' backed Commissioner Davignon by addressing a letter to him strongly underwriting the need for an ambitious Community initiative on which they made dependent the survival of the entire IT industries in Europe. Obviously, this letter was meant to exercise pressure on national governments, and it did so quite successfully. In return, the big companies were given large powers to define and shape the programme.

While other Community programmes such as BRITE, EURAM and RACE also deserve attention, ESPRIT is of particular importance. Not only did ESPRIT serve as the flagship and strategic lever for the breakthrough of Community-based R&D policies, which have been dominated by I&C technologies in the last decade as witnessed by their 40 per cent share in the second and third framework programmes. Also, ESPRIT served as a model for future, industry-oriented Community programmes, for example, as far as administrative procedures and rules of funding are concerned.

In sum, the opposition of national governments was eventually eroded by the transnational co-operation of private economic actors and the entrepreneurial role played by the Commission. Thus, the neo-functionalist logic of transnational co-operation, rather than patterns and benefits of intergovernmental co-operation, let alone the much-acclaimed 'Franco-German engine', lent support to the emergence and expansion of EC/EU-level research and technology policies.

Adapting national interests to new realities: Franco-German convergence in European technology policy

The above results clearly contradict intergovernmentalist claims in the literature about the crucial, and more or less benign, role played by the Franco-German 'axis' in the advancement of European integration, such as the recent statement made by Wood (1995: 221) that 'the engine of European integration has been and continues to be the Franco-German partnership, and the national governments remain the chief but not the only players'. On the other hand, a purely neo-functionalist explanation of European integration in technology policy would equally run the risk of over-simplification.

Despite the relative success of the functionalist and supranational logic, national interests and conflicts between member states continue to loom large in today's EU research and technology policy. The fact that a proper supranational (and transnational) dynamic has progressively been set in motion should by no means be interpreted as the demise of national interest representation. As dominant actors on the European scene, France and Germany, once they had more or less grudgingly accepted the idea of a supranational policy in research and technology, were able to shape the rules of the game and bring their specific (national) interests to bear on the (supranational) policy process. Here again, we encounter the interplay of strategic or institutional, material and ideological conflicts, now within the framework of EU research and technology policy.

One case in point is the principle of subsidiarity on which the German Federal Research Ministry had insisted in particular. It was enshrined in the context of the first (five-year) Framework Programme and reflected the larger members' interest in obstructing any automatic transfer of national R&D powers to the European level. Any policy transfer was to be justified according to several criteria (cf. Grande 1996).

This example shows that national interest formation and conflict resolution in EU technology policy do not primarily hinge upon Franco-German consensus or dissent per se. Rather, France and Germany both belong to the club of the large and rather prosperous countries whose interests diverge from small and less endowed member states. The former would like EU policy to concentrate on high-tech excellence important to their national industries and therefore defend the subsidiarity principle. The latter, by contrast, expect the Commission to give them support for R&D capacity building and consequently would welcome an enhanced role for the Commission and redistributive R&D policies (cohesion principle) in general.

A closer look at the distributional consequences of EU programmes such as ESPRIT and RACE shows the heavy concentration of EU funding on the five larger member states where the 'Big Twelve' are domiciled. They received 89 per cent of ESPRIT I and 84 per cent of ESPRIT II funding, while their share in RACE accounts for 83 per cent (Grande 1994: 272, 291). Peterson (1996: 232) points to the fact that Britain, France, Germany and Italy alone 'received more than three quarters of all EU funding for IT and communications technologies under Framework II'.

However, some big countries fare better than and at the expense of others. For France in particular the strategy to 'go European' paid off, with 26.3 per cent of ESPRIT I and 24.4 per cent of ESPRIT II France scored the highest national rate of funding. More important, France is a net beneficiary of the I&C programmes whereas Germany and Italy 'pay the bill' (see Grande 1994: 273, 293). Thus, redistribution occurs rather within the prosperous club of large member states than between them and the less endowed nations.

But also on the strategic and the ideological dimension, France and Germany had some incentives to play the European card, once the EU research and technology policy arena had been firmly established. This is related to the fact that not only national interests continue to bear upon the EU policy process, but also national positions and strategies have, in turn, been affected by the expansion of European policies. As to the French and the German positions, there has been considerable development since the early 1980s on both the strategic and ideological dimension. As we have demonstrated, both France and Germany initially opposed ambitious EC-level, industry-oriented policies and thus took a similar stance on the strategic issue of national control. However, with the progressive expansion of EC/EU policy dynamics, some important changes occurred.

For France, the decision to pursue the goal of French technological competitiveness at the European level turned out to be much more than a strategic cover-up of 'hidden techno-nationalism' on a larger scale. In addition to the financial benefits accruing from European policies, France realised that European programmes (both EC/EU and intergovernmental ones like EUREKA) could play an important strategic role in the necessary transformation of its own research system. In the context of the general shift away from state dirigisme, national-champion and *grands-programmes* strategies (Schmidt 1996), European collaboration helped to break the traditional isolation and business aversion of the French research system and pushed new and rewarding methods and avenues of technological research (Larédo and Callon 1990). The European policy approach nicely fitted the new, less 'mission' and more 'diffusion-oriented' agenda of French innovation policies emerging in the mid-1980s (Mustar 1994): encouraging R&D activities in much more French firms including SMEs (small and medium-sized eenterprises), a stronger emphasis on broad environmental support for innovation to the detriment of direct state subsidies, transnational co-operation and the promotion of regional technological development (Eberlein 1996, 1997). Consequently, France went some way to harmonising its domestic innovation policies with European programmes and, to some extent, tied its national innovation system to the dynamics of European-level policies. In sum, domestic policy changes effectively contributed, over time, to a much more pro-European position, even if, of course, France continued to pursue national ambitions.

These institutional changes clearly express underlying transformations on the ideological axis: the decline of interventionist policies resulted in a certain ideological rapprochement with market-oriented countries like Germany. Germany, in turn, also adapted to the new realities of international and supranational dynamics of research and technology policy which had complemented (but by no means superseded) national programmes and strategies.

Concerning the ideological dimension, Germany settled for a type of 'market-based industrial policy' at the Community level, which, though developed by German Commissioner Martin Bangemann, seemed to entail some concessions on the liberal stance of German economic and industrial policy. However, German practice, resulting from a compromise between the liberal Federal Ministry of Economics and the more interventionist Federal Research Ministry, has never quite matched the laissez-faire rhetoric. Thus, the European concept, situated, on the face of it, some way between fragments of old-style French interventionism and the German hands-off principle, was, in reality, a notion imported from German practice. Nevertheless, there was pragmatic reorientation of policy approaches on both sides which helped somewhat to reduce traditional ideological tensions and to increase the common 'win set' of France and Germany in Community-based technology policy.

In sum, we see a certain convergence of French and German positions, with both countries now, more or less, seeking actively to participate in and adapt to – rather than simply obstruct – European-level decision-making processes and policies.

Conclusion

In much of the relevant literature, the Franco-German couple is portrayed as the driving force or 'engine' of European integration. Simonian (1985: 361–362) diagnoses, at least for the time after 1974, a 'Franco-German "axis" in Europe' and asserts the 'indispensability of agreement between them (Paris and Bonn) for wider progress in the EEC'. In his foreword to the study written by Friend (1991) who sees European integration revolving around a Franco-German 'linchpin', A.W. DePorte qualifies the Franco-German partnership over the last forty years as a 'remarkably stable and constructive pattern of co-operation, the most important fruit of which is the European Community'.

To be sure, some authors, stressing the weight of diverging national interests, realise that Franco-German co-operation cannot be taken for granted and should rather be interpreted as a permanent 'struggle to co-operate', with 'spurts of co-operation and the ebbs that follow them' (McCarthy 1993: 23). Also, authors like Bulmer and Paterson (1987: 229) point to important divergences between France and Germany in the field of economic policy-making, creating obstacles to co-operation. On balance, however, the picture of the Franco-German partnership as 'engine of European integration' (Wood 1995: 221) seems to prevail.

Our argument is that in the particular field of research and technology policy we find the opposite pattern or logic at work. Franco-German co-operation at the supranational level is not the cause but rather the result of Community policies. At least initially, France and Germany acted as a brake on the emergence and expansion of EC/EU research and technology policies and rather preferred other, less demanding forms of international co-operation instead. The opposition of national governments to supranational integration was eroded by the transnational co-operation of private economic actors and the entrepreneurial role played by the Commission. Thus, in our case, we did not have a Franco-German driving force or engine but rather an engine that, so to speak, needed to be driven.

This does not detract from the importance of the Franco-German 'engine' for European integration in general. And it would be quite presumptuous to try and do so on the basis of a single case study. However, the different logic revealed in research and technology policy should alert us to the importance of sectoral variation of co-operation patterns. While in some sectors the Franco-German axis is a prime prerequisite and determinant of European integration processes (see, for example, the contribution by Webber in this volume), in other policy fields we need to focus much more on different factors and players beyond the important role played the French and German governments. This has important implications for integration theory, since it seriously calls into question inter-governmentalist claims about the pervasive and crucial weight of national govern-ments' preferences and interests across different sectors or policy fields.

However, national interests continue to play an important role in European technology policy. But they do not exclusively revolve around the Franco-German axis. Rather, they take the form of strategic, material or ideological conflicts between member states and within the EU system and combine to produce a very complex, multidimensional structure of conflicts.

In the context of this new EU arena, there has been some convergence of the French and German positions towards European policies. France in particular tends to benefit materially from European programmes, and there has also been a certain ideological rapprochement between French interventionism and German free market economics due to a pragmatic reorientation of economic policy approaches on both sides.

This convergence, however, should not raise high hopes of a bright future for a Franco-German 'engine' in European technology policy. This is because of the outstanding importance of economic globalisation, which, in this policy area, will have a greater impact on the development of Franco-German co-operation than German unification. To be sure, on the one hand globalisation blocks the way back to national-oriented economic policies, thus favouring patterns of co-operation between France and Germany. But on the other hand, globalisation constitutes a threat to privileged Franco-German economic co-operation (and, for that matter, to European co-operation in general) on the company level: the cosy Franco-German couple (if it ever existed) could be – and in fact partly has been – ousted by the ever-increasing weight of global alliances (cf. Muldur and Petrella 1994).

Notes

1 For similar statements, see Layton (1969).
2 The preface to the German edition of Servan-Schreiber's book was written by Franz-Josef Strauss, then Minister of Finance in the Federal Government, and it almost goes without saying that Strauss supported both the author's recommendations and conclusions.
3 In other words, the joint activities agreed upon in the early 1970s were another example of the non-committal way of co-operating 'which leads nowhere', as criticised by Servan-Schreiber (1968: 162).

References

Aked, N.H. and P.J. Gummet (1976) 'Science and technology in the European Communities: the history of the cost projects', *Research Policy* 5, 270–94.

Bulmer, Simon and William Paterson (1987) *The Federal Republic of Germany and the European Community*. London: Allen & Unwin.

Cawson, Alan *et al.* (1990) *Hostile Brothers: Competition and Closure in the European Electronics Industry*. Oxford: Clarendon.

Cohen, Elie (1992) *Le Colbertisme 'high-Tech': Economie des Télécom et du Grand Projet*. Paris: Hachette.

Cohen, Elie and Michel Bauer (1985) *Les grandes manoeuvres industrielles*. Paris: Belfond.

Eberlein, Burkard (1996) 'French center-periphery relations and science park development. Local policy initiatives and intergovernmental policy-making', *Governance* 9, 351–74.

—— (1997) *Abschied vom Unitarismus? Regionale Innovationspolitik und 'Technopole' in Frankreich*. Opladen: Leske + Budrich.

Ergas, Henri (1987) 'Does technology policy matter?', in R. Bruce (ed.), *Technology and Global Industry: Companies and Nations in the World Economy*. Washington DC: National Academy Press.

Esser, Josef, Boy Lüthje and Roland Noppe (eds) (1997) *Europäische Telekommunikation im Zeitalter der Deregulierung*. Münster: Westfälisches Dampfboot.

European Commission (1979) *Die europäische Gesellschaft und die neuen Informations-technologien: Eine Antwort der Gemeinschaft*. Brussels: KOM (79) 650 endg.

—— (1981) *Wissenschaftliche und technische Forschung der Europäischen Gemeinschaften: Vorschläge für die achtziger Jahre*. Brussels: KOM (81) 574 endg.

—— (1982) *Europäisches Strategieprogramm für Forschung und Entwicklung auf dem Gebiet der Informationstechnologien*. Brussels: KOM (82) 287 endg.

—— (1994) *The European Report on Science and Technology Indicators 1994*. Luxembourg: Office for Official Publications of the European Communities.

Eurostat (1994) *Forschung und Entwicklung: Jährliche Statistiken 1994*. Luxembourg: Amt für amtliche Veröffentlichungen der EU.

Friend, Julius W. (1991) *The Linchpin: French–German Relations, 1950–1990*. New York: Praeger Publishers.

Grande, Edgar (1993) 'Die neue Architektur des Staates: Aufbau und Transformation nationalstaatlicher Handlungskapazität – untersucht am Beispiel der Forschungs- und Technologiepolitik', in Roland Czada and Manfred G. Schmidt (eds), *Verhandlungs-demokratie, Interessenvermittlung, Regierbarkeit. Festschrift für Gerhard Lehmbruch*. Opladen: Westdeutscher Verlag, 51–71.

—— (1994) *Vom Nationalstaat zur europäischen Politikverflechtung. Expansion und Trans-formation moderner Staatlichkeit – untersucht am Beispiel der Forschungs- und Technologiepolitik*. Habilitationsschrift Universität Konstanz.

—— (1995) 'Forschungspolitik in der Politikverflechtungs-Falle? Institutionelle Strukturen, Konfliktdimensionen und Verhandlungslogiken europäischer Forschungs- und Techno-logiepolitik', *Politische Vierteljahresschrift* 36, 460–83.

—— (1996) 'Die Grenzen des Subsidiaritätsprinzips in der europäischen Forschungs- und Technologiepolitik', in Roland Sturm (ed.), *Europäische Forschungs- und Technologiepolitik und die Anforderungen des Subsidiaritätsprinzips*. Baden-Baden: Nomos, 131–42.

Grande, Edgar and Jürgen Häusler (1994) *Industrieforschung und Forschungspolitik. Staatliche Steuerungspotentiale in der Informationstechnik*. Frankfurt a.M.: Campus.

Hayward, Jack (1986) *The State and the Market Economy: Industrial Patriotism and Economic Intervention in France*. New York: New York University Press.

Krige, John and Luca Guzzetti (eds) (1995) *History of European Scientific and Technological Co-operation*. Brussels: European Commission.

Larédo, Philippe and Michel Callon (1990) *L'impact des programmes communautaires sur le tissu scientifique et technique français*. Paris: La Documentation française.

Layton, Christopher (1969) *European Advanced Technology: A Programme for Integration*. London: Allen & Unwin.

McCarthy, Patrick (1993) 'Condemned to partnership: the Franco-German relationship, 1944–1983', in Patrick McCarthy (ed.), *France-Germany, 1983–1993. The Struggle to Cooperate*. New York: St. Martin's Press, 1–25.

Muldur, Ugur and Ricardo Petrella (eds) (1994) *The European Community and the Globalization of Technology and the Economy*. Luxembourg: Office for Official Publications of the European Communities.

Mustar, Philippe (1994) 'La politique d'innovation en France: le colbertisme entamé', in Frédérique Sachwald (ed.), *Les défis de la mondialisation: innovation et concurrence*. Paris: Masson, 321–65.

Mytelka, Lynn Krieger and Michel Delapierre (1988) 'The alliance strategies of European firms in the information technology industry and the role of ESPRIT', in John Dunning and Peter Robinson (eds), *Multinationals and the European Community*. Oxford: Blackwell, 129–51.

OECD (1994) *Main Science and Technology Indicators*. Paris: OECD.

Peterson, John (1993) *High Technology and the Competition State: An Analysis of the Eureka Initiative*. London: Routledge.

—— (1996) 'Research and Development Policy', in Hussein Kassim and Anand Menon (eds), *The European Union and National Industrial Policy*. London: Routledge, 226–46.

Reger, Guido and Stefan Kuhlmann (1995) *Europäische Technologiepolitik in Deutschland*. Heidelberg: Physica.

Sabatier, Paul A. (1988) 'An advocacy coalition framework of policy change and the role of policy-oriented learning therein', *Policy Science* 21, 129–68.

Sandholtz, Wayne (1992) *High-Tech Europe: The Politics of International Co-operation*. Berkeley: University of California Press.

Schmidt, Vivien A. (1996) 'The decline of traditional state dirigisme in France: the transformation of political economic policies and policymaking processes', *Governance* 9, 375–405.

Servan-Schreiber, Jean-Jacques (1968) *Die amerikanische Herausforderung*. München: Hoffmann und Campe.

Sharp, Margaret and Peter Holmes (eds) (1989) *Strategies for New Technologies: Six Case Studies from Britain and France*. Oxford: Allan.

Sharp, Margaret and Claire Shearman (1987) *European Technological Co-operation*. London: Routledge.

Simonian, Haig (1985) *The Privileged Partnership: Franco-German Relations in the European Community 1969–1984*. Oxford: Clarendon Press.

Wood, Pia Christina (1995) 'The Franco-German relationship in the post-Maastricht era', in Carolyn Rhodes and Sonia Mazey (eds), *The State of the European Union, vol. 3 Building a European Polity?*. Burnt Mill: Longman, 221–43.

Zysman, John (1983) *Governments, Markets, and Growth: Financial Systems and the Politics of Industrial Change*. Ithaca NY: Cornell University Press.

7

AGRICULTURAL POLICY
The hard core

Douglas Webber

Introduction

Industrial trade liberalisation excepted, the Common Agricultural Policy (CAP) was the first common policy adopted by the EU. For a long time it remained the only significant common policy and consumed a good two-thirds of the EU budget. Even today it accounts for roughly half of the Union's expenditure and there are few policy areas where the EU's competences are as extensive as in agriculture. The agricultural ministers meet more often in Brussels than any other ministers except foreign ministers and spend more time there than any others: the 'marathon' meetings of the Agricultural Council, which may extend over several days and nights and in which the participants negotiate themselves to exhaustion over the annual farm prices, have long since become a part of the reality and image of the EU.

It was by no means inevitable or God-given that agricultural policy should come to occupy such a central role in the European integration process. Historically, it has proved harder, not easier, to subordinate trade in agricultural products to international disciplines than that in other goods and services; national traditions of agricultural protectionism died – and still die – hard. The emergence of the CAP in the 1960s can be explained only in terms of the particular constellation of interests and power that existed in the EU at the time. The 'founding decisions' in agricultural policy were almost invariably taken at the climax of political crises in which the very existence or survival of the EU was, or at least was alleged to be, at stake.

Almost without exception, the French and German governments were the chief protagonists in these as well as in later crises surrounding EU agricultural policy. In agricultural policy, France and Germany are certainly not natural allies with parallel agricultural structures, interests and policy preferences. On the contrary – their divergences are legion. Whereas France is a net food-exporting country, Germany is a net food importer; whereas, despite considerable interregional diversity of structures of agriculture in both countries, France has, overall, a relatively strong and efficient agricultural sector, Germany's is relatively weak and inefficient; whereas France is a big exporter of agricultural produce to non-EU markets, Germany is not; whereas France produces 'Mediterranean' as well as 'continental' products, Germany, apart from wine, does not; whereas France is an important net beneficiary of CAP spending, Germany is by far the biggest contributor; whereas Germany is a densely settled country with extensive non-agricultural employment opportunities in or close to rural or semi-rural areas, France is much more sparsely populated, so that workers displaced from agriculture are more frequently forced to 'desert' the countryside, and so on.[1]

These structural differences translate into different national agricultural policy concerns and discourses, with France, for example, stressing the importance of its 'exporting mission' (*vocation exportatrice*) and Germany the need to maintain the 'family farm' (*bäuerlicher Familienbetrieb*), and into opposed positions on issues such as the maintenance or reduction of subsidies for agricultural exports beyond the EU and the relative weight assigned to price cuts and administrative measures as instruments for the containment of EU agricultural production, with Germany on the latter issue pleading more strongly than France for an essentially 'planned' agricultural economy.[2] It is only on policies that benefit French and German farmers at the expense of third parties, such as high levels of external protection, that the agricultural ministers in Bonn and Paris have normally been able to agree easily.

The frequently deep conflicts of interest between France and Germany on agricultural policy issues means that their relationship in this sphere is essentially antagonistic and conflictual. Nonetheless, the centrifugal forces created by these conflicts have been contained in such a way as not to prevent the conception, implementation and maintenance of the CAP and not to imperil the overall 'special relationship' between Bonn and Paris. The extensive 'Europeanisation' of agricultural policy, the concentration of decision-making competences at the level of the EU, has created powerful pressures for the two governments to try to mediate their differences and co-ordinate their policies on agricultural issues.

According to Lequesne (1990: 132), the French and German agricultural ministries conduct an exchange of information across the 'entire spectrum' of such issues that is 'without any equivalent' in other policy areas. Bilateral co-ordination takes place across all levels of the ministries: between the ministers themselves, who normally meet, for example, at the biannual intergovernmental consultations foreseen by the 1963 Elysée Treaty; between the state secretaries, who call each other occasionally; between the agricultural attachés in the embassies in Bonn and Paris, who regularly visit the German and French agricultural ministries respectively; and between officials in the sections of the two ministries, who are in more or less daily contact with each other (interview). If there is not necessarily a marked difference between the volume of bilateral contacts and those that the two governments maintain with other EU member states, the importance which they attach to the Franco-German relationship is greater than that of any other bilateral relationship they maintain. In practice, the 'privileged' or 'special' nature of the Franco-German relationship expresses itself in the will to go to greater lengths to avoid a confrontation than in relations with other EU member states, to forge as 'broad an agreement as possible between the German and French positions' on 'all important issues' (interview).

Franco-German conflict mediation attempts on agricultural policy issues are by no means always successful. Given the frequently opposed positions from which the two governments depart, this is hardly unexpected. What is surprising and needs to be explained is rather the fact that the two governments do usually manage to reconcile their differences and reach an agreement on mutually important issues before they are discussed in the Agricultural Council (interview). Moreover, whether the two governments do succeed in finding a common position and whether this is in favour of or opposed to a given project is typically decisive for the outcome of major agricultural policy conflicts in the EU.

In this chapter, we shall try to show that if France and Germany remain divided over a major project, the outcome – until such time as their conflict is resolved – tends to be deadlock and crisis in the EU; that when they are jointly opposed to such a project, it fails; and that when they jointly support the project, it is adopted as EU policy. The analysis will focus on two sets of such conflicts: the first set relates to the 'founding decisions' taken concerning the CAP in the first half of the 1960s, the second to the reform of the CAP and the GATT Uruguay Round agricultural trade negotiations in the first half of the 1990s. The choice of two sets of conflicts separated by a time span of three decades makes it possible to control for the effects on the role and impact of the Franco-German relationship of the enlargement of the EU's membership and changes in its constitution and decision-making rules in the intervening period. I shall discuss these issues in the conclusion along with the questions of why France and Germany can normally find a modus vivendi on agricultural issues and why they seem to be able to exercise so powerful an influence on major EU agricultural decisions.

The 1960s: creation of the CAP

The CAP was created in a series of decisions stretching from 1960 to 1965, of which the most important were those relating to the organisation of the common agricultural market(s) in 1961–62, common cereals prices in 1964, and the joint financing of CAP expenditure, which became entangled with the scheduled transition from unanimous to qualified majority voting in the Council of Ministers, in 1965–66.

Conflict over Organisation of Common Agricultural Market 1961–62

The inclusion of agriculture in the common market was a controversial issue from the start among the original six EU member states. In general, the states with strong agricultural sectors and a net agricultural trade surplus, especially

Holland and France, wanted a common agricultural market, while those with weak agricultural sectors, especially Germany, but also, to a lesser extent, Belgium and Luxembourg, were opposed. Within the German government, however, there were divergences of attitude between the Agricultural Ministry, which, like the DBV (Deutscher Bauernverband, the German Farmers' Association), was hostile to the idea of a CAP, and the Economics Ministry, which favoured exposing German farmers to stiffer international competition. These conflicts had regularly to be mediated by the Chancellor, who had to balance external pressures on the government to make concessions to the 'pro-CAP' member states against domestic ones – from the numerically strong and politically extremely well-organised farming lobby – to resist the liberalisation of agricultural trade.

The Commission's proposals for organising the common agricultural market were considered at a series of no fewer than forty-five council meetings between December 1961 and mid-January 1962. The proponents of a common agricultural market, France and Holland, linked their acquiescence in the scheduled transition to the second stage of the industrial common market on 1 January 1962, a step that required the unanimous support of the member states, to the other states' acceptance of the CAP. For de Gaulle, the realisation of the CAP was indispensable to solving the 'peasant problem' in France, which he regarded as a potential 'second Algerian question on our own soil' (quoted in Peyrefitte 1994: 302).[3] He attached particular importance to the common financing of the policy, as otherwise, in his view, French industry would be too heavily burdened by the cost of agricultural subsidies to compete in the industrial common market. He told Adenauer before the final phase of the council negotiations that, without a CAP, France would block any further evolution of the EU.

French pressure weighed heavily on Adenauer and the German government, more heavily than the Dutch, because Adenauer had made the Franco-German 'friendship', designed first and foremost from his perspective to pre-empt any encirclement of the Federal Republic by a Franco-Soviet coalition, a cornerstone of his foreign policy and the participation of France in the EU was more indispensable than that of any other member state. After the clock for the transition to the second phase had been stopped in Brussels and other reluctant governments had abandoned their opposition, the German government finally acquiesced to the CAP in mid-January 1962. The last contentious issue, the (temporary) financing of the policy, was resolved in bilateral negotiations between the heads of the French and German delegations and the bilateral Franco-German solution pushed through the council as a whole by the German presidency, it 'long since' having emerged in Brussels that a Franco-German agreement was 'the most important pre-condition of an agreement among the six' (Couve de Murville 1971: 317; Lahr 1981: 354–55).[4]

An important motive for Germany's acceptance of the CAP was the hope that France would no longer oppose British entry to the EU, a hope that, a year later, de Gaulle was to dash. Not only the adoption of the CAP, but also its terms represented a considerable victory for France, not only vis-à-vis Germany, which became the principal financial contributor to a policy whose creation it had hitherto opposed, but also the Commission, whose competences, such as setting agricultural prices, were reduced to a minimum to the benefit of the Council.[5] Like the German government, the Commission accepted the CAP as the price of further progress in the integration process.

Battle over common cereals price 1964

By the time the most important and politically most explosive common price, that for cereals, came up for decision in the EU Council, the Franco-German relationship had endured a number of crises and Adenauer had been succeeded as German Chancellor by the much less Francophile and much more 'Atlanticist' Erhard. Cereal prices diverged widely between the member states: the French price was the lowest and the Italian highest, with the German price only just below the Italian. The Commission proposed a common price at the Belgian level, 'in the middle, between the French and the Germans' (Mansholt 1974: 110).

As with the CAP in 1961–62, the German government contrived to postpone a cereals price decision as long as possible. Ideally, it would like to have avoided a decision being taken before the German elections scheduled to take place in September 1965. Erhard had secured his election as Chancellor by promising the farmers in his CDU/CSU Parliamentary party not to take any decision 'against or without them' (Gerstenmaier 1981: 521). He and his government, in which his coalition partner, the liberal FDP, was even more hostile to a common cereals price than the CDU/CSU, feared that a prior decision in Brussels could alienate critical electoral support among German farmers. At German insistence, a Council decision, due to be taken in April 1964, was delayed until December and the government began to lobby its partners for a further postponement. Again as in 1961–62, however, the German government's prevarication encountered fierce French resistance. In October 1964, de Gaulle threatened to withdraw France from the EU if the common cereal price was not adopted as agreed by the end of the year.

While the German government did not take this threat at face value, it did fear that, if it were to prevent a decision in the EU, France would block any agreement in the GATT Kennedy Round trade liberalisation negotiations that were in progress and to which Bonn attached great importance. As Italy began to climb down from its opposition to a common price and Germany was again in danger of becoming completely isolated in the EU, Erhard overruled his agricultural minister, negotiated with the DBV over the conditions under which it might accept lower cereal prices and signalled his government's preparedness in principle to accept a common EU price in December. Despite the Chancellor's U-turn, the critical negotiations in Brussels reached an impasse that was broken only when the Commission proposed a new compromise package (containing, however, the same cereal price proposal) that, during an absence of the German agricultural minister and with Erhard's approval, the German economics minister then accepted.

Financing of the CAP and 'empty chair' crisis 1965–66

The third and most profound crisis relating to the creation of the CAP broke out over the proposals made by the Commission for the long-term financing of the policy in 1965. The Commission combined these proposals with others that implied a considerable strengthening of the supranational character of the union, evidently calculating that de Gaulle, facing elections later the same year, would accept the latter in exchange for a CAP financing regulation very favourable to France. However, this calculation, misfired. De Gaulle rejected the proposals out of hand. While most of the other states, including Germany, objected to aspects of the proposals, they were much more sympathetic to their 'integrationist' thrust. Following its experience with de Gaulle over the British entry issue in 1962–63 and its acquiescence on the common cereal price, the German government was loath to make any concessions to France on the financing of the CAP without simultaneous French concessions on other issues.

Bilateral talks over the package at a Franco-German summit a few weeks before the scheduled Brussels Council meeting broke down, the French side insisting that the CAP financing regulation be adopted as originally agreed by the end of June 1965 and the German that the negotiations on the issues where it expected French concessions could not be terminated successfully in the time still available. Although the German government believed to have found a modus vivendi with Paris in consultations between the foreign offices on the eve of the Brussels meeting, the Council culminated in a stand-off between the French delegation, on the one hand, and the Commission and the most of the other delegations, notably the Italian, but also the Dutch and the German, on the other. While the latter reckoned on the clock being 'stopped' and negotiations continuing as they had done in 1961–62, the French foreign minister declared the negotiations to have failed. The French government subsequently decided to 'boycott' the EU organs.

The other five member states surmised, almost certainly correctly, that the French boycott was motivated less by agricultural policy concerns than by the desire to avert the scheduled transition from unanimous to qualified majority voting in the Council and, in general, to stifle a strengthening of the supranational character of the EU. Among them, the German government took a relatively uncompromising position, calculating that France could not afford to leave or destroy the EU and that France would exploit any sign of weakness on its part to extract bigger concessions from the other member states as the price of its abandonment of the boycott. The French foreign minister of the day later accused it of having done nothing to facilitate a settlement of the crisis (Couve de Murville 1971: 263).

The German delegation was the principal player among the five and interlocutor of France at the negotiations which, in early 1966, produced the 'Luxembourg Compromise'. This 'agreement' in fact recorded the disagreement between France and the five over the EU's constitution. There were no changes in the Treaty of Rome of the kind that de Gaulle was looking for at the debut of the crisis. However, the deal struck on the financing of the CAP at Luxembourg was very favourable to France and, to the extent that, in practice, unanimous voting continued to be the norm in the Council of Ministers for the following two decades or more, de Gaulle also won the 'constitutional' conflict with the other member states and the Commission.

Thus, in the first three big conflicts over the CAP, France and Germany always found themselves in opposing camps. They were not the sole protagonists in all of them since Holland was as strongly in favour of the CAP's creation as France; Italy fought against the common cereal price alongside Germany; and Italy fell out more strongly than Germany with France over the CAP financing issue in 1965. But France and Germany were the chief protagonists, whose actions had more bearing on the course and outcome of the successive conflicts than those of the other four member states. When they succeeded in reconciling their differences, their joint position was multilateralised, i.e. transposed into the policy of the EU; where they did not, the outcome, until such time as they did find a modus vivendi, was crisis and deadlock.[6] After they had mediated their conflict over the CAP in January 1962, the Franco-German agreement was rapidly piloted through the Council as a whole, while, in the battle over the common cereal price, the conflict was mediated by the Commission, which split the difference between the French and German prices and embedded its proposal in a larger package containing a range of concessions designed to enhance the acceptability of the common price to the agricultural ministers, especially, it seems, the French and German (Mansholt 1974: 112–13).

The difficulties experienced by France and Germany in reaching a modus vivendi contributed to the outbreak of the 1965 crisis, albeit de Gaulle may in any case have been resolved to precipitate a confrontation to prevent a shift of decision-making power away from the member governments to the Commission and the European Parliament. One cannot be certain that if Bonn and Paris had reached an agreement over the Commission's proposals at their summit in June 1965 that this would have been acceptable to all the other member states. But such an agreement would certainly have created a centripetal force that, going by the impact of previous Franco-German agreements, the other member states would have found difficult to resist.

Apart from the dominant influence of France and Germany and their relationship on their course and outcomes, the other striking – and interrelated – features of the above conflicts were, first, the regularity with which Germany bowed to French pressure and, second, the extent to which the resolution of Franco-German conflicts depended on the arbitration of conflicts within the German government by the Federal Chancellor, prioritising foreign policy over domestic-electoral objectives. In the first two conflicts, the German government ultimately made extensive concessions to France, from which, in return, it expected concessions in the future.[7] In 1961–62, it acquiesced on the CAP's foundation in the hope that France would not veto British entry into the EU; in 1964, it accepted the common cereal price in the expectation that the 'other member states' (meaning, first and foremost, France) would subsequently agree to an 'expansion of economic and political co-operation' (Akten 1964: 1396).

The frustration of these expectations in both cases precipitated the crisis in 1965 to the extent that Germany was consequently more loath than hitherto to make concessions to France that were not balanced by simultaneous French concessions to Germany. In all three cases, there were also more or less profound differences of opinion between the Bonn ministries. In particular, his stance aligned with the DBV's, the agricultural minister was hostile to the creation of the CAP and the common cereals price. The economics and foreign ministers, on the other hand, were more conciliatory. In each case, the Chancellor, Adenauer the first time and Erhard the second, arbitrated the conflict in favour of foreign policy priorities, i.e. of the promotion of the European integration process and, in Adenauer's case at least, the Franco-German relationship.

With Germany occupied and divided after World War II and the Federal Republic being located at the front line of the Cold War, dependent for its security on the West, West German leaders perceived themselves as having too strong an interest in promoting European economic and political integration to let this project fail on agricultural policy issues. But neither did they want de Gaulle to destroy this process or crush it in its infancy – which partially explains the tougher stance that they adopted against the French government in 1965. By this time, the political will at the highest governmental levels in Bonn to subordinate domestic-sectoral interests to the requirements of the Franco-German 'partnership' was too weak to avert a crisis, not least because the two governments' foreign policy priorities could in any case no longer be reconciled.

The 1990s: GATT Uruguay Round and CAP reform

After the formative decisions had been taken in the first half of the 1960s, the prevalence of unanimous voting in the Agricultural Council following the 1965-6 crisis raised very high political barriers to any reforms of the CAP. The Commission's role was largely reduced to that of an 'honest broker' between the member states.[8] German farming interests and the German agricultural minister, who exercised the strongest pressure in favour of higher guaranteed prices, developed into ardent supporters of the CAP. The German and French ministers formed a 'strong mutually protective alliance' in the council, whereby France acquiesced in the high internal prices demanded by Germany, and Germany in the export subsidies consequently required by France to be able to sell its agricultural produce on the world market (Moyer 1993: 11).

The bill for the CAP was met largely by German taxpayers, on the basis of a long-term agreement negotiated between the German Chancellor Brandt and the French President Pompidou as a quid pro quo for French acceptance of British entry into the EU in 1973. Aspirations harboured by Brandt's successor, Schmidt, to reform the CAP as the cost of the policy began to explode came to nothing, as they ran or would have run into the opposition of his agricultural minister and coalition partner, the FDP, on the one hand, and the French government, on the other. Under the centre-right coalition led by Chancellor Kohl, Bonn's enthusiasm for CAP reform dwindled: as late as 1985, the German agricultural minister, supported by Kohl, invoked the 'Luxembourg Compromise' to try to veto a Commission proposal to cut the guaranteed cereal price by 1.8 per cent. Reform of the CAP did not become politically feasible until the second half of the 1980s, when the existing policy came under simultaneous internal and external pressure, internally from the rapid growth of spending, which threatened to 'break' the EU budget, and externally from the demands for reductions in EU agricultural protection and export subsidisation by other agricultural exporting states in the GATT Uruguay Round.[9]

Failure of the Brussels GATT summit 1990

The EU's very acquiescence in the launching of the Uruguay Round in 1986 was the product of an essentially Franco-German bargain, whereby the French government agreed not to veto the EU's participation in exchange for the German government supporting it on the round's agenda (Odell 1993: 247).[10] The internal conflicts over trade, especially agricultural trade, liberalisation in the EU, in particular French opposition, dissuaded the Commission from seeking a formal negotiating mandate for the round until autumn 1990, just a few months before the round's scheduled conclusion. In the Agricultural Council, the proposed mandate for the agricultural trade negotiations was supported by Britain, Denmark and Holland, but rejected by Germany, whose minister was initially the ringleader of the opposition, Ireland and France, which together possessed a blocking minority.

In the last of seven Council meetings that discussed the mandate, the German minister was allegedly under instructions from Chancellor Kohl to back French demands 'to the hilt' since Kohl was loath to unsettle German farmers with agricultural trade liberalisation plans so close to first all-German federal elections (*Frankfurter Rundschau*, 7 November 1990; Paemen and Bensch 1995: 178; interviews). The Franco-German-Irish front so tied the Commission's hands that it had virtually no leeway to make the USA and the 'Cairns Group' of agricultural-exporting states a serious negotiating offer at the Brussels GATT summit in December 1990. The positions of the major states and groups of states affected by agricultural trade liberalisation were so far apart that the summit was virtually condemned in advance to failure.

CAP Reform 1992

The publication of proposals to reform the CAP on the day that the Brussels GATT summit began was no coincidence. More than the internal fiscal pressures, which the proposals would do little to alleviate, the pressures exerted on the EU by its trading partners, most of all the USA, dictated the thrust and especially the timing of Agricultural Commissioner MacSharry's project. Essentially, the aim of the proposed reform was, without rendering small farms economically unviable, to make the CAP internationally more acceptable by reducing European agricultural surpluses and hence the volume of produce that the EU 'dumped' on the world market and to protect the policy from future attack under international trade dispute procedures (see Legras 1993: 331).

The proposals included more radical price cuts (35 per cent for cereals) than had ever been proposed previously, the introduction of compensatory direct payments to farmers in place of price support and, obligatory for farmers receiving direct payments, 'set-aside' measures to take land out of production. In general, member states with small farms, predominantly those in Southern Europe, greeted the proposals, while those with big and/or very productive farms, notably Britain, Denmark and Holland rejected them. The authors of the MacSharry Plan (so named after the Agricultural Commissioner), which had been formulated 'in consultation with the important member states', calculated that they could do without the support of the three North Sea states, which did not have a blocking minority in the council, but they needed that of France and Germany which, allied with Ireland, did (interview; Moyer 1993: 15).

Different aspects of the project attracted and alienated the French and German ministers: the French minister welcomed price cuts, which his German counterpart rejected, and opposed compulsory land set-aside, which the German minister supported. The Franco-German conflict 'dominated' the debate over the reform in the Agricultural Council (interview). While both ministers, albeit for diametrically opposed reasons, held out against the proposed reform, the pressure on them mounted within their respective governments to acquiesce in a CAP reform. In fact, in early 1991, Kohl and Mitterrand had reached an informal deal whereby Germany would not veto a cereal price cut and France would not veto a new GATT treaty (interviews). In autumn 1991, the German Cabinet, which had been split over CAP reform and the Uruguay Round between the agricultural and economics ministers, signalled that it would accept price cuts provided that they were compensated by direct payments; soon after it was reported that the French government, too, was no longer opposed to a CAP reform (Lemaître 1991). The adoption of the reform finally appears to have been facilitated, prior to the decisive council negotiations, by a bilateral Franco-German agreement involving a trade-off linking cereals and beef price cuts (Le Theule and Litvan 1993: 776; interviews). Even so, the French and German ministers may have to have been instructed to accept the reform by Mitterrand and Kohl respectively (interviews; *Die Welt*, 24 May 1992). Only Italy opposed the reform in the final council vote.

Blair House accord 1992

Implying as it did a reduction in EU agricultural production and surpluses that had to be dumped on the world market, the CAP reform substantially increased the Commission's negotiating flexibility in the Uruguay Round. A rapid revival and conclusion of the Uruguay Round negotiations was stymied, however, by French President Mitterrand's decision to stage a referendum on the Maastricht Treaty. As the CAP reform had already antagonised French farmers, the Uruguay Round had to be kept on hold for fear that their opposition could bring about a referendum defeat. After the referendum, however, the pressure on the Commission intensified to try to reach an agreement with the USA over agriculture. It came first and foremost from the German government, which was worried about the impact on the economic conjuncture of a collapse of the GATT negotiations and under growing pressure from industrial lobbies to push for a settlement. Once the German 'bandwagon' started rolling, the Commission 'jumped aboard' (interview).

The last impetus to the conclusion of the Blair House accord was provided by a US threat to impose penal tariffs on a range of EU, especially French, agricultural exports if the EU did not implement a GATT disputes panel recommendation concerning EU oilseed subsidies. France failed to obtain a qualified majority in the General Affairs Council for a threat of counter-retaliation: the German delegation joined the northern member states and Italy in pleading for a conciliatory approach to the USA that would not destroy the chances of reaching a GATT settlement. 'For the first time,' the German economics minister was reported as saying, 'a decision went against France' (*Der Spiegel* 47, 16 November 1992: 154).

The Blair House accord was clinched shortly afterwards, in the interregnum between the Bush and Clinton presidencies. On the one hand, the responsible Commissioners believed that the accord corresponded to the mandate they had been given by the last European Council meeting, namely to improve on the agricultural trade provisions of the Dunkel Paper.[11] On the other hand, they made concessions to the USA for which they estimated that they would not have found a majority in the council if they had consulted it before the talks.

Given the external pressure being put on the EU and the internal pressure being exerted by business interests in favour of trade liberalisation, they reckoned, however, that, after the accord had been concluded, the Council would not reject it. Whereas most of the northern member states, including Germany, approved the accord, numerous southern member states, together with Belgium and Ireland, were worried that it would increase the sacrifices imposed on farmers by the CAP reform, but not to the point that they rejected it. Only the French government declared its outright opposition to the accord, demanding, without finding any allies in the council, that the GATT agricultural talks be suspended until agreement had been reached on all other issues – a demand that, if backed by the Council, would likely have led to the collapse of the Uruguay Round altogether.

The proximity of parliamentary elections four months away meant that the accord was immediately and inevitably whipped into the maelstrom of French domestic politics. The Socialist government, which was deeply unpopular, could not afford to be seen to be 'soft' on agricultural trade. It declared that it would veto the accord if it were put before the council. In order not to risk this scenario, and since it was in any case an informal bilateral agreement on which the council would not have to vote until and insofar as it was incorporated in a final draft GATT treaty, the Commission refrained from submitting it to the Council. It counted ultimately on the pro-European Mitterrand not to provoke a crisis in the EU by authorising the government to try to veto Blair House and an overall GATT agreement. Mitterrand's political authority and capacity to avert a crisis over the Blair House accord was diminished, however, by the crushing victory of the right in the March 1993 elections. Although Mitterrand appointed a Prime Minister (Edouard Balladur) with known pro-European and liberal economic sentiments, the government which now wielded day-to-day control over French GATT policy was composed of parties more vociferously opposed to agricultural trade liberalisation than the Socialists.

Since the collapse of the Brussels GATT summit in 1990, there had been a realignment of forces on the issue of agricultural trade liberalisation in the EU. The CAP reform adopted in 1992 gave the Commission greater latitude to make concessions to the other GATT member states on agricultural trade. Meanwhile, the Franco-German bloc that had then prevented the EU making a negotiable offer to its trading partners had also disintegrated. Germany had begun to push harder for a Uruguay Round settlement, encouraging the Commission to negotiate an agreement with the USA at the risk of alienating and isolating France. It had not succeeded, however, in taking France with it. As in 1965–6, France was in conflict with a coalition of most, if not all, of the other member states headed by Germany, the EU decision-making process appeared to be deadlocked and a crisis seemed to be brewing – this time in transatlantic relations as well as in the EU itself.

Revision of the Blair House accord 1993

Soon after coming to office, the Balladur government affirmed that the Blair House accord was 'not acceptable in its present form' (*Le Monde*, 14 May 1993). This formulation implied that it could accept a revised agreement, but also, of course, that the existing agreement must be renegotiated, a demand which the USA had hitherto strictly rejected. Within the EU, the government mounted an 'intense diplomatic effort' to win allies for its position, focusing in particular on Bonn, which had hitherto proved impervious to French pressure on the issue (interview).

At a Franco-German summit a month before a special Council meeting on the Uruguay Round demanded by Paris, Balladur succeeded, at least partially, in turning Kohl around. The Chancellor announced, apparently entirely unexpectedly in Bonn, that his government too had 'problems' with the Blair House accord and that a compromise must be found on the issue that was 'acceptable to everyone', i.e. to France as well as to the other member states (*Financial Times*, 27 August 1993). Balladur and Kohl resolved to try to reach as 'similar a position as possible' on Blair House in time for the Council meeting and, to this end, scheduled a series of meetings of high-level officials from their respective offices, the foreign offices and economics and agricultural ministries (*Le Monde*, 28 August 1993).

Kohl's shift of position was motivated by two, if not three, considerations: first, the objections of the German Agricultural Ministry to certain provisions of the Blair House accord, which it feared would displace French cereals exports from the world to the German market; second, and more importantly, the fear, impressed upon him by Balladur, that his government would fall in a parliamentary rebellion if it dared to approve Blair House without its having been changed, to be succeeded, presumably, by a more nationalistic and protectionist right-wing administration that could destroy the Uruguay Round and with it, in the worst-case scenario, imperil the EU internal market and the Franco-German relationship; third, as the agricultural press speculated, Kohl may have wished to trade German support for France on Blair House in exchange for French support in the Agricultural Council for measures to safeguard German farmers' incomes against the prospective negative impact of an appreciation of the DM in the wake of the crisis in the European Monetary System that broke out in July–August 1993 (*Agra Europe*, no. 1561, 24 September 1993: P/1).

'To demonstrate Franco-German cohesion', joint French and German delegations met the Commission and the Belgian Council presidency before the Council meeting (interview). The Belgian presidency encouraged the two governments to try to develop a common position. The consultations between Bonn and Paris led to some convergence of attitudes towards Blair House, but not a complete agreement. The presidency detected differences within the German government – between the Chancellor's office and the economics minister – over how far it should go to accommodate France. Before the meeting, the French delegation was uncertain of the outcome: in the meeting of the 113 Committee that prepared the Council session, Ireland was the only other member state to put its weight fully behind France. The council meeting opened with a sharp clash between the French Foreign Minister Juppé, who demanded the renegotiation of the Blair House accord, and EU Trade Commissioner Brittan, who did not refuse to talk with the USA about it again but did not want the EU to demand a formal renegotiation of the accord or to send him to the USA with a 'shopping list' of proposed changes.

France won some support for its stance from Ireland, Belgium and the southern member states, whom, in lobbying for the meeting, it had promised to back on issues that concerned them in the Uruguay Round and CAP. The turning point in the meeting came, however, when Juppé climbed down from his demand for a formal renegotiation of the accord, declaring that the actual conduct of new talks with the USA and their outcome were more important than terminological issues. At this indication of the French delegation's preparedness to compromise, and fearful that otherwise the meeting might collapse, the German delegation, which had sided more with Brittan at the outset than Juppé and in which Kohl's advisers appeared to exercise a dominant influence, swung in behind France.

The number of member states that did not want the Blair House accord reopened shrank to four: Britain, Holland, Denmark and Luxembourg. They could not block a qualified majority decision in favour of reopening Blair House, but could block the unanimous decision that the Belgian presidency and the Commission wanted from the meeting. Two long 'restricted' sessions pitted the views of the French and German delegations against those of the British delegation and the Commission before the latter acquiesced in a joint Franco-German text that listed almost all French as well as numerous southern member states' demands for changes in Blair House and the CAP. The British delegation took with it the other three small North European states and banked on Brittan ensuring that the EU's push for a revision of Blair House would not destroy the Uruguay Round. The agricultural press declared the outcome of the Council meeting to be an unequivocal victory for France.[12]

At each stage of the EU policy-making process on the Uruguay Round and the CAP reform, the Franco-German relationship exercised a determining influence. First, Germany was instrumental in overcoming French resistance to the opening of the round. Second, their joint opposition prevented the Commission from making a negotiable offer on agricultural trade liberalisation in the GATT summit at Brussels in 1990. Third, an informal understanding between Kohl and Mitterrand and a bilateral Franco-German deal linking cereal and beef price cuts appear to have facilitated the adoption of the CAP reform. Fourth, when France and Germany fell out over the Blair House accord in 1992, the decision-making process was deadlocked. Fifth, it was not 'unblocked' again until Kohl returned to 'rescue' France in summer 1993. In the final months of the Uruguay Round, Germany helped France to gain a number of concessions on other issues that facilitated French acceptance of a revised Blair House accord and the French government, despite still strong domestic resistance, approved the new GATT treaty.

Conclusion

Much changed in the EU between the early 1960s and the early 1990s. In the early 1990s, the Union contained twelve member states, twice as many as thirty years earlier. The successive enlargements, for example, the entry of the UK, the Iberian states and Greece, had greatly increased the diversity of agricultural structures in the Union. There had been a significant increase in the frequency of qualified majority, as opposed to unanimous, voting in the Council, although the formal procedure for making agricultural policy decisions, the consultation procedure, which tightly circumscribed the powers of the European Parliament, had not changed. The EU was also a much more consolidated entity. The idea that any member state could decide to leave it was much more improbable and, to that extent, threats to leave or to veto decisions by member states were less credible than they had been three decades previously.

None of these changes seemed, however, to have significantly altered the centrality of France and Germany and their relationship to agricultural 'high politics' in the EU. In both eras, in almost all major agricultural policy conflicts, France and Germany initially took opposing sides. When their differences were not mediated and they remained divided, the outcome was a crisis or deadlock in the decision-making process, as in 1965–66 or following the conclusion of the Blair House accord.[13] If they were united in opposing a given project, such as an EU offer of substantial agricultural trade liberalisation prior to the Brussels GATT summit in 1990, it was still-born. If they reached a modus vivendi on a given project, such as the launching of the CAP in 1962, the common cereals price in 1964, the CAP reform in 1992 and the revision of the Blair House accord in 1993, the EU embraced the joint Franco-German position. Thus, whether divided over or united in opposing or supporting a given initiative, the role of France and Germany and the Franco-German relationship in the EU agricultural crisis politics has been decisive. Together they indeed constitute the 'hard core' in the EU agricultural policy-making process.

In most of the big agricultural policy conflicts in the EU, France and Germany have been leading or indeed, albeit more frequently in the early 1960s than the early 1990s, the chief protagonists. This being the case, their record of mediating their conflicts has been striking – the successes clearly outnumber the failures and the failures were, in any case, interim ones, in as far as the 1965–66 crisis was settled, if only by an 'agreement to disagree', and the deadlock over the Blair House accord was ultimately overcome in a way that averted a crisis and facilitated a successful conclusion to the Uruguay Round. Overall, it seems therefore that, on agricultural policy issues and despite often very divergent interests and policy preferences, Franco-German co-ordination functions 'pretty well' (interview).

How can one explain this at first glance paradoxical pattern of characteristically contradictory or polarised interests and, compared with other policy sectors, close and, in terms of conflict mediation, 'efficient' bilateral co-ordination? First, it may be important that agriculture belongs to the most highly 'Europeanised' policy sectors, i.e. one of those where the competences of the EU are the most extensive and the scope for national policy solutions is most tightly circumscribed, although by no means non-existent. The pressure on and incentive for a government to engage in inter-state co-ordination is higher if the 'default condition' of non-agreement with one's 'partners' is not the pursuit of an 'independent' national policy, but rather the implementation of an EU policy that may, depending on the majority relations in the Council, disregard or contradict its interests and if, moreover, the non-mediation of a conflict with an important 'partner' government and the 'defeat' of the one by the other threatens to destabilise the overall bilateral relationship.

Second, agriculture is the policy sector which has longest been 'Europeanised'. Consequently, among the 'technical' or 'sectoral' ministries at least, the agricultural ministries have accumulated the longest experience in inter-state policy co-ordination, both bilateral and multilateral. Franco-German conflict mediation processes in agricultural policy have become more highly intensive, routinised and institutionalised and, as a result more efficient, than in other policy areas: 'practice makes perfect'. The impact of the 'age' of the 'Europeanisation' of agricultural policy may be reinforced by the frequency and longevity of agricultural ministers' and their officials' EU meetings – no other ministers and high-ranking officials from any other ministries see each other so often and for so long as those from agriculture (see introduction).

Third, as the above case studies testify, agricultural policy issues may be politically extremely salient and the conflicts surrounding them so explosive that they affect the fate of the entire integration process. This is, in turn, a product of the high level of political organisation and mobilisation of farmers in both Germany and, especially, France, where farmers' organisations have developed and maintain a high capacity to exert pressure on the government by means of (actual or threatened) electoral sanctions, protests, demonstrations, civil disobedience or violence. The high salience and conflict potential of agricultural policy conflicts has led political leaders on both sides of the Rhine to invest commensurately high resources in their mediation. Indeed, despite the relatively highly routinised conflict mediation processes between the agricultural ministries, numerous major Franco-German conflicts over the CAP have not been settled at this level, but could be resolved only through the intervention of the heads of government, typically by the German Chancellor ruling in favour of concessions to France so as not to imperil the Franco-German 'partnership' and the integration process. It is notable that the biggest agricultural policy related crisis of those portrayed above broke out at a time (1965–66) when the foreign policy strategies of the French and German governments diverged strongly and neither the French president nor the German chancellor (and foreign minister) attached the same importance to the bilateral relationship as had been the case while Adenauer had been Chancellor and as did later Giscard and Schmidt and their respective successors, Mitterrand and Kohl.[14]

If cases of failed Franco-German conflict mediation efforts on big agricultural policy conflicts are rare, instances of the failure of the transposition of Franco-German bargains or deals into EU policy are rarer still. It is standard practice for the Council presidency to seek an agreement in the Council on the basis of a joint Franco-German position where one has been formulated (interview). When the two states do act jointly in the Council, according to a former EU commissioner, 'it always works' (interview). In this sense, nothing seems to have changed fundamentally in the role and influence of the French and German ministers in the Agricultural Council since the first half of the 1960s, when the French Minister Pisani observed that everything went smoothly in the Council when his German counterpart Schwarz and he were in agreement and nothing could be decided when they were not (see note 6).

Realist theorists of EU politics typically ascribe the centrality and bargaining power of France and Germany in EU decision-making to the structural dependence of some member states on the French and German economies and the financial dependence of others on French and, especially German, contributions to the EU budget, which enable them to buy off possible dissenting states with side payments (Moravcsik 1991; Garrett 1992). Especially when they are mobilised and deployed jointly, resources of this nature may indeed confer considerable influence upon France and Germany in the EU, although they may not always be deployable in conflicts over agricultural policy. However, this analysis suggests that there is an additional, arguably more important, factor that facilitates the multilateralisation of Franco-German bargains. It is, as de Gaulle's foreign minister once remarked, the fact that they represent 'to a certain extent the opposed poles of the Community' (Couve de Murville 1971: 262).

The 'multilateralisability' of Franco-German agreements is, in this perspective, directly linked to their being so often the chief or leading protagonists in agricultural policy conflicts, because, when they do reach a modus vivendi, the solution, provided it is located, as it usually will be, somewhere between their originally opposed positions, is unlikely to be very far away from what most other member states will find acceptable.[15] In agricultural policy conflicts, as happened in the Council meeting on the Blair House accord and the Uruguay Round in September 1993, France tends to bring with it the 'southern' member states (plus Ireland and Belgium) and Germany the 'northern' member states. It is easier to explain from this than from a realist perspective why, among other member states, there is not stronger opposition to collective Franco-German leadership in the EU and why, despite their frequently ambivalent attitudes towards the Franco-German relationship, these states prefer France and Germany to co-operate with each other rather than to be irreconcilably divided.

Notes

1 German reunification has considerably changed the structure of German agriculture by adding a large area of potentially very productive and competitive farming in former East Germany. The effect has been to reduce the structural differences between French and German agriculture and increase the probability that, in the future, Germany will support EU agricultural policies that favour big competitive farms versus small unproductive ones.

2 Hence, the German Agricultural Minister from 1982 to 1993 argued that 'you can't compensate for the difference between the Paris basin and the [German] alpine foothills through the market' (Kiechle 1992: 85–7).

3 In May 1961 France had been hit by the most extensive and violent farmers' protests in its modern history (see Willis 1968: 287).

4 Lahr, Permanent State Secretary in the German Foreign Office, and Couve de Murville, French Foreign Minister, were two of three participants in the last round of bilateral Franco-German negotiations. Lahr also chaired the final Council meeting for the German presidency.

5 During the first three years of application of the CAP financing regulation agreed in January 1962, France contributed 25 per cent of the CAP budget and, thanks to the large volume of its agricultural exports to non-EU states, benefited from 85 per cent of the expenditure.

6 The central role of France and Germany in the Agricultural Council of Ministers was expressed by the French Minister, Edgar Pisani, who told his colleagues in the French government in November 1963: 'When we, my colleague Schwarz [the German Agricultural Minister] and I, are in agreement, everything is fine. If not, the whole machine is jammed' (quoted in Peyrefitte 1997: 248).

7 One might argue, of course, that, in exchange for German acceptance of the CAP in 1961–2, France acquiesced in the second stage of the transition to the industrial common market, but this would be to overlook the fact that France, too, had benefited from industrial trade liberalisation, so that this was a costless 'concession'.

8 The fate of the Mansholt Plan, which aimed at a structural modernisation of European agriculture, but was disfigured beyond recognition in the Agricultural Council, principally at the behest of the French and German ministers, was symptomatic of the Commission's limited influence on CAP decisions (see Pinder 1991: 83–5).

9 A first attempt to reform the CAP was undertaken in 1988, with modest results, attributed by Patterson (1997) primarily to the resistance of the French and German governments, each of them fearful that a radical CAP reform would have negative domestic political repercussions.

10 The following analysis of EU agricultural politics in the 1990s rests to a considerable extent on interviews conducted with more than forty participants in the EU agricultural and trade policy-making process, including officials of ministries in several national governments and farmers' associations as well as of the European Commission and the Council of Ministers.

11 The Dunkel Paper was a draft Uruguay Round treaty named after and containing proposals made by the then GATT secretary-general.

12 Thus, *Agra Europe* wrote (no. 1561, 24 September 1993: P/1–2): 'A combination of French determination and German chicanery resulted in the Council ordering Trade Commissioner Sir Leon Brittan to go to Washington to seek "clarification" of the Blair House agreement … French politicians have been at pains to present the Council outcome as a victory for their re-negotiation demands – which of course it is. The Commission has been forced to re-open the agricultural issue, which both Washington and Brussels had hitherto regarded as settled … Juppé had every reason for claiming … "We got exactly what we wanted".'

13 A similar case was that of the banana trade, where, in 1992, Franco-German conflict mediation efforts failed and the Agricultural Council, against German opposition, adopted an extremely protectionist regulation favouring European, French and former British Caribbean producers and traders of these bananas against North European importers of Latin American bananas. German commercial interests pursued the issue through the European and German courts to the point where, in 1998, it was still possible that the conflict might jeopardise the hitherto sacrosanct principle of the primacy of European over national law, leading legal commentators to speculate that Europe might 'slip on a banana skin'. Even a World Trade Organisation verdict declaring the regulation to be illegal did not bring about a swift end to the conflict.

14 Schmidt and Giscard actually had an explicit agreement to try to reach joint positions on issues that they regarded as important, while retaining a 'degree of flexibility' on issues that they rated secondary (See Gerbet 1990: 103).

15 Britain, whose agricultural structure is very different from that of almost all the continental EU member states, may constitute an exceptional case here. With its radical critique of the CAP, it has remained relatively isolated in EU agricultural politics.

References

Akten zur auswärtigen Politik der Bundesrepublik Deutschland 1964 (2 vols), Hauptherausgeber: Hans-Peter Schwartz; wissenschaftlicher Leiter: Rainer A. Blasius; Bearbeiter: Wolfgang Hölscher and Daniel Kosthorst. Müunchen: R. Oldenbourg, 1995.

Couve de Murville, Maurice (1971) *Une politique étrangère 1958–1969*. Paris: Plon.

Garrett, Geoffrey (1992) 'International co-operation and institutional choice: the European Community's internal market', *International Organization* 46:2, 533–60.

Gerbet, Pierre (1990) 'Le rôle du couple France–Allemagne dans la création et développement des Communautés Européennes', in Robert Picht and Wolfgang Wessels (eds), *Motor für Europa? Deutsch-französischer Bilateralismus und europäische Integration.* Bonn: Europa Union Verlag, 69–119.

Gerstenmaier, Eugen (1981) *Streit und Friede hat seine Zeit: Ein Lebensbericht.* Frankfurt-am-Main/Berlin/Vienna: Propyläen.

Kiechle, Ignaz (1992) 'Ich bin gegen den Markt' (interview), *Der Spiegel* 31, 27 July, 85–7.

Lahr, Rolf (1981) *Zeuge von Fall und Aufstieg: Private Briefe 1934–1974.* Hamburg: Albrecht Knaus.

Legras, Guy (1993) 'L'Uruguay Round et la réforme de la PAC', *Politique étrangère*, 2, 325–31.

Lemaître, Philippe (1991) 'La France ne s'oppose plus à la réforme de la politique agricole commune', *Le Monde*, 20–21 October.

Lequesne, Christian (1990) 'Formulation des politiques communautaires et procédures de consultation avec la RFA en France', in Robert Picht and Wolfgang Wessels (eds), *Motor für Europa? Deutsch-französischer Bilateralismus und europäische Integration.* Bonn: Europa Union Verlag, 123–44.

Le Theule, François-Gilles and David Litvan (1993) 'La Réforme de la PAC: Analyse d'une négociation communautaire', *Revue française des sciences politiques* 43:5, 755–87.

Mansholt, Sicco (1974) *La crise.* Paris: Stock.

Moravcsik, Andrew (1991) 'Negotiating the Single European Act: national interests and conventional statecraft in the European Community', *International Organization* 45:1 (Winter 1997), 19–56.

Moyer, H. Wayne (1993) 'EC decision-making, the MacSharry reforms of the CAP, Maastricht, and the GATT Uruguay Round', unpublished paper presented at the Third Biennial Conference of the European Community Studies Association, Washington DC, 27 May.

Odell, John S. (1993) 'International threats and internal politics: Brazil, the European Community and the United States', in Peter B. Evans, Harold K. Jacobson and Robert D. Putnam (eds), *Double-Edged Diplomacy: International Bargaining and Domestic Politics.* Berkeley/Los Angeles/London: University of California Press, 233–64.

Paemen, Hugo and Alexandra Bensch (1995) *From the GATT to the WTO: The European Community in the Uruguay Round.* Leuven: Leuven University Press.

Patterson, Lee Ann (1997) 'Agricultural policy reform in the European Community: a three-level game analysis', *International Organization* 51:1, 135–65.

Peyrefitte, Alain (1994 and 1997) *C'était de Gaulle*, 2 vols. Paris: Fayard.

Pinder, John (1991) *European Community: The Building of a Union.* Oxford/New York: Oxford University Press.

Willis, F. Roy (1968) *France, Germany, and the New Europe 1945–1967.* Stanford/London: Stanford University Press/Oxford University Press.

8

AN AWKWARD ALLIANCE
France, Germany and Social Policy

Martin Rhodes

Introduction

This chapter seeks to delve beneath the surface of what is, superficially, a harmonious Franco-German relationship in support of a European 'social dimension' and to examine the preferences and motivations of the two countries. It reveals an awkward alliance between the two from the early years of the integration process. Although there have been phases of close co-operation, there has also been frequent conflict. The relationship has evolved within a policy 'environment' that has been politically and institutionally 'structured' by both countries as leaders, but in unequal fashion and alongside other, significant non-state actors: while each has contributed via intergovernmental bargains to the legislative development of the social dimension (although with France often setting the pace), the Commission (especially during the years of the Mitterrand–Delors axis) has been a major, although controversial, contributor to legislative advances, as well as a tactical ally of the European labour movement (and especially its powerful German component) in building the industrial relations 'social dialogue'.

Beyond the details of the relationship itself, this inquiry raises a number of issues about the nature of policy preferences and the integration process. These broadly challenge the following assumptions of both governmental (Lange 1992, 1993) and liberal intergovernmental (Moravcsik 1993) approaches: that the pursuit of narrow self-interest (costs for interest groups, the impact of decisions on short-term electoral popularity) is more important than ideology, or adherence to a set of beliefs about the desirable nature of governance; that relations between domestic organised interests and governments is a national affair in which demands are transmitted upwards to political bargains – the liberal intergovernmental 'rational state behaviour' assumption (Moravcsik 1993: 480); and that the policy sphere at the supranational level is relatively unstructured by the influence of supranational actors, consisting of a metaphorical 'bargaining table', in which past decisions are relatively uninfluential.

In contrast, the following analysis argues that ideology and broad preferences are as important as national self-interest narrowly defined, with actual choices reflecting complex amalgams of both. Equally, the role of organised interests (in this case the European, but especially the German, labour movement) is no longer that of lobbying governments: they have become key actors at the supranational level, making significant inputs into both policy and changes in the architecture of decision making, as has the European Commission when it has been able to distance itself from member state control and the Court of Justice in interpreting the Treaty in labour mobility cases. Together with more classical intergovernmental activity, the Commission, the Court and organised interests have contributed to a highly structured decision-making system with significant sunk costs and lock-in effects, in which even the powerful French and German governments have found their hands tied.

The context: interests, ideology and policy preferences

This is a policy area in which intergovernmental bargaining has figured prominently, but also one where the Commission as entrepreneur, umpire and broker has played a key role in spurring forward often reluctant and hesitant member states, among them Germany (Rhodes 1995). There has also been a far from coherent process of policy formation. As a result, and despite the predictions of the early theorists of the European Community that the integration of social security and labour market organisation would follow from the integration of the European market, social integration has proven to be anything but spontaneous. Nor, indeed, has there ever been any agreement as to its desirability. Instead, the various components of a weak regime of social policy and labour market regulation have been put in place amid conflict over the direction and extent of reform. This conflict has not simply been over the defence of self-interest; it has also been about conceptions of the market and the nature of Europe.

Ideology and European social policy

From the very beginning, any attempt by the European Commission to set an agenda for the harmonisation or approximation of rules and regulations, or promote supranational decision-making, has provoked a two-way conceptual clash: between the competing philosophies of highly and loosely regulated labour markets; and between 'solidarity' and 'subsidiarity' in the framing of European policies. Neither of these clashes represent the pursuit of pure self-interest: they are shaped by national political traditions, patterns of economic organisation and the ideology of parties in power. From the late 1970s, there appeared to be a clear division between the continental countries and the British government over the promotion of a European system of employment rules and industrial relations. This has been related both to contrasts between the Anglo-Saxon and Roman–Germanic legal traditions and to competing notions of national sovereignty and economic organisation. At the same time, there has been a clear clash of interests and ideology between Europe's employers and trade unions. The subsequent conflict has made the European regulatory project more complex still. In terms of government positions, the two-way clash is especially acute in labour policy. This is closely linked to the diversity of Europe's national systems of labour market regulation which generates different conceptions of regulation and makes policy implementation and enforcement problematic.

This clash, which has become particularly acute since the 1987 Single European Act (SEA), has underpinned an ongoing debate and conflict of interests within a heterogeneous and fragmented policy community. It has been complicated still further by the diversity of Europe's national labour market regimes, among which there has been little hard evidence of genuine convergence (Rhodes 1992, 1995). The result has been a sporadic although increasingly important process of institution building and legislation at the European level. This has followed two paths: rule making and the establishment of minimum standards in a broad range of areas, from health and safety standards, through equal opportunities, entitlements in the workplace and, most recently, the establishment of rights to consultation in transnational companies; and the creation of a process of bargaining at the European level through the social dialogue, initially as a process of forging agreement on general issues between still weakly organised European employers' organisations and trades unions.

An examination of these two areas reveals the first distinction between France and Germany as key players in the development of European social policy. As argued below, the main thrust behind movement along the first path has been French commitment, for different reasons in different phases, to a relatively high, law-based floor of social rights and entitlements, a project which Germany has supported only with reluctance, belying its usual image of a member state 'self-interested' in exporting its social costs to the rest of Europe. The main force behind progress along the second path, by contrast, has been the Commission, especially under Jacques Delors, in alliance with the European labour movement. In practice, this has very often meant that the German trade union movement, which, frequently in opposition to other European unions, has always lobbied for the inclusion of German principles of consensus policy making and company co-determination at the European level.

With the Maastricht Treaty and the appended Social Protocol and Agreement, these two paths have come closer together, with the possibility of the social partners reaching agreements that can then be transformed into legislation or implemented nationally via collective bargaining. In bringing the two paths together in a form of multi-level governance, the possibility of social and labour market innovation at the EU level escaping from clearly intergovernmental bargains becomes real, even if still heavily constrained by the member states.

Explaining policy preferences

But how have countries divided at the bargaining table? Does the fact that Germany and France originate broadly from within the same 'camp' of European social and labour market regulation (the Roman–German), and that both fund generous welfare states from social charges rather than purely from taxation, mean that they have similar interests? Is there a rich, high-regulation country position? Ostensibly, the approach of the French and Germans to European social policy should be close, since they are both members of the same broad continental model of 'co-ordinated' or 'network' capitalism, sharing many features of corporate governance and welfare state arrangements and a certain idea of the state as a legitimate actor in: 'slowing down sectoral change in the interest of preserving economic activity, preventing social degradation and making change acceptable ... underpinned by a strong sense of public responsibility for the social situation of their citizens' (Deubner 1997: 25).

At the same time, following the 'rational actor' model of governmental action, one would expect Germany to take the lead in the quest for a European social dimension because of lobbying by the powerful German labour movement, the strength of its social market economy and a desire to defend it against 'competitive' deregulation. Neither assumption is entirely correct.

First, there are critical differences between the French and the German models of 'networked' capitalism, even if they are closer to each other than to the distinctive Anglo-Saxon system of Great Britain (Rhodes and van Apeldoorn 1997). This is true of both the external environment of the firm and the system of corporate governance itself. The most important differences are the importance of public ownership and influence over the banking system in France (compared with a largely private basis for German finance) and the weakness of French trade unions (outside the public sector), compared with a strong labour movement and a highly institutionalised system of industrial relations in Germany. To a large extent, France is closer to the Latin model of networked capitalism than the German model. This has a number of implications for the position of France in European policy-making. First, it has been much less constrained or supported by domestic coalitions and interests than Germany where trade unions have had a powerful, if waning, influence on government policy. Second, combined with the centralisation of the French polity and a strong statist tradition, this difference appears to predispose governments of both the left and the right in France towards a more interventionist stance on social and labour market issues, not just at home but in Europe.

Germany, by contrast, with its federal system and less interventionist 'social market' economy, has been resistant to a high level of state social regulation at both national and European levels. On occasion, as in the case of equal pay and equal treatment, the implementation of European directives has clashed with German conventions of *Tarifautonomie* (autonomous collective bargaining between employers and trade unions) and elements of its legal tradition. As a result, the German approach to Europe has generally been less ambitious and less 'state-protectionist', in terms of its position on the two critical axes of social intervention – regulation and deregulation in the labour market and the architecture of European governance: i.e. the strength of supranational versus national rules and decision-making. In brief, although the French and Germans have been allies in propelling forward a European 'social dimension', this partnership has clearly been an awkward one, with Germany frequently pulled along, often reluctantly, by its commitment to the Franco-German alliance, and pushed forward by its own trade union movement.

Thus, while the French position on Europe has been fairly consistent since the 1950s, when it first made clear its concern to protect its own levels of social regulation by encouraging higher standards in the rest of Europe, the German position has been much more complicated. Its federal system and coalition governments have made Germany's European social policy position much more subject to divergent domestic views (even when compared to French phases of president–prime minister 'cohabitation'); and clashes have been common between Christian Democrat labour and Liberal FDP economics ministers. This is just part of a wider constraint on the role of the German government in the European integration process: decision-making with regard to EU issues is based on the principle of autonomy, allowing each ministry to justify its point of view as defending the national interest. Thus, while the influence of Germany within the EU is strong, it is also fragmented and diffuse, and does not lend itself readily to a leadership role.

Role of organised interests

In this context, the role of the German trade unions has been of great importance, with regard both to domestic and European policy-making. In domestic politics, a distinctive feature of the German labour movement has been its commitment to European integration from the 1950s. In the early years of the European project, they were the pro-European component of the German left, since the Social Democrats (SPD) remained highly sceptical if not fully opposed to integration from the Treaty of Paris through to the Treaty of Rome. This position contrasts sharply with the long-standing animosity towards Europe of the largest French union, the Confédération Générale du Travail (CGT), because of its Marxist, anti-monopoly capitalist view of the EC and its consequent alienation from the European Trade Union Confederation (ETUC). In recent years the German unions have been a major spur in compelling often reluctant German labour ministers (the CDU's Norbert Blüm over the most recent period) to take firmer positions on EU social issues.

In European politics, the German labour movement has been critical in a number of ways in both lobbying for legislative advances and in contributing to the industrial relations component of the 'social dimension' (Barnouin 1986; Streeck 1991) – a phenomenon that a purely intergovernmental approach to integration cannot capture. The French Confédération Française Démocratique du Travail (CFDT) – the more European-minded of the two major French unions – has wielded influence much more through former officials and allies in the Commission, including Jacques Delors and his social policy advisor Patrick

Venturini from the Directorate for Employment and Social Affairs (DG 5), creating a network of interests that also defies simple intergovernmental explanations (Risse-Kappen 1996). Even if their lobbying strength has been less powerful than the German agricultural lobby or business interests, and their objectives in building a European industrial relations system constrained by the power of business and member state opposition, the German unions have helped provide a counterweight to the general tendency for business interests to predominate in Brussels (Visser and Ebbinghaus 1992; Kohler-Koch 1993).

The German unions are distinctive first in the strength of their national power base compared with other European unions (especially the French), and their wealth: the Deutscher Gewerkschaftsbund (DGB) is by far the largest financial contributor to the ETUC and reputedly the only member with de facto veto rights in ETUC decision making (Ross 1995). But they have also been distinctive in their determination to use this strength since the 1950s to build up labour movement capacities, overcome fragmentation at the European level and institutionalise a 'social dialogue' with a reluctant employers organisation, the Union of Industrial and Employers' Confederations of Europe (UNICE). In part, as Streeck (1991) argues, the aim has been to use Europe as an additional arena for the pursuit of the German labour movement's national interests, although, increasingly, national and transnational interests are becoming more difficult for such actors to disentangle. In any event, the ETUC and union influence in the sectoral European Industry Committees owe much to the superior financial resources and capacity for political action of the German unions. Although this enthusiasm has frequently been tempered by a concern to balance their European role with national objectives, and while critics have called for them to play a still stronger role (Streeck 1991; Turner 1996: 330–1), they have nevertheless been the main union force behind some of the key developments since the 1950s. These include the early sectoral dialogue, the Val Duchesse European social dialogue – in which their influence combined with the commitment of Jacques Delors – and, after a period of preoccupation with German unification, the recent reorganisation and relaunch of the ETUC.

France, Germany and social policy before Maastricht

The awkward nature of the partnership between France and Germany in social policy is actually enshrined in the Treaty of Rome, due to early disagreement on the desirability of a European role. The French wanted decision-making powers built unambiguously into the Treaty of Rome, due to a combination of self-interest and a defence of French constitutional rights: they believed that without some form of social security harmonisation their high social charges would create competitive disadvantage; and that gender equality provisions in the French constitution would have to be transferred to the Treaty. But the Germans, defending their distinct 'ordo-liberal' position, were opposed to any legal competence for the EEC in this area. The result was an awkward Treaty compromise, providing a section on social policy with no clear guidelines on the scope of its provisions or the means for their implementation.

The legal basis for a Community role in social and labour market policy (set out in Articles 117 to 123 of the Treaty of Rome) has therefore been ambiguous, forcing the Commission, which has always adopted a broad interpretation of its powers, to forge alliances with member state governments and, where possible, interest groups, to fill the gap between formal competence and actual influence (Holloway 1981: 11–39). The Commission has also had to make a creative use of Treaty articles in order to push forward legislation, given that Article 118 gives the Commission the task of promoting close co-operation between the member states in training, employment, working conditions, social security and collective bargaining, without specifying how. Only Article 119, which met the demands of the French in defining the equal pay principle, Article 121 on social security measures for migrant workers and Articles 123–8 on the European Social Fund were more explicit (Holloway 1981; Hantrais 1995). If alliances with interest groups and member states and the creative use of the Treaty has occasionally allowed the Commission to make great leaps forward with 'social action pro-grammes' (the most ambitious of which after 1987), it has also heavily constrained it and fuelled battles over the appropriate type, level and voting basis of Community regulation (Rhodes 1995).

Explaining policy differences

Throughout the history of the European 'social dimension', French and German positions have been based on complex combinations of principle and self-interest. The French position has always been that the creation of 'social Europe' at a high level is essential if standards are not to diminish. This position has been shared with the German trade unions, although the latter have also accepted from the outset a logic of national diversity (see Streeck 1991: 322) and the fact that German standards cannot be exported wholesale to the rest of Europe. The German government position, however, has been more nuanced – due in part, as discussed above, to the distinction between a more market-oriented economics ministry and a more welfare-oriented social affairs ministry. This conflict has reinforced a primarily reactive German policy making style, and allowed the French, especially in the Mitterrand–Delors era, to take the lead.

To the extent that there is a discernible German government position which unites even quarrelsome ministers, it is this: that while there is a role to be played by pan-European legislation, giving full social policy competence to the Community would be wrong since high national standards are best defended at home. This has been manifested in the legacy of the initial and early quarrel over gender equality provisions: in the 1970s and 1980s there was a protracted battle over the implementation of Community equal pay and equal treatment law in Germany, because they conflicted with the principles of free collective bargaining and the assumptions underpinning Germany's male breadwinner oriented gender regime (Ostner and Lewis 1995: 186ff). Also, and contrary to the 'rational actor' view that it is in the interests of high social standard nations to harmonise rules across Europe, there has been a more *communautaire* consensus in Germany that it is far from desirable to 'export' the German social model, given the diversity of European industrial relations and social policy traditions.

By contrast, the French view has often been that European regulation, overriding if needs be traditional domestic industrial relations, is essential precisely to prevent a regulatory race to the bottom which would threaten its own social achievements. The German view has been somewhere between the French and the British positions (the latter could be characterised as 'what is good for us is good for Europe'), including the appropriate level of EU regulation. In the late 1980s, Germany often opposed the predilection of the Commission towards a 'creative' use of Treaty provisions (the 'Treaty base game') to evade the single-country veto. This was made possible by unanimous voting in the Council and exploited extensively by the British government (Rhodes 1995). In the mid-1990s, the Germans have even allied with the British in opposing an extension of European intervention, not because they have shared the former's blanket opposition to an EU role, but because of the subsidiarity principle and a commitment to more flexible rules.

These differences were important even between the mid-1980s and the early 1990s when the Germans became close partners of the French in developing a new phase of EC social policy. France's position was relatively unambiguous. Mitterrand's domestic policies were based on clear social democratic principles, while the energy put into the European 'social dimension' by the French Socialist government was also a reflection of its own domestic weaknesses – its inability to expand its own social programme, its shift in 1983–84 towards an economic policy of austerity and a failure to deal effectively with increasing unemployment. Thus, the early years of Delors as Commission President saw a clear attempt to elevate French national priorities to the EC level, in both 'statist-protectionist' industrial policy, in the old 'Christian socialist' ideas of *autogestion* in the Val Duchesse social dialogue, and in the 1989 Social Charter which, in its mix of the rhetorical and the bland (its vague set of principles was called 'a solemn declaration') bears all the hallmarks of French policy-making style, that is, the combination of 'heroic' statements with incremental change (Hayward 1982).

In this context, the agreement of the French Socialist and German centre-right governments on reconciling borderless trade with a commonly regulated 'social space' was important. The Mitterrand–Delors version of moderate socialism that emerged from the capitalist 'cold shower' of 1982–83 dovetailed, at a general level, quite nicely with the 'social market' inclinations of Helmut Kohl (Allin 1993: 34). Moreover, French impetus behind the social policy relaunch in 1989 was also due to the need to dispel criticism that France was too weak to hold her own against Germany, and led to greater co-operation in getting the 1989 social action programme off the ground. Nevertheless, although Kohl backed the initiatives of the late 1980s, the German position remained much more cautious, based on a quite different view of the Community's role in social affairs.

From the Social Charter to Maastricht

Relations between France and Germany in the late 1980s, and the role played by the Commission and German trade unions, reveal the complexity of constraints and pressures in translating preferences into policy. The original drafts of the Social Charter were highly diluted due to opposition not just from Britain but also from Portugal, Spain and Ireland to certain clauses (Rhodes 1991: 262). German backing for a stronger, less vague list of principles had faltered: internal divisions in the government between the Labour Minister Blüm and the Economics Minister Haussman had forced the former to withdraw a number of Social Charter proposals he had advanced in the Council of Ministers. Nevertheless, the German position hardened when French Labour Minister Soisson submitted a final anodyne text to be approved by the December 1989 Strasbourg summit. It had become clear even to German employers that the Charter would do nothing to protect them from 'social dumping': the alliance of Britain and the poorer member states had forced the exclusion or dilution of most clauses limiting labour flexibility and maximum working hours, as well as those encouraging equality of treatment for foreign contract workers.

In response, the DGB and the BDA (Bundesvereinigung Deutscher Arbeitgeberverbände, Federation of German Employers' Associations) issued a joint statement about the need for a less ambiguous commitment to the 'European social model',[1] followed by a more specific nine-point declaration signed by German employers, unions and the Labour Ministry in Bonn.[2] This brought important pressure to bear on the Commission where officials were convincing a hesitant Jacques Delors to push ahead with a more detailed set of commitments in the new action programme (*Financial Times*, 31 October 1989 and Ross 1995: 374ff). Union pressure on Blüm led to a public agreement by Blüm and his French counterpart Soisson to put their collective weight behind a programme of legally binding rights for employees (*Handelsblatt*, 21 October 1989). The following week, the German unions launched a more radical manifesto for social and employment rights: this was the first step in a new phase of activism by the German unions that would also lead to a reorganisation and reinvigoration of the ETUC's leadership, giving it a much more aggressive role in pushing for pan-European initiatives (see Visser and Ebbinghaus 1992 and Ross 1995: n. 60).[3]

But this did not mean that the long-standing antipathy of the Germans to state-interventionist social policy had changed. At one level, the period between 1989 and the Maastricht Treaty in 1992 is often caricatured as one in which Britain fights a lone battle against the rest of Europe in resisting attempts by the Commission to introduce new legislation, often by deceptive means (manipulating the Treaty base of directives). Equally, the creation of a new set of decision-making rules for the Maastricht Treaty, involving a significant extension of qualified majority voting (QMV), can be seen as an attempt by the broad anti-British coalition to eliminate the latter's veto on European social policy for good (Rhodes 1995). In fact, the attempt at Maastricht to build on the social dimension and change the Treaty basis for policy-making also bore the marks of French boldness and German caution, with smaller member states (the Belgians and the Dutch) – and, once again, the Commission – mediating between them and the British. The Germans, in fact, continued to moderate the French and rein in the Commission: shortly after the Social Charter battle, and the apparent hardening of German support, Blüm attacked the Commission's extension of its powers beyond the limits set by the Treaty, especially in shifting the legal basis for European labour law and trying to transfer as much legislation as possible from unanimity to QMV. The Germans sought to compromise between British opposition to any extension of QMV and the desire of the French and the Commission to use it as widely as possible. Instead, they advocated a modified QMV system which would prevent a single-country veto but also obviate the need for broad alliances to oppose particular pieces of legislation (*Handelsblatt*, 6–7 October 1989; *Frankfurter Allgemeine Zeitung*, 7 October 1989).

Germany was also opposed to the imposition of high levels of regulation across the Community. An example was in the negotiations on atypical working conditions – the subject of three highly controversial draft directives – where it joined with Britain in blocking parts of the package, including the requirement that part-time employees who worked more than eight hours per week become liable to social security contributions, instead of fourteen. Blüm took this opportunity to accuse the Commission of interfering in areas of social insurance, labour law and collective bargaining where it had no competence to act. Blüm again declared himself to be against the use of full QMV, and was backed in this view by German employers (*Die Welt*, 24 September 1990).

Maastricht and after: a broken or renewed relationship?

The Maastricht compromise: Social Protocol and Agreement

Acknowledging the critical stance of the German government towards the Delors–Mitterrand position is important, because it helps explain why Maastricht did not innovate as extensively in social policy as many had wished. In brief, the draft 'social chapter' of the Maastricht Treaty was drawn up in 1991, largely under the Luxembourg and Dutch presidencies, and aimed to extend QMV to several areas, among them 'working conditions' and 'the information and consultation of workers'. The Germans initially seemed keen to ensure that redundancy conditions and the representation and collective defence of workers, including co-determination, were also brought under EC jurisdiction. The fact that the latter were finally excluded from QMV (which was restricted to health and safety, work conditions and equality at work) is usually attributed to British intransigence, which meant that the 'social chapter' could not be integrated into the new Treaty but was appended as a 'Social Agreement' among the other eleven member states. In fact, the German position also remained fairly consistent in opposing a radical shift in the nature and content of European social policy; and its initial support for the inclusion of industrial relations under QMV should be seen as a sop to the German trade unions, for this had little hope of acceptance by other member states, least of all the British.

In November 1992, Blüm, in a speech to the CDU, again warned that it would be dangerous to impose high German standards on the rest of Europe. So why did the Germans buy the Social Agreement package? Their acceptance of the extension of QMV at Maastricht, despite their past opposition to it, owed much to the limits placed on EU legislation in other parts of the Agreement: an 'upward harmonisation clause' was dropped between the initial and final draft stages; Article 1 stated that national diversity (an evocation of 'subsidiarity') and the needs of competitiveness would be observed; and Article 2(2) warned against the imposition of standards that would prevent the creation or damage the development of small and medium-sized firms. There was, in fact, little chance that the new arrangements would allow either rapid or widespread innovations in European social policy.

Confirmation that the Germans remained the reluctant partner in their relationship with the French came in 1993 in a dispute between the two in negotiations on the introduction of a maximum working week. This was an innovation they broadly agreed on (in contrast to outright opposition from the British) but differed in the details and motivation. In a major row at a meeting of EC social ministers in Luxembourg in June, the German Secretary of State, Horst Gunther, threatened to block all other decisions, including the European Works Council Directive, if France did not compromise on the working hours reference period. Germany wanted the rules on the working week to be as flexible as possible, with a forty-eight hour week averaged over six months, as against a British demand for twelve months. The French, backed by the Commission, wanted a much shorter period of three months, arguing that the forty-eight hour maximum was already sufficiently flexible (*Süddeutsche Zeitung*, 2 June 1993). Apparently trivial, this example illustrates again the point that, while France has frequently attempted to equalise the conditions of competition at its own level, Germany has been much more concerned with minimum standards, leaving ample scope for national variation.

A new Social Policy agenda: 'flexibility' and 'subsidiarity'

While many of the more ambitious of the Commission's social action programme measures from the late 1980s and early 1990s remained unimplemented, a clear switch in 1993 was discernible in Commission policy language in the direction of 'flexibility', a notion which implies a degree of labour market and social policy deregulation. This was a radical departure in Commission thinking, first put forward in its *White Paper on Growth, Competitiveness and Employment* (CEC 1993) and reflecting a shift in the position of governments in the main European capitals, especially with the election of a right-wing government in France.

One key element in the meeting of minds between Germany and France in the early 1990s had been parallel labour market developments, including the search for new forms of work sharing as a solution to unemployment and the proliferation of European works councils initially in French (public sector) and German companies, giving greater credibility to the Commission's attempts to pass a European Works Council Directive. However, the inability of both economies to come to terms with their employment crises had led to a redefinition of self-interest and signs of a gradual labour market paradigm shift. The British view had, of course, remained consistent that what Europe needed was less not more regulation. But from 1993, both the French and Germans – but especially the latter – began to embrace some elements of the deregulatory agenda and stepped back from shifting more responsibility to the EU.

A rational actor approach to European integration would see these developments in terms of a pursuit of national self-interest in a changed international context. However, even recent attempts to back away from commitment to the 'social dimension' represent complex amalgams of ideology and self-interest: indeed, the 'new' ideology or paradigm of flexible labour markets is probably the driving force, rather than any rational calculation of the costs of European social measures (European wide surveys of employers reveal that they are relatively unconcerned by their impact). At the same time, there has been a growing awareness by governments that they no longer have the process of integration fully under control, and that the European Court of Justice (ECJ), even more so than the Commission, has become a quasi-independent actor. A further cooling of German support for the social dimension can also be explained by a series of conflicts with the ECJ from the early 1990s over the latter's interpretations of labour mobility provisions in the Treaty, concerning in particular beneficiary control, spatial control over the use of benefits and the exclusivity (application to all those in a given state) of benefits. Germany has been affected more than most member states by such rulings because of higher levels of inward migration, leading to heavy criticisms of the 'imposition of foreign authority' in German social policy (Leibfried and Pierson 1995). The very existence of such criticism is proof that, although not lost, national sovereignty has been significantly encroached upon.

Together, the emergence of a new labour market paradigm and growing resistance to EU social policy intervention have contributed to new positions and new alliances. The German government's 1994 proposal for a deregulation group at the level of the EU to help cope with unemployment was part of this shift in thinking, attracting stiff opposition from some countries but gaining the support of the British and the Dutch. Germany, like Britain, wanted an expert group to examine secondary legislation of the Community concerning unnecessary rules and find ways of facilitating enterprise activities (*Handelsblatt*, 17 May 1994). This shift in Germany towards a new type of agenda for the labour market was also revealed in a debate between Delors, Klaus Zwickel (the head of *IG Metall*) and FDP Economics Minister Gunter Rexrodt at the Hans-Bockler-Stiftung in Bonn in April 1994 where the latter came under fire for his deregulatory proposals. This position was supported by the German employers' organisations who found the emphasis of the Commission's White Paper on Competitiveness wanting, given its focus on increasing demand and modifications to social charges. rather than cost reductions for firms. The dispute between Delors and Rexrodt continued through 1994, while Helmut Kohl made his own 'Euro-sceptic' attack in declaring that the priority of that year's German presidency was 'to free ourselves from the notion that everything that has a European dimension automatically falls under the jurisdiction of Brussels' (*Financial Times*, 17 May 1994). This reflected a general shift away from the old pattern of the alliances in the earlier part of the decade, as well as the diminishing power of the Commission from mid-1993, above all in its role as power broker and umpire in the EU policy-making process.

Once again, a complex amalgam of national self-interest and ideology was at play. While the June 1994 Corfu summit confirmed in symbolic terms 'the importance of the social dimension as an indispensable corollary to the single market', the deregulators, led now by Germany and Britain, got their deregulatory task force as well. If there was new common ground between Germany and Britain, the differences remained clear: if the former wanted greater flexibility in working hours regulations, for example, it remained fully behind the need for an EU framework, while the British Conservative government wanted to remove the 'threat' of a European role altogether. The relationship between France and Germany was also changing, rather than breaking down. French politicians like Lionel Jospin attacked Kohl for wanting to deregulate (*Libération*, 6 June 1994) – a conflict which was accentuated in the early weeks of the Jospin government elected in 1997; and there were signs of a loss of faith among French union leaders in the ETUC – because it lacked real bargaining partners, employers were pushing their own deregulatory agenda with more determination and because it seemed paralysed by the need to compromise between the interests of different countries (*Le Figaro*, 2 June 1994).

But at the same time, reflecting the more general paradigm shift referred to above, there were early signs of a new coalition of interests between the two countries in the results of a report commissioned by both governments. Written by Johann Eckoff (Rexrodt's number two at the Bonn Economics Ministry) and former Socialist industry minister, Roger Fauroux, this report recommended a controversial shake up of both country's labour markets if they were to create more employment. However, there are also powerful forces ranged against such a shift in the social policy paradigm.

Alongside these indications of a shift in ideology and policy, the major political/ institutional change was the demise of the Mitterrand–Delors axis and its replacement with a more centrist Commission president and a right-wing (although paternalist) French president. This seems to have allowed the German government of Helmut Kohl to shift back towards a position with which it is much more comfortable – one less constrained by the need to back a maximalist French line. This produced some new alignments in EU policy-making and a sentiment in the Commission that the Paris–Bonn relationship had moved closer to the British position and would block any substantial new initiatives. In the deregulation debate, Germany and Britain forged ahead with the announcement of new initiatives and a greater independence from Commission thinking (although the shift away from prioritising social protection in favour of the elimination of labour market rigidities was also in line with the position of the then Commission chief Jacques Santer).

Meanwhile, other countries, notably Belgium and Portugal, have warned that efforts to roll back Brussels legislation risked damaging both the single market and the Commission's authority. France, whose right-wing coalition government was struggling to balance a commitment to privatisation and liberalisation without incurring higher unemployment, sat on the fence. In 1994, the German government rejected, with the support of the British and Dutch delegations, the Commission's programme to fight against social exclusion: according to the Labour Ministry's state secretary, the programme was not congruent with the social programmes of the German states (Länder) and the experience of EU poverty programmes had not been very positive. Then in 1995, the German delegation rejected the draft directive on social exclusion, both because of alleged misuse by the Commission of its legal basis (Article 235) – one of the major means of Commission initiative – and on the grounds of subsidiarity. The Germans opposed the Commission's new fourth action programme on equal opportunities for similar reasons. In 1996, Germany joined forces with Britain to block Santer's proposal for a 'confidence' pact on employment.

However, this illustrates less a convergence on a neo-liberal position than a more confident opposition by the Germans to the surrender of national sovereignty – something they had always resisted but seldom with the vehemence of the British. British and German positions on social policy issues remained different. For, despite Kohl's call for a major shift in thinking on the role of Brussels, Bonn proved its continuing commitment to minimum European standards during its 1994 Council presidency. Specifically, it pushed forward with key pieces of stalled legislation against the wishes of the British, especially those extending the rights of full-time to part-time workers, widening parental leave rights, regulating the rights and obligations of workers outside their own country and reversing the burden of proof, from the complainant to employer, in sex discrimination cases. There has since been success in several of these areas with directives covering posted workers, parental leave and the burden of proof, in addition to a diluted transnational works council directive, using Social Agreement procedures.

At the same time, while the German union movement is very much on the defensive, it remains the most powerful single pressure group for new initiatives: a declaration of demands by the DGB in 1996 called for the inclusion of social rights, as well as the adoption of the complete Social Agreement into the EU treaty, an extension of qualified majority voting to all areas covered by the Social Agreement, excluding only social security; a stronger EU labour market policy, more competence for the standing committee for employment, and international (EU-level) co-ordination of economic and financial policy (Kaufmann 1996: 135–7). The German unions have been unable to consolidate an alliance around these demands since it depends on alliances among the member states. For the moment the latter are split, with no clear leadership on these issues.

Conclusion

Since 1993–94, the impetus behind EU initiatives has clearly been reduced and this has much to do with a new meeting of minds between Paris and Bonn on a reduced role for Europe in social affairs. To some extent the new hesitancy and apparent deadlock on these major issues represents a change in mood that has swept across Europe in the post-Maastricht era: rising unemployment has shifted concern from employment protection (which the Commission has proven capable of fostering) to employment promotion (where it faces much bigger problems). It is also due to a new realism in a difficult economic conjuncture when minds are very much focused on macro-economic developments and EMU convergence. But it is also due to the absence of the alliance which, despite its difficulties and differences, brought Kohl, Mitterrand and Jacques Delors together through the important years of European social policy innovation between 1987 and 1992.

The return of a Labour government in Britain and a Socialist Prime Minister, Lionel Jospin, to the Matignon Palace in 1997 failed to tip the balance back in favour of a more interventionist stance in finding solutions to Europe's ongoing unemployment crisis. Thus, despite the accurate appraisal by the German foreign minister during the Amsterdam IGC negotiations that 'as so often, Franco-German solidarity will be decisive in the final round of the conference' (*Financial Times*, 12 June 1997), the final compromise (essentially a statement of intent) papered over a continuing conflict between the two governments (and two philosophies) over the appropriate means and decision-making levels in European social policy.

The Germans, backed by Britain, were implacably opposed to French calls for a new European spending initiative on jobs, stressing the need to stay true to the budgetary rigour enshrined in the EMU stability pact signed six months earlier in Dublin and emphasising the desirability of a national rather than European focus on employment policy. Although the guidelines for European employment policy agreed at the Luxembourg unemployment summit in November 1997 prioritise job creation for the young and long-term unemployed, and require member states to submit national action plans to cut unemployment, they also call on them to simplify the rules on small business, develop more flexible markets and reverse the trend towards higher taxes and charges on labour. From this loose amalgam of liberal and social market objectives, governments could draw quite different conclusions: while the French saw it as the first step towards a European co-ordination of all aspects of macro-economic policy, Germany (again in alliance with Britain) stressed that it secured the primacy of national decision-making (*Financial Times*, 21–22 November 1997). The return of the Social Democrats to power in Germany in autumn 1998 does not seem to have altered the equation, especially given the early departure of Oskar Lafontaine from the government.

But despite the fragility of the alliance behind an expansion of the European social dimension, and the ongoing clash of philosophies over the level and content of social policy initiatives, it is instructive to step back and survey the results of four decades of joint activity in this domain. In doing so, it is important to acknowledge that the interaction of France, Germany and other member states has created a European sphere of labour law and social legislation that is 'European' in character and not simply the amalgam of the traditions of particular member states (although it certainly reflects them) or one, moreover, that they are fully able to control. To this extent, the Franco-German partnership at the heart of social policy is now structured, if not locked in place, by a series of mutual obligations and responsibilities linking these two countries to each other and to other member states.

This can be seen by highlighting three themes running through the above analysis. First, and contrary to the argument that rich states seek to sustain their competitive status by imposing their social standards on others, the German position in particular reveals a more sophisticated policy design accommodating self-interest and altruism, as well as an interest in what can only be described as *politique communautaire* (i.e. 'what is good for Europe is good for us').

Second, in contrast to the intergovernmental view, domestic interests do not only lobby governments which then forge bargains at the supranational level. They also strike alliances with supranational actors, successfully bypassing the national sphere, and when these relationships are institutionalised, as in the social dialogue provisions of the Maastricht Social Agreement, introduce important elements of multi-level governance. Thus, what is striking about the social policy area is the extent to which French, and especially German, non-state actors (principally labour unions) have played a critical role in creating and structuring the social policy 'space' at the European level.

Third, there are sunk costs and lock-in effects once original concessions have been made (Pierson 1996), while the complexity of decision-making, the accommodation of diverse positions and attempts to resolve Treaty anomalies, create enormous potential for unintended consequences. They also strengthen non-state actors, especially the Commission and the Court of Justice as illustrated in the German case by the protracted battles over the implementation of equal pay and equal treatment directives in the 1970s and 1980s. All of these developments reduce the autonomy of member states: hence their recent attempts, via the new enthusiasm for 'subsidiarity', to rein in powers that have often unwittingly been surrendered.

Notes

1 The declaration made the following points: the Single European Market will be incomplete if social standards are not harmonised at a high level, but harmonisation is not required in all fields of social policy; European minimum social standards should be supported, but only if they are in the interest of the creation and the functioning of the single market; a European guarantee of social rights, freedom of association and freedom of collective bargaining (*Tarifautonomie*) is seen as necessary (the BDA claimed that the concrete arrangements/shape of the systems should be mainly the responsibility of the individual member states, while the DGB demanded that they should be set by EU law); a high

level of protection in safety and health should be reached, and the levelling down of national social standards should be excluded 'in principle' (*im Grundsatz*), implying that in certain cases deviations might be justified. But there was no agreement on protecting the German system of co-determination, although a transfer of the system to the rest of the EC was seen as unrealistic (see Kohler-Koch 1990).

2 This declaration advocated that a set of minimum rights and entitlements be appended to the social charter, including a minimum four weeks holiday per annum, fourteen weeks paid pregnancy leave, a minimum full-time working age of fifteen, a forty-hour working week limit for those under eighteen, sick pay, paid days off for national holidays, protection for contract workers, the integration of the disabled into the workforce, health and security in the workplace and the right to employment advice (*Financial Times*, 31 October 1989).

3 This manifesto included demands for co-determination rights with veto power over some management decisions; an unqualified right to strike (including solidarity strikes or 'secondary picketing'; unemployment benefit starting at 68 per cent of previous net income (and falling no lower than 60 per cent); a two-week 'training holiday' per annum; a forty-hour, five-day week; and a limit on overtime of fifteen hours per month and 120 hours per annum (*Financial Times*, 3 November 1989).

References

Allin, D. H. (1993) 'Germany looks at France', in P. McCarthy (ed.), *France–Germany 1983–1993*. London: Macmillan, 27–47.

Barnouin, B. (1986) *The European Labour Movement and European Integration*. London: Frances Pinter.

CEC (Commission of the European Communities) (1993) *White Paper: Growth, Competitiveness and Employment*, 700 Final.

Deubner, C. (1997) 'The Franco-German relationship: from Europe to bilateralism', in *The Future of Franco-German Relationship: Three Views*, Discussion Paper No. 71, London: Royal Institute of International Affairs.

Hantrais, L. (1995) *Social Policy in the European Union*. London: Macmillan.

Hayward, J. (1982) 'Mobilising private interests in the service of public ambitions: the salient element in the dual French policy style', in J. Richardson (ed.), *Policy Styles in Western Europe*. London: Allen and Unwin, 111–40.

Holloway, J. (1981) *Social Policy Harmonisation in the European Community*. Farnborough: Gower.

Kaufmann, I. (1996) 'Vor Maastricht II oder hat die europäische Sozialpolitik noch eine Perspektive?', *Soziale Sicherheit* 45:4, 135–7.

Kohler-Koch, B. (1990) 'Binnenmarkt '92: Herausforderungen von sozialer und politischer Sprengkraft', in H. Böhme and A. Peressin (eds), *Sozialraum Europa: Die soziale Dimension des Europäischen Binnenmarkts*. Frankfurt.m.M: Lang, 11–35.

—— (1993) 'Germany: fragmented but strong lobbying', in M. P. C. M. Van Schendelen (ed.), *National Public and Private EC Lobbying*. Aldershot: Dartmouth, 23–49.

Lange, P. (1992) 'The politics of the social dimension', in A. M. Sbragia (ed.), *Euro-Politics: Institutions and Policy making in the 'New' European Community*. Washington DC: The Brookings Institution, 225–56.

—— (1993) 'Maastricht and the social protocol: why did they do it?', *Politics and Society* 21:1, 5–36.

Leibfried, S. and P. Pierson (1995) 'Semisovereign welfare states: social policy in a multitiered Europe', in S. Leibfried and P. Pierson (eds), *European Social Policy: Between Fragmentation and Integration.* Washington DC: Brookings Institution, 43–77.

McCarthy, P. (1993) 'France looks at Germany, or how to become German (and European) while remaining French', in P. McCarthy (ed.), *France–Germany 1983–1993.* London: Macmillan, 51–71.

Moravcsik, A. (1993) 'Preferences and power in the European Community: a liberal intergovernmentalist approach', *Journal of Common Market Studies* 31:4, 473–524.

Ostner, I. and J. Lewis (1995) 'Gender and the evolution of European social policies' in S. Leibfried and P. Pierson (eds), *European Social Policy: Between Fragmentation and Integration,* Washington DC: Brookings Institution, 159–93

Pierson, P. (1996) 'The path to European integration: a historical institutionalist analysis', *Comparative Political Studies* 29:2, 123–63.

Rhodes, M. (1991) 'The social dimension of the Single European Market: national versus transnational regulation', *European Journal of Political Research* 19, 245–80.

—— (1992) 'The future of the "Social Dimension": labour market regulation in post-1992 Europe', *Journal of Common Market Studies* 30, 23–51.

—— (1995) 'A regulatory conundrum: industrial relations and integration', in S. Leibfried and P. Pierson (eds), *European Social Policy: Between Fragmentation and Integration.* Washington DC: Brookings Institution, 78–122.

Rhodes, M. and B. van Apeldoorn (1997) 'Capitalism versus capitalism in western Europe', in M. Rhodes, P. Heywood and V. Wright (eds), *Developments in West European Politics.* London: Macmillan, 171–89.

Risse-Kappen, T. (1996) 'Exploring the nature of the beast: international relations theory and comparative policy analysis meet the EU', *Journal of Common Market Studies* 34:1, 53–80.

Ross, G. (1995) 'Assessing the Delors era and social policy', in S. Leibfried and P. Pierson (eds), *European Social Policy: Between Fragmentation and Integration.* Washington DC: Brookings Institution, 357–88.

Streeck, W. (1991) 'More uncertainties: German unions facing 1992', *Industrial Relations* 30:3, 317–49.

Turner, L. (1996) 'The Europeanisation of labour: structure before action', *European Journal of Industrial Relations* 2:3, 325–44.

Visser, J. and B. Ebbinghaus (1992) 'Making the most of diversity? European integration and the transnational organisation of labour', in J. Greenwood, J. R. Grote and K. Ronit (eds), *Organised Interests and the European Community.* London: Sage, 206–37.

9

FRANCO-GERMAN CO-OPERATION IN FOREIGN AFFAIRS, SECURITY AND DEFENCE

A case study

Amaya Bloch-Lainé

Introduction

The concept of 'closer co-operation', introduced in the revised version of the Maastricht Treaty at the Amsterdam summit of July 1997, echoes the more informal one of 'hard core': indeed, it allows some member countries of the European Union (EU) to go further on the road of European integration without being hindered by the other partners. The insertion of this provision in the treaty followed a debate engaged on the German side as early as 1994 and later joined by Paris: Chancellor Kohl and French President Chirac sent two joint letters to the then presidents of the European Council, in December 1995 and October 1996, proposing the introduction of such a clause. Indeed, France and Germany share the idea that, in an enlarged EU, it will be increasingly difficult to take decisions by the unanimity rule, especially in fields where the notions of national interests and sovereignty are at stake: this is particularly true in the context of Common Foreign and Security Policy (CFSP).

Such a common vision on the part of Paris and Bonn came after years of strong bilateral partnership and co-operation in foreign affairs, security and defence: formally inaugurated with the Elysée Treaty in 1963, this co-operation was reaffirmed and deepened with the adoption of a 'common strategic concept' at the bilateral summit of Nuremberg in December 1996. Moreover, the willingness of Paris and Bonn to put their bilateral relationship at the heart of a broader European endeavour was also made very clear over the years. Hence most of the provisions which found their way into the CFSP in the Maastricht Treaty were initiated jointly by Paris and Bonn. In the 1980s, France and Germany were at the origin of the Eurocorps, intended to give some operational credit to the political project of a European defence. Last but not least, the changes made in the CFSP at the Amsterdam summit also stemmed from a joint Franco-German approach.

It thus seems indisputable that, against the background of a strong political willingness to give Europe a voice in international and strategic affairs, France and Germany worked hand in hand to push such a project. However, that does not mean that both countries succeeded in building what is called a 'hard core', likely to act as the main decision-making and operational centre of European policy in security and defence. The existence of a hard core supposes that three conditions are met: first, a strong commonality of security interests; second, operational and military credibility; and finally, other partners' acknowledgement of such credibility.

It will be argued here that if, after years of progressive rapprochement between France and Germany expressed both at the political and institutional level, the first condition is about to be met, the second and third conditions are far from being fulfilled, for reasons linked both to the ambiguities of Franco-German co-operation itself and to the other partners' reluctance to admit the validity and credibility of such co-operation.

An enduring political and institutional co-operation

The story of Franco-German co-operation in security and defence should be placed in a broader political context. Indeed, behind all the major initiatives taken in common by Bonn and Paris, be it at the bilateral or European level, lies one fundamental common goal: to get both countries definitively reconciled, at the heart of Europe. As stated by Yves Boyer:

> There is obviously the feeling on both sides of the Rhine that European stability can no longer be guaranteed if basic agreement is not maintained between France and Germany. Without such an agreement, Western Europe may return to a balance of power game, a game that can verge on latent civil war which, in the longer run, is synonymous with collective suicide.
>
> (Boyer 1996:249)

It should be kept in mind, then, that only such a strong political commitment on both sides explains how and why, despite very different, if not asymmetric security and military status, France and Germany have always sustained a deep and constant dialogue and co-operation on security and defence. The choice to promote constant co-operation on such issues was not casual – insofar as security and defence represents the essence of national sovereignty and national interests, they have a strong symbolic value. Moreover, it should be remembered that both countries decided to establish a special relationship in foreign affairs, security and defence prior to France opting for an autonomous security and defence policy. By the early 1950s, Chancellor Adenauer decided definitely to anchor Germany in the Western community: such a fundamental choice had to use Franco-German close co-operation as one of its main paths. On the French side, apart from the willingness to be reconciled with Germany, the goal was also to keep control of Bonn and to embed Germany within the framework of European construction.

From the outset, Franco-German co-operation in security and defence has thus been linked to the broader logic of European construction and integration. Indeed, one of the clearest elements of continuity in the Franco-German relationship is the commitment of both countries to consider their bilateral links as the starting point of a broader European project, namely the building of a political Europe. There has been permanent back and forth movement between the bilateral dynamics and the broader European picture. Indeed, failures to organise security and defence co-operation at the European level have been most of the time followed by the strengthening of bilateral co-operation. In turn, there are numerous examples of France and Germany having tried to transpose their model of the bilateral co-operation on to the European Communities and later the EU.

The failure in 1954 of the European Defence Community project, aimed at avoiding the resurgence of a German army, did not prevent Franco-German co-operation from developing. Actually, the 1954 agreement over Germany's integration in the NATO was facilitated by an agreement between Pierre Mendes-France and Adenauer. The new impetus given to the European construction in the mid-1950s and leading to the Rome Treaty was largely due to a Franco-German initiative. In 1957–58 talks about military affairs between France and Germany took place. In the same way, the failure in 1962 of the Plan Fouchet, which proposed a European political union among the six member states of the European Communities, relaunched the bilateral dynamic and led directly to the 1963 Elysée Treaty – the realisation of the Plan Fouchet at a bilateral level.[1]

Very ambitious in goal, the Elysée Treaty came at a time of asymmetric positions between both countries as far as the organisation of European security was concerned.[2] Indeed, whereas France, under the impulse of Charles de Gaulle, was already seeking a security system which could have allowed the Europeans, or at least France and Germany, to distance themselves from the USA, Germany was clearly politically and militarily embedded in the Atlantic Alliance and considered the NATO as the only viable European security structure. By making that very clear in the added preamble to the treaty, the German Bundestag deprived it of any chance of concrete application. Later on, the American Multilateral Force (MLF) project aggravated disagreements between Bonn and Paris. When France left the integrated military structure of NATO in 1966, the Elysée Treaty's hopes regarding military co-operation were put to rest.

It was not until the early 1980s that bilateral co-operation found a new impetus. It is also during this period that Franco-German co-operation witnessed its greatest operational achievements. In 1982, François Mitterrand and Helmut Kohl decided to deepen co-ordination in foreign affairs and security through regular meetings between their foreign affairs and defence ministers. In October 1983 Mitterrand and Kohl announced their willingness to promote greater interaction between their military doctrines. Informal discussions began concerning nuclear deterrence, based on the French idea of 'extended deterrence'. This process of close consultation found a new momentum in the late 1980s, with the establishment in 1988 of the Franco-German Defence Council which involved the addition of a new protocol to the Elysée Treaty.

At the operational level, the creation of the Eurocorps, decided at a bilateral summit in La Rochelle in May 1992, led to the development of an army corps composed of French and German units, later joined by Belgian and Spanish ones. It is essentially from the Franco-German bilateral dynamic in security and defence that most of the initiatives to develop a European policy came, as exemplified by the central role played by France and Germany in the framework of European Political Co-operation (EPC), and, in the post-Cold War context, by the elaboration of the provisions concerning Common Foreign and Security Policy (CFSP) in the Maastricht Treaty, largely under the impulse of Paris and Bonn.

The debate in the mid-1990s about 'hard cores' (Europe Documents 1994: 1895/96) and 'reinforced co-operation' within the EU, which would essentially revolve round the Franco-German couple, is largely the consequence of the difficult process of the development, at the EU level, of a CFSP. The Maastricht Treaty, as revised at Amsterdam in 1997, actually contains, as far as the CFSP is concerned, most of the Franco-German ideas, such as the creation of a High Representative for CFSP (who is actually the Council General Secretary), a planning cell to assist the Council, and the introduction of the rule of 'closer co-operation'.

This brief historical overview of the links between the bilateral dimension and the European exemplifies the central role played by France and Germany in the progressive definition and institutionalisation of a security and defence role for the European Union. But most of the results of such a common endeavour are of an institutional nature – at the operational level, the picture is much less clear. Indeed, Franco-German co-operation is also about a gap between words and deeds as far as operational and military issues are concerned.

Lack of operational credibility

Franco-German co-operation in security and defence developed at the political level between two countries of asymmetrical operational and military status, with concrete co-operation almost impossible at the time of the signing of the Elysée Treaty, given France's opting for an autonomous policy outside the framework of NATO's integrated military structure and Bonn's exact opposite stance. As a result, only the provisions of the Elysée Treaty regarding co-operation in armaments production were really developed.[3]

The 1980s and 1990s became a test for operational co-operation between the two countries. Indeed, the new parameters of European security confronted France and Germany with difficult political and security dilemmas.[4] On the German side, the end of East–West military confrontation on the European continent and German reunification inevitably raised the issue of a new international status for Germany, and the question of a more active involvement by Bonn in the political and military sides of foreign, security and defence issues.[5] The time had come for Germany to 'normalise' its foreign and security policy, but such a normalisation initially caused and continues to cause uneasiness in Bonn.

One of the clearest signs of this was the indecisiveness of the German government concerning the participation of German troops in peace-keeping missions abroad. In 1994 Chancellor Kohl decided to let the Federal Constitutional Court deal with such a political issue. The verdict was that sending German troops on peace-keeping missions abroad was not anti-constitutional, even if such a decision would have to be approved by the Bundestag. Germany's security and defence policy needs to be adapted all the more since multilateral security structures, and especially the Atlantic Alliance, are also witnessing dramatic changes in their mission and posture. Inaugurated in 1991 with the adoption of a new strategic concept, NATO's evolution has been remarkable. From being an essentially military defensive organisation against the Soviet threat, it is progressively becoming an East–West forum where every issue related to security is debated and whose new missions are directly connected with peace-keeping and humanitarian action. The catchwords of the 'new' NATO are crisis prevention and peace-keeping operations – such a global role will inevitably affect German security and defence policy.[6]

On the French side, the end of the Cold War also led to a revision of traditional security and defence orientations, beginning with the last years of the Mitterrand presidency and developed further by Jacques Chirac. This aggiornamento finds its roots in various considerations. First, German reunification profoundly disturbed the traditional French position in Europe, precisely by raising the issue of a new political status for Bonn. In order to deal with this, and to retain political influence over a strong economically reunified partner, France endorsed the aim of European political integration alongside Economic and Monetary Union (EMU), deciding to accelerate European integration in foreign affairs, security and defence. Again, as in the past, the idea was and largely remains to tie Germany within a 'constraining' framework called Europe, to avoid any temptation on the part of Bonn to develop an autonomous foreign policy on the continent.

Second, and especially since Chirac's arrival in power, Paris modified its policy towards the development of a European identity in security and defence. The mixed experience of the EU in the Yugoslavian war, the confirmation of the inescapable political and military role of the USA and NATO in such events, and the reluctance, not to say the opposition, of other major countries within the EU, especially Great Britain, to any development of 'purely' European responsibilities in security and defence, moved Paris closer to the Atlantic Alliance. In December 1995, President Chirac announced that Paris would fully participate in the integrated military structure of the alliance that it had left in 1966 – under the condition that NATO would reform itself in order to allow its European members to make their own identity more visible, both in political and operational terms.[7]

Therefore, as Axel Sauder (1996: 584) stated: 'The German bet which consisted in maintaining, with patience, the links between France and NATO in order to favour a progressive rapprochement has been won. But at the same time, France has succeeded in Europeanising German security policy more than was the case before.' Such a political context could be expected to have produced renewed operational co-operation between the two countries, as expected in the aftermath of the publication of French and German white papers on defence in 1994 – both of which were largely based on a process of bilateral consultation, analysing the new strategic environment in almost identical terms. However, the gap between words and deeds remains, given the profound difference in attitudes towards the potential usefulness of the military in the European Union context are concerned.

Such divergences have been further aggravated by recent French defence policy reforms. Indeed, major French defence policy decisions have apparently been made outside the framework of Franco-German dialogue, particularly regarding the reform of the army, announced on 22 February 1996 by Chirac, which will lead to a military priority for the prevention and management of regional crises. The decision to put an end to conscription was also taken without prior consultation with Bonn. How is it that France took such essential decisions, to a greater or lesser extent affecting Germany's own defence policy and Franco-German co-operation mechanisms, without prior consultation with Bonn?

There are two lines of argument: first, the domestic factor – Chirac had to show his majority that decisions in such matters as security and defence were still taken on a national and independent basis, without 'asking' for the approval or even advice of foreign countries, even such close allies as Germany. Second, Chirac may have considered this a way to compel Germany to go further in its own defence reform in order to keep up with France's agenda – this would not be the first time Paris reasserted what it still considered its leading role in bilateral security and defence co-operation with Bonn.

Germany itself has used this kind of tactic in its relationship with Paris, as exemplified by the debate about hard cores within the European Union launched mainly by Bonn in 1994. Such an initiative, taken by high-profile members of the ruling coalition in a 'national' document, was also a way of pushing France to adopt the concept. This mutual process reveals the mechanisms of Franco-German co-operation in political matters – not reacting or responding to unilateral initiatives by the other partner could severely endanger Franco-German co-operation in all its facets. That is why the potentially negative consequences of unilateral moves on the part of Paris or Bonn should not be overestimated. Such moves are usually aimed at sending signals to the other party to modify its own position.

The changes in French defence policy may nevertheless be at odds with the traditional orientation of Germany.[8] Where France is currently aiming its military forces towards crisis management missions, Germany is still attached to territorial defence and collective defence in the framework of the Atlantic Alliance.[9] Where France is moving towards a professional army, Germany and its public opinion are still attached, for historical but also political reasons, to the principle of conscription, even if it is also starting to be questioned in Germany. Such differences could complicate any day-to-day co-operation between the two armed forces. Lastly, both countries are developing divergent attitudes to the Eurocorps – while France still considers it a tool for European military intervention in limited crises, Germany remains attached to the principle of its serving collective defence purposes within the NATO framework.

Aware of these remaining ambiguities, Paris and Bonn tried to overcome them by giving a new political and institutional impetus to their co-operation. At the December 1996 Nuremberg summit they adopted a 'common concept in security and defence'. Starting from a common assessment of security risks in Europe, Paris and Bonn decided to accelerate the process of achieving complementarity between their respective armed forces – both operationally and in terms of military doctrine. In the context of crisis prevention and management, which is recognised as one of the central features of international security, they decided to reinforce their co-operation in two particular fields: airlift capacities and intelligence – precisely the areas in which European armed forces are weak, making them almost totally dependent on American assets within NATO. Finally, it remains to be seen whether the political and institutional will apparent in the declaration that 'our countries are ready to open a dialogue concerning the role of nuclear deterrence in the context of European defence policy' will be translated into operational reality.[10]

External constraints: reluctant partners and NATO's central role in European security

Diverging conceptions about security and defence within the EU

It is not clear that member countries share the same views about what exactly the role of the EU should be on the world stage, especially in political and security terms. The main issue seems to be that of a real defence role for the union. While countries such as France and Germany are advocating that such responsibility be given to the EU in the medium to long term, other countries, particularly the UK, forcefully question this approach. The UK stance consists of differentiating between two notions of security and defence – one encompassing diplomatic, economic and 'social' aspects already within the EU's remit (be it through EU's external policies as applied in the first pillar or within the CFSP); the other believing that defence aspects should be dealt with outside the EU framework, within the Atlantic Alliance. All official British declarations tend in this latter direction. Tony Blair's government has maintained the same position as John Major (*Le Monde,* 8 November 1996: 15) who stated that:

> I do not recognise, at the time being, any capacity for the European Union to endorse responsibilities in the defence field. Europe should certainly reorganise its capacities. But the only framework in which she

can really carry out such reorganisation is the WEU (Western European Union), and ultimately, NATO.

Other countries, such as Sweden, are receptive to this argument given their historical background, and also emphasise the role which the EU could play in terms of conflict prevention by political, diplomatic and economic means rather than military.

The British position is motivated by several considerations. The first relates to 'high politics' – London clearly does not easily accept the idea of a political Europe. This difference of perspective between Great Britain, on the one hand, and France and Germany, on the other, is not new, but today appears even more acute than it was formerly. The second consideration is much more pragmatic – in the context of severe budgetary constraints, why should European countries duplicate operational and military resources already available through NATO, which has Combined Joint Task Force mechanisms enabling the Europeans to act alone if they choose?

Moreover, London is convinced that the commonality of security interests between Europe and the USA, at least on the European continent, is so strong that it is unrealistic to think there could be situations where European countries would have to act militarily without US participation. Starting from such an assumption, it is clear that the European Union does not need to develop its own security and defence policy. London considers also that, in defence policy, the only way to act in an efficient way is to form ad hoc coalitions of various partners, as opposed to any formal and institutionally binding decision-making process. Lastly, there is the general uneasiness that Great Britain feels towards the Franco-German couple, be it in the economic or political field. It is still very difficult for London to accept the idea of a Franco-German engine within the European Union.

The marginalisation of CFSP

Given the lack of common political vision among EU's members, and the relative inadequacy of CFSP in responding to crises, the tendency in recent years has been to assemble ad hoc groups, gathering 'big' actors in security and defence, to deal with such situations. Examples include the Contact Group for Bosnia, gathering the USA, Great Britain, France, Germany and Russia outside any existing institutional framework, such as the EU or NATO; France and Great Britain (later joined by the Netherlands) forming the Rapid Reaction Force in Bosnia, again outside the institutional framework of the EU and CFSP; and in 1996 the Paris proposal for a summit between the USA, Russia, France, Germany and Great Britain to deal with the issue of Russia's reaction to NATO enlargement.

Even within the legal framework of the EU and CFSP, European countries, France and Germany in particular, tend to emphasise the weight of bilateral co-operation – whether Franco-German, Franco-British or Franco-Spanish – without being clear how to translate such bilateral processes into a multilateral dynamic associating all members of the EU. As put by two EU practitioners:

The intergovernmental character of CFSP has produced a tendency to sacrifice the institutional framework to ad hoc structures, where only a few members are represented and where issues concerning the European Union as a whole are debated. In that respect, one of the worrying lessons of the Yugoslav crisis is the tendency of various member states which took part in the Contact Group (France, Germany, Great Britain) to ignore existing organisations which they consider inefficient, rather than to try to make them more effective. CFSP is replaced by the Contact Group policy, the latter apparently itself replaced by more and more obvious bilateral relationships.

(Willaert and Marqués-Ruiz 1995: 86–7)

The issue of ad hoc groups raises a difficult dilemma – the ad hoc group can seem the more efficient solution in terms of flexibility in decision-making and the fact that they usually gather the countries best able to influence specific issues or crises. On the other hand, such a system, outside any existing institutional framework, may condemn the EU and CFSP to play no role in security and defence, either in the mid or long term.

Again, there is a clash of visions among European countries. What a country like Great Britain is questioning is not the possibility of European countries gathering their political and operational means to deal with security issues and specific crises, but the willingness of some of its partners to give such a process a permanent institutional framework.

Shared responsibilities between EU and NATO: the unresolved issue

The third issue is that of role sharing between the EU and NATO. Many questions remain unanswered in this respect, such as the nature of the necessary institutional links between these two entities that play a role in security and defence; how to combine CFSP, which is theoretically supposed to develop a defence dimension, and the development of a European security and defence identity within the Atlantic Alliance. If the Western European Union is meant to provide such a link, how does it sit with the Franco-German idea of integrating the WEU into the EU? Is it conceivable that decisions with potential defence and military implications will be taken by the European Council and realised within the framework of NATO? Will the USA accept such a European caucus within the alliance?

Conclusion

A strong political and institutional core, a hollow operational one: this could be a blunt but realistic assessment of Franco-German co-operation in security and defence. If there is no doubt that both countries have never failed to express their common willingness to build a political Europe, notably through the very symbolic nature of security and defence, they have not yet succeeded in transposing the model of their co-operation on to the EU. This only partial success is due both to the ambiguities of bilateral co-operation, notably at the operational level, which have been perceived by other partners as lacking credibility, and to their own reluctance regarding the very idea of a genuine European security and defence identity.

Two basic scenarios can be mooted regarding the future of Franco-German co-operation in security and defence and its capacity to trigger a wider European project. One could think that it is essentially a matter of time – France and Germany will in the long run resolve the ambiguities of their bilateral co-operation, making it more credible and convincing for their European partners. Or, given the symbolic nature of security and defence, one could also imagine Franco-German co-operation taking other routes to a political Europe.

As recent events show, economic aspects of the European integration process, and especially European Monetary Union (EMU), have taken priority. Where political initiatives, such as the many taken by France and Germany in the CFSP, were supposed to be the engine of further European integration, EMU has become the strategic vehicle for such integration. The real issue now is whether the agreement and willingness to move towards a single currency will, in turn, lead to a political Europe, with France and Germany playing a major role.

Notes

1 For a synthetic historical view of Franco-German co-operation, see Soutou (1993: 17–25) and Gerbet (1993: 27–58).

2 Both countries committed themselves to favouring the rapprochement between their respective strategic and tactical concepts, in order to achieve 'common conceptions'. Regular meetings of defence ministers and chiefs of staff were instituted. Co-operation was also supposed to take place at the earlier stages of the armaments procurement process.

3 This did not prevent both countries from maintaining co-operation in the armaments procurement sector. During the fifteen years following the Elysée Treaty, common projects were developed, in particular the Hot, Roland and Milan systems, and the Alpha-Jet and Transall airplanes. See Manfrass-Sirjacques (1993: 103).

4 For a very good review of such dilemmas, see Leimbacher (1995: 37–58).

5 As explained by Reinhardt Rummel: 'Bonn was confronted with the assumption of its neighbours that German policy, supported by nationalist and neutralist forces particularly in the East of the country, would turn more inward-looking, a fear which has partly materialised ... The opposite assumption was also made: that Germany would conduct a more independent outward-looking foreign policy ... Each of these extremist ideas would have meant the end of the concept of a communitarian foreign policy' (Rummel 1996: 44, 59).

6 Finally, some of the new goals of Bonn's foreign policy need to be pursued more than ever in multilateral structures. This is especially the case with EU enlargement eastwards. As the main proponent of the EU's inclusion of such countries as Poland, the Czech Republic and Hungary, Germany cannot act 'alone', for both political and economic reasons. Politically speaking, any German 'solo' in the region would be considered by both other EU members and Central European countries as potentially dangerous, given past experiences and the potential for German hegemony. In this framework, and as a proof of the good health of the Franco-German couple, Paris and Bonn joined to form what is now

called the Weimar Triangle with Poland. It consists of a mechanism of regular political and economic co-operation among the three countries, in order to facilitate Poland's accession to the EU. Germany, then, needs the EU, both to share in the burden of the reconstruction in the former Communist part of Europe, and in terms of political legitimacy.

7 Domestic considerations also played a role in the French move towards NATO. In a context of severe budgetary constraint, especially in the field of defence, it was clear that no supplementary expenses would be devoted to the development of 'purely' European military capacities (except in the field of intelligence, a point which will be addressed later). The opportunity, then, to develop a European security and defence identity against the background of existing capacities within NATO remains to be exploited.

8 Most of the following points have been taken from Sauder (1996: 585–7).

9 This difference did not prevent Germany from building military units supposed to react to crises. According to the Bundeswehrplan 1997, Germany should in future be able to have a 12,000-man contingent dedicated to military operations outside German territory.

10 Such a common position comes after the remarkably low profile maintained by the German authorities when in 1995 Chirac decided unilaterally to resume French nuclear tests. In an international context of severe criticism, and against the pressure of some segments of German public opinion and political forces, Chancellor Kohl decided not to argue with Paris. The chairman of the CDU parliamentary group, Wolfgang Schäuble, outlined perfectly the official German position in declaring that 'the announcement of a new campaign of nuclear tests complicates the debate on a common foreign and security policy in Europe ... But in order to make progress, we have to minimise problems between Paris and Bonn, whose respective positions on this topic are so different' (Schäuble interview, *Le Monde*, 5 July 1995).

References

Boyer, Yves (1996) 'France and Germany', in Bertel Heurlin (ed.), *Germany in Europe in the Nineties*. London: Macmillan, 241–56.

Europe Documents (September 1994), no. 1895/96, *Documents du groupe parlementaire CDU/ CSU du Parlement allemand sur l'avenir de l'unification européene*.

Gerbet, Pierre (1993) 'Le rôle du couple franco-allemand dans les Communautés européennes', in Henri Ménudier (ed.), *Le couple franco-allemand en Europe*. Paris: Pia, 27–58.

Leimbacher, Urs (1995) 'La co-opération franco-allemande dans le cadre de la Politique étrangère et de sécurité commune de l'Union européene', in Hans Stark (ed.), *Agir pour l'Europe: les relations franco-allemands dans l'après-guerre froide*. Paris: Masson, 37–58.

Manfrass-Sirjacques, Françoise (1993) 'La co-opération militaire depuis 1963', in Henri Ménudier (ed.), *Le couple franco-allemand en Europe*. Paris: Pia.

Monde, Le (1995) 'Interview with Wolfgang Schäuble', 5 July.

—— (1996) 'Oeuvrer avec la France à bâtir l'Europe', 8 November, 15.

Rummel, Reinhardt (1996) 'Germany's role in the CFSP: Normalität or Sonderweg?', in Christopher Hill (ed.), *The Actors in Europe's Foreign Policy*. London: Routledge, 44–59.

Sauder, Axel (1996) 'Défense française et co-opération franco-allemand', *Politique Etrangère* Autumn, 584.

Soutou, Georges-Henri (1993) 'France–Allemagne 1870–1963', in Henri Ménudier (ed.), *Le couple franco-allemand en Europe*. Paris: Pia, 17–25.

Willaert, Philippe and Carmen Marqués-Ruiz (1995) 'Vers une politique étrangère et de sécurité commune: état des lieux', *Revue du Marché Unique Européen* 3, 86–7.

10

FRANCE, GERMANY AND IMMIGRATION POLICY

A paradoxical convergence

Patrick Weil

Introduction

Historically, France and Germany have adopted different approaches to immigration. France has welcomed large numbers of immigrants since the second half of the nineteenth century, whereas Germany has consistently refused to recognise itself officially as a country of immigration. Yet, despite this divergence, the two countries are increasingly co-operating on immigration, a process that culminated in the Schengen agreements of 1985 and 1990. This increased co-operation reflects a broader development in German and French immigration policy – although this process is still underway, it is possible to speak of an emerging convergence in the two countries.

This chapter will trace the rise of the convergence, and will argue that the process has two features. First, despite the contrasting historical approach to immigration taken by France and Germany, the institutionalisation of international norms has placed similar constraints on policy makers in both countries. Second, while the two countries have different interests in managing immigration, they have come to co-operate in the implementation of immigration control.

The rise of normative constraints on immigration laws

Before World War II, the arrival of large numbers of immigrants in countries such as the USA or France placed the issue of 'selection' on the political agenda. At the time, Western nations retained a large degree of autonomy in immigration policy. Broadly speaking, the merits of two forms of selection were debated: an 'egalitarian' and a 'universalistic' selection, based on individual qualifications (physical, mental, moral and eventually educational) or a 'racialist' selection based on national or racial affiliation. Starting in the 1920s, the USA implemented a policy of selecting immigrants based on nationality and race (Divine 1957).

Although the racialist approach was never publicly chosen in France, it was nonetheless implemented in practice. Following World War I, 'undesirable' colonial soldiers and workers, who had been brought to France during the war, were deported to their colonies of origin. In addition, France deported numerous Poles in 1934–35.

Since World War II, these policies have increasingly been viewed as unacceptable. While the rapidity with which international standards have been internalised has varied from country to country, the experience of Nazism stigmatised all forms of 'racial science' in public policy. This had an important consequence: the selective welcome or naturalisation of immigrants based on racial criteria or national origins was progressively eliminated from the legislation of liberal democracies.

The debate surrounding France's approach to immigration illustrates this development. At the end of the 1930s France was on the verge of adopting a national and racial quota policy similar to that used in the USA. In fact, even after the war, the government, with the approval of Charles de Gaulle, considered implementing such a policy. However, some key French civil servants opposed the project, arguing that an immigration policy based on a hierarchy of racial or national origins would too closely resemble Nazi ideology (Weil 1995: 74–99). Likewise, in Germany, the guest worker (*Gastarbeiter*) programme established after the war explicitly rejected the selection of workers on the basis of national or racial origin.

In fact, in both Germany and France, the status of 'temporary worker' was a mean of managing the flow of undesirable immigrants. In the 1970s, however, both countries were forced to recognise that the categorisation of immigrants into various groups (temporary, permanent, refugee, guest workers, and so on), has little impact on the actual duration of the stay, and a de facto right to stay emerged during the 1970s for legal foreign residents.

In France, this lesson originated in the failure of a political project: President Valery Giscard d'Estaing attempted a forced repatriation of the majority of legal North African immigrants, especially Algerians, between 1978 and 1980 (Weil 1991: chapter 5). Due to a strong reaction from the political left, the labour unions, the Gaullist and Christian Democratic parties, however, the initiative failed. Giscard's repatriation proposal also provoked a vivid reaction from the French Administrative Supreme Court (le Conseil d'Etat). In its decision, the Court, which primarily based its decision on republican values and constitutional principles, also referred to the damaging effects of such a policy on France's image abroad. The force of this rebuttal caused the government to retreat and to recognise the ethical and practical impossibility of repatriating 'undesirable' foreign workers by force. In June 1984, the French parliament passed an Act that guaranteed permanent residence for all foreign citizens living legally in France, regardless of their origin.

In Germany the result was similar, but the process different. The German courts were at the centre of a policy revolution that was only belatedly accepted by the political elite. The German government officially maintained that it was not a country of immigration, and that the workers recruited in the 1950s were to return to their countries of origin after no more than a few years in Germany. In keeping with this logic, a Bavarian administrative court ruled in 1970 that a foreign worker's sojourn of more than five years was sufficient grounds to deny further residency (authorisation), as each extended residency (authorisation) would tend towards settlement, which ordinarily ran counter to state interests because the Federal Republic of Germany was not a country of immigration (Miller 1986: 71).

This decision was overruled by the German Federal Constitutional Court, and in 1972 the federal government stated that 'the limitation of the duration of the stay of foreign employees will not be regulated through repressive measures under the law related to foreigners'. Basing itself on the Preamble of the Basic Law, which recognises and protects fundamental human rights and is considered a 'spiritual–moral confrontation with the previous system of National Socialism' (Kanstroom), the German court extended the rights and privileges associated with the principle of 'basic constitutional rights for everyone' (*Jedermanns Grund-rechte*), not only to German citizens but also to aliens resident in Germany. In 1978 the court recognised that 'an alien acquires a constitutionally protected reliance interest to remain in Germany as a result of prior routine renewals of his residence permit and his integration into German society' (Kanstroom: 171).[1] After the failure of the voluntary return policy which, in 1983–84 tried to encourage foreign residents to return to their countries of origin, this legal right resulted in a massive sociological reality: a large, permanently resident population of non-citizens in Germany.

Since World War II, liberal democracies have been unable to select immigrants according to race or national origin; they have accepted that any foreigner autho-rised to take up residence has to be considered by the state as a potential permanent immigrant.[2] Post-war international standards have also transformed perceptions of legitimate behaviour in another policy area: asylum (Martin 1990: 1254). The creation of an individual international status for the 'refugee' is the product of a complex process which was codified in the 1951 Geneva Convention. Article 1 defines a refugee as a person who is unwilling or unable to return to his or her country 'owing to a well-founded fear of persecution for reasons of race, religion, nationality, membership of a particular group or political opinion'. To a degree, the Convention constituted a setback for efforts to secure individual human rights against arbitrary state power since the requirement that nation states admit unconditionally to their territory those who claim refugee status was rejected (Norek and Doumic-Doublet 1989: 35). Admission to national territory remains the jurisdiction of each nation, which is sovereign in determining the conditions under which asylum seekers are admitted (Goodwin-Gill 1983).

The Convention did not guarantee that an applicant would be granted asylum if his or her case merited it: it simply stated that he would not be returned 'to the frontiers of territories where his life or freedom would be threatened' (Article 33).

Although all the countries involved in this study now recognise and claim to obey the Convention, refugee policy varies greatly from one nation to another.

Founded in 1949, the Federal Republic of Germany far surpassed the requirements of the Geneva Convention, which it signed in 1951. The inclusion of a provision related to a right for individual territorial asylum in the 1949 Basic Law was seen by its drafters as an important commitment to human rights in the aftermath of the war, not only symbolising the rejection of National Socialism, but also responding to political persecution in Eastern Europe (Kanstroom: 194). Article 16, paragraph 2, sentence 2 of the German Basic Law provides that 'the politically persecuted shall enjoy asylum'. Three kinds of applicants, and therefore refugees, are recognised by the German system: Article 16 refugees, Geneva Convention refugees, and de facto refugees. The last lack clear proof of the well-founded fear of persecution needed to obtain Geneva status but are nonetheless permitted to remain on humanitarian grounds, under the implicit rule of *non-refoulement* (non-repatriation) (Neuman 1993: 509–11).

In France, the distinction between political refugees and other types of immigrant is centuries old. After World War II, France ratified the Geneva Convention, including a restrictive option clause which was not repealed until 1971.[3] The French Office for the Protection of Refugees and Stateless Persons, created in 1952, is in charge of recognising refugee status. The Preamble of the 1958 French Constitution specifies that 'any person persecuted on account of his actions in favour of liberty has a right to asylum within the territories of the Republic'. In addition, de facto refugee status and permission to remain on French territory can be provided, at the discretion of the state, to refugees who lack any individual proof of the well-founded fear of persecution necessary to claim Geneva status.

Apart from refugees' access to their territory, France and Germany accepted family reunification: the right to normal family life was progressively recognised by French and German jurisprudence. The French Conseil d'Etat recognised it in a Groupe d'Information et de Soutien des Travailleurs Immigrés (GISTI) decision in 1978. In Germany, the Federal Constitutional Court has extended the protection of the family provided for by Article 6 of the Basic Law ('marriage and family shall enjoy the special protection of the state' and 'the care and upbringing of children are a natural right of, and a duty primarily incumbent on, the parents') to immigrants (Motomura 1995: 517). In France, as in Germany, alien residents who wish to be joined by their family members must satisfy three requirements: legal residence, sufficient living space, and adequate means of financial support.

Formally, three categories of immigrants are authorised to enter France and Germany with relative ease: foreign-born spouses of citizens, political refugees, and families of foreign residents. Progressively, without having predicted or desired it, French and German immigration law has converged and is based on the same principles of admission and restriction. Nevertheless, despite these common rules, despite relatively small differences in the size of their populations (55 versus 80 million) or their economies, France and Germany welcomed markedly different numbers of foreign nationals in 1993 (99,200 and 986,900 respectively) (SOPEMI/

OECD 1994: 205). In the last decade, Germany has received the majority of immigrants to Western Europe. The French–German decision to co-ordinate the implementation of their control policies, through the Schengen agreement, has been taken in spite of their very different experiences of immigration.

Franco-German co-ordination despite divergence

Despite the globalisation of the world economy, increased population movements, the spread of telecommunications, and the comparable economic and demographic conditions in the countries of Western Europe, rates of immigration in both absolute and proportional terms vary greatly from one country to another and from one year to the next.[4] To explain these differences, it is necessary to consider both geographical and historical factors. A nation's geographical position has a tremendous impact on immigration flows. As land borders are more difficult to control than sea borders, it is easier for France, which only has land borders with developed countries, to control immigration than it is for Germany which shares borders with several East European nations.

The historical image of a country's treatment of refugees or immigrants (foreign or colonial) can also have a significant influence on the types of policies that can be considered legitimate. Paradoxically, it was France's image as the birthplace of human rights which made it conceivable to organise the forced repatriation of several hundred thousand resident immigrants to their countries of origin, a measure which no other European country considered. By contrast, Germany is limited in matters of civil and human rights to a greater degree than any other country, by moral constraints stemming from the experience of Nazism. It was impossible for Germany to organise the forced repatriation of temporary foreign workers following the 1973 oil shock.

Given that the two countries are facing significantly different immigration 'problems', and given that the focus of Germany's concern is on Eastern Europe, one may ask why the two countries have sought to secure a treaty ensuring French co-operation on Germany's western border. Several factors are relevant. First, international co-operation in Europe has been perceived by some European governments as a potentially effective tool in preventing illegal immigration, as reflected by the inclusion of migration issues in the Maastricht Treaty. This treaty states that rules of entry, temporary visits by foreigners, the issuing of visas, the granting of asylum, and measures taken to stop illegal immigration fall within the jurisdiction of the European Union. Decisions taken by the Union in this domain nonetheless still require the unanimous vote of member states. It is the Schengen agreement, signed originally by Germany, France and the Benelux countries on 14 June 1985, and in particular the 'technical application agreement' signed on 19 June 1990, that represents the truly decisive step in European co-operation in the domain of immigration.[5]

These accords create a common external border around the signatory nations, thus securing 'free travel' within this 'enlarged border', while provisions apply primarily to citizens of Schengen countries. The elimination of control posts on the common borders between these countries requires the harmonisation of visa policies for citizens of non-member countries. They also require common deportation policies allowing, for example, an illegal immigrant arrested in France to be sent back to Germany or Belgium if he or she passed through that country prior to arriving illegally in France. In reality, the elimination of border control posts between the members of the Schengen group does not mean that all identity checks have been eliminated. On the contrary, if the regulations are obeyed to the letter, any citizen of a country which is not part of Schengen should fill out a declaration form upon entering France, and then be able to prove the visit is legal if a policeman asks to see identification. Before the Schengen accords, police checks were largely limited to the border. Today, border police can theoretically control identity papers anywhere on national territory.

Each country seeks different benefits from the Schengen treaty.[6] Germany's motivation for the agreement has always been, since the outset, political rather than technical. While the treaty could improve the control of immigration flows coming from France or Belgium into Germany, these flows have been, since 1989, much less substantial that those from Eastern Europe. In fact, German interest in European co-operation in this domain stems from two factors: principally, it represented a step towards further European integration, the first step in the 'communitarisation' of police and justice affairs. The Schengen agreement was a political project launched and personally supported by Chancellor Kohl, and later adopted by the German government – 'the Schengen agreement was a way of including what would later become the third pillar of the Maastricht Treaty'.[7]

Later, it facilitated a reform of the German constitution limiting access to its territory by asylum seekers. Through the instrumentalisation of the Schengen agreement in German politics, the conservative coalition succeeded in adopting a constitutional amendment restricting an extremely liberal asylum law, thereby aligning German laws with the laws and practices in other European countries and subsequently leading to a significant decrease in the number of demands for asylum (Neuman 1993: 503–15). Movement towards European unification has also permitted the German government to conclude agreements with Poland and the Czech Republic limiting the flows of asylum seekers from these countries.

France finds itself in the opposite situation. It had a 'technical' interest in the accords, and successive French governments found signing the treaty politically risky. During the parliamentary debate, the Schengen agreement, signed because of the personal involvement of Mitterrand, was criticised as an attack on the nation state in its traditional domains of sovereignty; as a result, leading members of successive governments, Gaullist but also Socialist, who had to implement the original agreement, were reluctant to do so.[8] Nonetheless, as all French land borders are with Schengen members (with the exception of Switzerland), the French police department had a strong technical interest in ensuring that the original agreement was implemented. If these countries were to enforce the accords rigorously, if German, Belgian, or Spanish police and customs agents were as strict with the papers of foreigners passing through their country on the way to France as they are with foreigners trying to enter their own country, the French police would greatly benefit by the accords: less work, more mobility and greater efficiency.

The manner in which the negotiations were conducted reflected the different aims of the two countries. In France, the negotiations took place at the Ministry of Interior and it was Charles Pasqua (Interior Minister 1986–88 and 1993–95) who played the decisive role in the last stages of the agreement (interviews). In Germany, by contrast, a director at the Chancellor's Office would welcome the negotiators at the Chancellor's Office. French primary concern was technical – ensuring the effective policing of its border – while Germany's was political – further integration in Europe.

Germany has already seen the benefits of the agreement: the Basic Law was changed to restrict territorial asylum and negotiations have been developed with neighbouring Eastern states to include them in a Schengen agreement model. For France, the results have to be demonstrated practically. If the border controls were to be lax, France would be the country with the most to lose. This is especially true in light of the current debate over immigration in France – increased immigration across France's eastern or southern borders could increase support for the French extreme right. Still, if the accord is properly implemented, France will be the primary beneficiary in terms of immigration flows, with the border police of the other Schengen nations essentially screening all incoming visitors before they reach France's land borders.

Conclusion

The Schengen agreements can be represented as a bargain between France and Germany, a model of intergovernmentalism (Moravcsik 1993: 507). For Germany, it has permitted a change in the constitutional provision relating to asylum and is a first step in the Europeanisation of police affairs. For France, the bargain was acceptable when the 1990 technical application treaty focused on and reinforced border control (Bigo 1996: 129–45) with the aim of increasing the efficiency of restrictive immigration policies, without involving a large transfer of responsibilities to a supranational level.

This accord will also be a test for European co-operation. Its success will reside in reciprocal involvement and confidence in each nation's border police properly implementing control for the benefit of other members. If this co-operation works we could expect further institutional developments, such as the creation of a European police – not written in the treaties nor forecast by its creators.

Notes

1 It is the judgment of 26 September 1978, 49 BverfGE 169; see also the judgment of 10 May 1988, 78 BverfGE 179, 196–7.

2 This is not to say that all immigrants who enter will stay indefinitely, since every year there is a significant number who spontaneously return to their country of origin and are often not counted in official statistics.

3 The Convention permitted each signatory state not only to implement the general time limit laid down by the Convention (which specified that a person could only acquire refugee status 'as a result of events occurring before 1 January 1951') but also to impose a territorial limit by inserting after the word 'events', the optional words 'occurring in Europe' prior to the critical date. On the French policy towards refugees after World War II, see Noiriél 1991: 139–52 and Cohen 1996: 92–101.

4 In Germany, asylum seekers represent the major part of these flows. The 1993 restrictive reform of the status of asylum seekers has therefore already produced a decrease in these flows.

5 Both treaties came into effect on 26 March 1995. On their history, see Bigo (1996: 115–45). The French and German governments had reached a prior agreement to abolish border controls between their two countries at Saarbrücken in 1984.

6 Great Britain had therefore much less to gain in entering the Schengen group, because abandoning identification checks at ports and airports would have required the British to carry out identification checks within their own borders, which is contrary to their political tradition.

7 Interview with Wenceslas de Lobkowicz, European Commission, 11 July 1996.

8 Interview with Jean Marc Sauvé, General Secretary of the French Government, former director of the French Ministry of Interior, Prime Minister's Office, 22 July 1996.

References

Bigo, Didier (1996) *Polices en Réseaux: l'Experience Européenne*. Paris: Presses de Sciences Po, 115–45.

Cohen, Daniel (1996) 'Insertion et transit: les réfugiés juifs de l'après-guerre 1945–1948', *Archives Juives* 29:1, 92–101.

Divine, Robert (1957) *American Immigration Policy 1924–1952*. New Haven: Yale University Press.

Goodwin-Gill, Guy S. (1983) *The Refugee in International Law*. Oxford: Clarendon Press.

Kanstroom, Daniel (1991) 'Wer Sind Wir Wieder? Laws of asylum, immigration and citizenship in the struggle for the soul of the new Germany', *The Yale Journal of International Law* 18:1, 194.

Martin, David A. (1990) 'Reforming asylum adjudication: on navigating the coast of Bohemia', *University of Pennsylvania Law Review* 138:5.

Miller, Mark J. (1986) 'Policy ad-hocracy: the paucity of co-ordinated perspectives and policies', *Annals AAPSS* 485, May.

Moravcsik, Andrew (1993) 'Preferences and power in the European Community: a liberal intergovernmentalist approach', *Journal of Common Market Studies* 31:4, 473–524.

Motomura, Hiroshi (1995) 'The family and immigration: a roadmap to the Ruritanian lawmaker', *American Journal of Comparative Law* 43:4, 511–35.

Neuman Gerald L. (1993) 'Buffer zones against refugees: Dublin, Schengen and the German asylum amendment', *Virginia Journal of International Law* 33:3, 503–15.

Noiriel, Gérard (1991) *La tyrannie du National: Le droit d'asile en Europe 1793–1993*. Paris: Calmann-Lévy.

Norek, Claude and Frédérique Doumic-Doublet (1989) *Le Droit d'Asile en France*. Paris: Presses Universitaires de France.

SOPEMI/OECD (1994) *Trends in International Migrations*. Paris: OECD.

Weil, Patrick (1995) 'Racisme et discriminations dans la politique française de l'immigration: 1938–1945/1974–1995', *Vingtième Siècle* July–September, 74–99.

—— (1991) *La France et ses étrangers*. Paris: Folio-Gallimard.

11

CONCLUSION

Douglas Webber

The conventional or orthodox view of the Franco-German relationship is that its quality and intensity depend critically on the engagement of the political leaders on both sides of the Rhine. According to this perspective that 'great men make history', the relationship has waxed and waned according to the identity or, more precisely, the foreign and European policy orientations of German chancellors and French presidents. Hence, the relationship was good and close under Adenauer and de Gaulle in the early 1960s, bad and distant under Erhard and de Gaulle in the mid-1960s, better, but still strained, under Brandt and Pompidou in the early 1970s, and good and close again not only while Schmidt was German Chancellor and Giscard French President in the second half of the 1970s, but also, save arguably for a short time during the German unification process, through most of the 1980s and early 1990s under Kohl and Mitterrand, before they cooled again with Mitterrand's succession as French President by Chirac.[1]

It is certainly not entirely misplaced to see French and German leaders as having played a central role in setting the 'compass' for the development of Franco-German relations at critical junctures in the history of the bilateral relationship and the European integration process. Projects such as the Coal and Steel Community, the Élysee Treaty and the Maastricht Treaty – which often encountered considerable domestic political resistance – may not have been launched, let alone implemented, but for the commitment displayed to them by, respectively, Adenauer and Schuman, de Gaulle and Adenauer and Kohl and Mitterrand. Moreover, political leaders in both states have often also played a critical role mediating bilateral conflicts over more mundane issues in 'day-to-day' EU politics, as the cases of agriculture and electricity liberalisation, for example, illustrate. Nonetheless, the emphasis in this perspective on the history-making role of 'great men' needs to be relativised in at least two ways. The first of these is that even French presidents and (more so) German chancellors are restricted in their decision-making autonomy by institutional (including normative) constraints that have accumulated over time and appear to make it less and less feasible for them to 'opt out' of the bilateral relationship. This may be seen in the fact that, no matter what new or different foreign or European policy accents and orientations newly elected political leaders have pledged in opposition and election campaigns, the length of time that they take, once elected, to convert or be converted to the indispensability of a 'special' Franco-German relationship has grown progressively shorter: from arguably two years in the case of Mitterrand to fewer than six months in that of Chirac and a matter of days in the case of the Jospin government in 1997 and that of the new German Chancellor, Schröder, in 1998.[2] The second is that Franco-German relations are not monopolised by the heads of state or government and that, beneath this level, many kinds of Franco-German relationships may exist and develop, not necessarily in synchrony or harmony with that of the political leaders. To focus only on the level of heads of government and state in analysing the Franco-German relationship is to overlook a large part of the daily reality of the relationship that exists, as in the case of an iceberg, 'below the surface'.

Inter-sectoral variations in the Franco-German relationship

The picture of the Franco-German relationship in the EU revealed by the above contributions is variegated. A large proportion of the issues or issue areas in which, as measured by the resources and efforts devoted to try to mediate bilateral conflicts, the relationship appears to be relatively intensive consists of 'constitution-making' issues handled in intergovernmental conferences (IGC) and involving the definition or extension of the EU's competences and determination of formal decision-making procedures. To this category belong the issues of monetary union, immigration policy, and foreign and security policy. In as far as it also has fundamental long-term implications, even if it is not itself an IGC issue, the Eastern enlargement of the EU is comparable to these 'constitution-making' issues. However, not all of the issues or issue areas in which the Franco-German relationship seems to be relatively intensive – for example, electricity liberalisation and agricultural policy – can be so defined. Thus, the bilateral relationship is or has evidently been less intensive in the spheres of social, telecommunications and research and technology policy (the development of the EUREKA programme excepted).[3]

To what factors can these inter-issue or inter-sectoral variations in the intensity of the Franco-German relationship in the EU be attributed? The most important seems to be quite simply the political salience of the issue or sector. For the two governments, salient issues are of two types. First, there are the 'constitution-making' issues referred to above. In as far as the way in which they are resolved determines the 'rules' of the game in the EU, and thus the governments' prospects for realising their political goals, for long periods, more is at stake for the governments in these conflicts, other things being equal, than in those that occur in day-to-day EU politics. Second, there are those issues that are salient because they are seen by one or other or both of the governments as significantly affecting their prospects of being re-elected or maintaining domestic political stability and order. On issues that are salient in one or other of these senses, other things being equal, the governments are more likely to co-ordinate their positions (and tactics) than on others, either because, in the case of the former set of issues, it is feared that a split between Bonn and Paris would damage the integration process and the bilateral relationship itself or, in the case of the latter set, the government for which the issue has a high domestic political salience appeals to the other to show 'solidarity' and to contribute to resolving it in a way that does not damage the government domestically. On issues of low political salience, by contrast, the prospective gains to be had by forging a common position are exceeded by the prospective costs in terms of diminished flexibility vis-à-vis other member governments and domestic constituencies. Most of the issues in the spheres of EU research and technology, market liberalisation and social policy analysed in the above contributions are of relatively low political salience. The greater intensity of Franco-German co-ordination on issues of agricultural policy, compared with the former policy areas, may be attributable to the fact that 'agriculture is high politics'[4] – that is to say, an issue area in which the German and especially the French government perceive the political stakes as being very high, not least because farmers are relatively well organised and possess a relatively strong capacity to sanction governments for EU decisions which they oppose (on this issue, see Keeler 1996).

A second factor influencing the intensity of the bilateral relationship in the EU is the role of the participating ministry or department in the political–bureaucratic division of labour. Given their respective roles or 'briefs', some ministries or departments are more strongly disposed than others to co-ordinate their positions on EU issues with their counterparts on the other side of the Rhine. The relevant distinction here is, in practice, between the offices of the heads of government or state (Federal Chancellor's office in Bonn and the President's office in Paris) and the foreign ministries, on the one hand, and the 'technical' or sectoral ministries, on the other. With few exceptions, the latter are oriented predominantly, if not exclusively, towards the management of domestic political issues and constituencies. They have, by and large, little need to co-ordinate, and only limited experience in co-ordinating, their positions with foreign governments. Their inclination to co-ordinate and make agreements with their counterparts on the other side of the Rhine is correspondingly weak. The remarks of an official in a Bonn ministry that the sectoral German ministries are 'not always happy' about Franco-German co-operation and sometimes find the weight given to it 'very unsatisfactory' may apply equally to the same kind of ministries in Paris.[5]

The foreign ministries are in both capitals those whose bilateral co-ordination is closest and the principal guardians of the Franco-German relationship. Whereas the 'domestic' ministries are inclined to prioritise the resolution of problems or issues according to domestic political priorities, the foreign ministries obey rather the logic of diplomacy, which prioritises the attainment of an agreement in international conflicts over the agreement's concrete contents.[6] The role of the foreign ministries as guardians of the bilateral relationship is strengthened by the fact that their ministers sit in the General Affairs Council and they provide the permanent representatives that sit in the COREPER, whose brief extends to virtually the entire range of EU policy. The French and German permanent representatives 'work closely together and try frequently to be allies', knowing that if it would 'not be good' for them in their respective foreign ministries if they were to clash (interview).[7] The closeness of the co-operation of the two foreign ministries in day-to-day Franco-German relations and EU decision-making is replicated by the Federal Chancellor's and the President's offices in respect of the biennial European Council meetings and intergovernmental conferences: in the importance that they attach to the Franco-German relationship, both offices lie closer to the foreign than to the 'technical' ministries in Paris and Bonn, whereby, in the 1980s and the first half of the 1990s at least, the co-operation was evidently facilitated by the stability and continuity of the political leadership and their foreign and European policy staff (see Védrine 1996: 407, 425–6). The Chancellor's and President's offices' competence for the intergovernmental conferences helps to explain the high level of Franco-German co-ordination on IGC issues. The Chancellor and the President (or, during periods of *cohabitation* in France, the Prime Minister) also exercise an important function in mediating intra-governmental conflicts where Franco-German relations are at stake.

The third factor which seems to influence the intensity (and effectiveness) of bilateral co-ordination is the extent to, and the length of time for, which policy-making competences in the issue area have been transferred to the EU, that is to say, 'Europeanised'.[8] Other things being equal, the stronger the competence of the EU for a given issue area, the stronger is the Franco-German co-ordination. Hence, Franco-German co-ordination is more intensive on issues of agricultural policy, which is strongly Europeanised and for which the EU's competence reaches back into the 1960s, than on issues of telecommunications, environmental or research and technology policy, where the EU has acquired significant policy-making powers only recently. While, for example, on agricultural policy issues, the participating French and German ministries routinely try to harmonise their positions, there is no convention of close co-ordination or the development of joint proposals between the ministries involved in telecommunications policy-making.[9] It is a case of the 'practice' of making decisions in the EU tending to make Franco-German co-ordination 'perfect' – or at least less imperfect than it would be otherwise.

By and large, the policy areas in which the EU's competences are strongest are also those in which ministers and officials of the member states interact most frequently with each other. Interaction between ministers and officials in EU decision-making organs in turn facilitates the development of mutual trust, which may be a prerequisite of a 'special relationship', in as far as this presupposes the willingness or capacity to forgo opportunities for short-term interest-maximisation at the partner state's expense. Of the 'sectoral' EU councils, the Council of Agricultural Ministers actually meets far more often than almost any other, rivalled only by the Council of Economics and Finance Ministers, the frequency of whose meetings has grown in the 1990s, mainly as a consequence of the preparations for the introduction of the single currency (Westlake 1995: 60, 252–9).Only the EU foreign ministers meet more frequently than the agricultural and economics and finance ministers. The frequency of their interaction is not related so much to the 'Europeanisation' of foreign policy as to the issue area overarching function that they perform in the guise of the General Affairs Council. For similar reasons, relating to the preparation of intergovernmental conferences (of which there have been three in little more than a decade), European Council meetings and their role of arbitrating conflicts that have not been able to be settled at lower levels, the offices of the heads of government (and the French President) in the EU almost certainly interact more with each other than do the 'sectoral ministries'. It is improbable that an official could describe the relationship between the staffs of the same 'sectoral' ministries in Bonn and Paris as having become 'daily, trusting, organic' during the 1980s as this has been done by the former secretary-general of the Elysée for the staff of the Elysée and the Federal Chancellor's Office in Bonn (Védrine 1996: 407).

Inter-sectoral variations in the influence of the Franco-German relationship

Most of the current models of European integration contain an implicit or explicit argument about the influence exercised by the member state governments in this process, if not of that of France and Germany in particular. Most of these arguments, are of a general or 'global' character and do not make any distinction between issues or sectors in terms of the influence wielded by these two governments. The preceding chapters show very clearly, however, that there are major inter-issue or inter-sectoral variations in the impact of the French and German governments on EU decisions. Broadly, it seems possible to distinguish between two sets of issue or policy areas: those that are governed by an *intergovernmental* and others that are governed by a *supranational* decision-making logic. In the former issue areas, given the prevalent decision-making rules, the council is the principal locus of decision-making and decisions are primarily shaped in bargaining between the member state governments. In the latter, the decision-making rules enable supranational actors to play a more decisive role and these actors – the Commission, the ECJ and coalitions or groups of transnational firms – have come to rival or even supersede the member state governments in terms of their impact on decisions. The issues handled in intergovernmental conferences, such as economic and monetary union, immigration and CFSP, other issues that can be resolved only with the consent of all the member states, such as the prospective Eastern enlargement, and those issue areas, first and foremost agriculture, for which the consultation procedure applies, exhibit an intergovernmental decision-making logic. A supranational decision-making logic is observable on those issues and in those issue areas in which, based on treaty provisions, favourable ECJ judgments or on the support of groups of transnational firms, the Commission has been able to achieve a large degree of autonomy from the member state governments – that is to say, first and foremost, on issues of market liberalisation (for example, telecommunications), but also, for example, research and technology policy.

Other things being equal, the influence of the Franco-German relationship on the outcome of 'intergovernmental' issues is strong. The chapters above contain, concerning these issues, no cases of a decision having been made to which both governments were opposed and few examples of joint Franco-German initiatives which (arguably) failed, in the sense that they were either not adopted or, in the process of being adopted, their content was substantially diluted. Examples of the latter phenomenon are arguably the 1989 Social Charter (see Chapter 8 by Rhodes) and the Maastricht Treaty provisions on a CFSP (see Chapter 9 by Bloch-Lainé), both projects that were resisted not only – strongly – by the British government, but also by several other member states. For this kind of issue at least, the observation of a former permanent representative to the EU that cases in which joint Franco-German proposals fail are 'few and far between' seems nonetheless to hold true (interview). When Franco-German conflicts on such issues remain unmediated, this tends to produce deadlock, if not crisis, in the EU policy process, such as occurred in 1992–93 on the GATT Uruguay Round (see Chapter 7 by Webber).

In 'supranational' issue areas, the Franco-German capacity to avert undesired outcomes or to secure desired ones is much more restricted. Among the issue areas analysed above, this applies notably to research and development policy for the information technology industry, to telecommunications liberalisation and, to a lesser extent, to the liberalisation of the electricity supply industry. In the latter two cases, backed by favourable ECJ jurisprudence, the Commission could use or threaten to use treaty provisions empowering it to eradicate public monopolies to soften the governments' resistance to market liberalising legislation. It broke the initial opposition to telecommunications liberalisation of both the French and German governments, which gradually came to accept the necessity or inevitability of this process; likewise, it was able to liberalise the electricity supply market, despite the same governments having initially rejected its proposals (see Chapter 5 by Schneider and Vedel and Chapter 4 by Schmidt). In the case of research and development policy, the big European information technology firms, half of them French or German, played a role as allies of the Commission functionally equivalent to that played by the ECJ on the market liberalisation issues. This is not to say that the French and German governments had no or even little influence on the outcome of these conflicts. Thus, the modalities of the EU research and development programmes for information technology were strongly shaped by member states, including French and German, reservations and the Commission was forced to make substantial amendments to its original electricity liberalisation proposals to accommodate French objections before the corresponding directive could pass the Council of Ministers. However, on these issues, much more than on 'intergovernmental' ones, the role of the French and German governments was predominantly reactive and, rather than their being the 'motor' or architects of integration, the impact of their co-operation was to modify the terms and tempo of implementation of projects that were sponsored by other actors.

The findings of the case studies thus support neo-functionalist and transnational exchange models of European integration in the latter set of issues and inter-governmentalist models in the former. In the one set, powerful coalitions of supra-national governmental and non-governmental actors have increasingly superseded the national governments, including the French and German, as the primary policy 'movers'. In the other, the national governments remain the principal actors and, among the national governments, the principal actors are frequently at least, but not always, the French and the German. In as far as this pattern is attributable to variations in decision-making rules, procedures and norms, it seems to be more compatible with institutionalist than with other interpretations of EU politics (see, for example, Pierson 1996; Armstrong and Bulmer 1998). The case of agricul-tural policy-making in particular suggests, moreover, that (formal and informal) decision-making rules and norms and the distribution of influence to which they contribute may prove very stable over time and that, contrary to neo-functionalist and transnational exchange theories (see introduction), there is no inexorable or irreversible process of the 'supranationalisation' of EU politics whereby national governments are condemned to forfeit control over the EU policy process to supranational actors. The Franco-German propensity to co-ordinate their positions more closely, the longer and more comprehensively an issue area has been 'Europeanised' points less towards the growth of supranational than towards that of 'interlocking politics' in the EU, with the member states granting an extension of the EU's competence in exchange for the consolidation or expansion of their rights of participation in the policy process, much as has been argued by Wessels (1997).

Intergovernmentalist theorists offer a different explanation of inter-sectoral variations in the distribution of influence between different actors in the EU. In general, their explanations of the perceived (dominant or co-dominant) role of France and Germany in the EU emphasise such variables as other member states' structural dependence on the French and German economies, the combined Franco-German contribution to the EU budget (and associated capacity to finance side payments who might otherwise oppose their projects), and the use of the credible threat of exclusion (see introduction). Intergovernmentalists would likely attribute deviations from the norm of the control of the EU policy process by the member states or a given subset of them to inter-sectoral variations in the extent to which the states have concurred to delegate sovereignty to supranational organs. In deciding to delegate sovereignty to 'semi-autonomous central institutions' (or to pool it through qualified majority voting), national governments accept an increased political risk of being outvoted or overruled on any individual issue in exchange for more efficient collective decision-making (Moravcsik 1993: 509–10). 'Independent actions by the Commission or outcomes that contravene the interests of a single Member State, taken in isolation, do not constitute decisive evidence against the intergovernmentalist view that the EC is grounded fundamentally in the preferences and power of Member States' (Moravcsik 1993: 514). Hence, if, other things being equal and as the preceding chapters suggest, the Franco-German relationship has been less influential on issues of market liberalisation than on others, this would be attributed by intergovernmentalists to the fact that the member states have simply delegated more sovereignty to the supranational organs on these issues. The observable inter-sectoral variations in the influence of the Franco-German relationship can be squared equally well with institutionalist and intergovernmentalist models. Which of the two models is more plausible turns on the empirical question of whether supranational organs such as the Commission and the ECJ have grown more autonomous of the member states than the latter intended when the treaties were negotiated or revised (the institutionalist position – see Pierson 1996: 132–9) or not (the intergovernment-alist one).

Franco-German influence in the EU also appears to be greater – paradoxically – the greater the initial divergence between their preferences on a given issue. The preceding chapters show that it is comparatively rare for the French and German governments to have convergent positions on EU issues. However, the kinds of issues on which they had at least partially convergent preferences – for example, research and technology, telecommunications and social policy – are precisely those on which, other things being equal, their impact on the way in which the analysed issues was resolved was weakest. By contrast, where they were the principal protagonists in conflicts, provided they managed to settle their bilateral differences, their influence on the conflicts' outcome, other things being equal, was very strong. This was the case, for example, in several of the big agricultural policy conflicts, economic and monetary union, and electricity liberalisation. The capacity of the Franco-German relationship to multilateralise bilateral bargains in the EU thus depends on the extent to which they represent 'opposed poles', around one or the other of which most of the other member states cluster. If from the outset French and German preferences are similar, it is improbable, assuming that the spectrum of preferences represented among the member states is similarly wide across different issues, that a Franco-German compromise will be close to the median position of the member states as a whole. Examples of the latter kind of issues include those that separate large and small or rich and poor member states.[10]

If, by contrast, France and Germany do represent 'opposed poles' among the member states, any agreement that they reach will probably be acceptable, or close to being acceptable, to the other member governments. In this scenario, the council presidency may take this as the basis for a proposal to the council, as is said to be the norm when the two governments have found a modus vivendi on issues of agricultural policy (see Chapter 7 by Webber). Or the council may indeed ratify a bilaterally negotiated Franco-German agreement without further ado, as seems to have occurred at the Dublin European Council meeting in December 1996, when, following heated talks between Helmut Kohl and Jacques Chirac over the so-called Stability Pact to flank the single currency, the Irish council president reputedly announced: 'If I understand correctly, an accord has been reached on the Stability Pact between the French and the Germans. Is there any objection? No? Good, then let's pass on to Bosnia' (Milesi 1998: 147). Basing a council decision on a Franco-German agreement that, with modifications made or added to accommodate the interests of other member states, arguably contributes to greater decision-making efficiency in the EU, in as far as it renders superfluous negotiations between all the member states on all aspects of an issue. Beyond such considerations, a certain Franco-German leadership role is also legitimised by their historical role in the foundation of the EU. A consequence of all the above factors combined is that the Franco-German 'tandem' enjoys a high degree of acceptance among the other member states and that the failure of the two governments to settle their disputes is more frequently lamented than their 'successful' co-ordination.

In effect, on issues where their preferences are very divergent, the French and German governments tend thus to be representatives of two groups of EU member states and their bilateral bargains to be bargains between these two groups. The most common cleavage on economic issues, such as external and internal trade and issues relating to the single currency, is determined by attitudes to the role of the state in the economy and divides the typically more 'mercantilist' southern member states, whose standard-bearer is France, from the more liberal, free trade-oriented northern member states, whose champion is Germany (cf. CDU/CSU Parliamentary Group 1994). A similar north–south cleavage, in this case underpinned by different geographical locations, manifests itself on issues relating to the prospective Eastern enlargement, on which member states' attitudes are shaped to an important extent by physical proximity to Central and Eastern Europe. However, the composition of the 'French' and 'German' blocs on issues where they represent 'opposed poles' among the member states is by no means always the same. Thus, on issues relating to European integration as such, Germany has typically lain closer to the (mostly) relatively pro-integrationist southern member states (as well as to the Benelux countries) and France to the member states more concerned to protect national sovereignty, among which northern member states are more numerous than southern. It is important, moreover, not to equate 'opposed poles' with the most extreme poles. Following the first enlargement in 1973, Britain adopted the most extreme position on numerous important issues, from those concerning the integration process to the EU budget and CAP reform. To the extent, however, that it failed to find allies for its positions among the other member states, no influential 'pole' of member states under British 'leadership' emerged.

German unification and the Franco-German relationship

Much of the scholarship on the Franco-German relationship has emphasised that the division of Germany and Europe was a pre-condition of the 'special' relationship that developed during the post-World War II period because it preserved a roughly equal balance of power between the two states, the one (Germany) stronger economically and financially and the other (France) stronger militarily, diplomatically and politically. According to the logic of this essentially realist analysis, the end of the Cold War and German unification would destroy this relationship because these radical changes in the political architecture of Europe would make Germany much more, and France much less, powerful than they had been under the Yalta order.[11]

So far as the European integration process is concerned, the predicted demise of the Franco-German relationship has not (yet) materialised. To be sure, the end of the Cold War has generated issues, such as the Eastern enlargement of the EU, intervention in the Balkan wars and future European defence and security arrangements, that are burdensome for the relationship as the tense and difficult negotiations over reform of the EU's budget and agricultural and regional policies ('Agenda 2000') in spring 1999 showed.. Neither collectively nor individually, however, do the preceding chapters suggest that the relationship is in crisis or that the capacity of the two governments to mediate bilateral conflicts over contentious EU issues has significantly declined. Rather, on the contrary, many of them (economic and monetary union, Eastern enlargement, immigration, security and defence policy, electricity liberalisation) tell a story of how major differences were gradually ground down and made way finally for a compromise with which both governments could live roughly equally well or badly. At the end of the 1990s, the French and German governments were interacting, within the EU on a wider range of issues and on a larger number of issues where the EU had important competences than had been the case before the Cold War had ended and Germany had been reunited.

The Franco-German relationship was and is not, of course, immune to confrontation and – to what appears, at least at the time of their occurrence to be – 'crises'. The confrontations or crises of the 1990s can not be attributed entirely, however, to the changes brought about by the end of the Cold War and German unification. They are always determined by short-term variables, such as the domestic political conjuncture in the two states and changes in the composition of the political leadership (such as the succession of Mitterand as French president by Chirac) as well as by longer-term, structural shifts in the underlying relationship. It is important, in any case, to see and to analyse conflicts such as those that took place over the first ECB president in 1998 and the Agenda 2000 in 1999 in historical perspective. Viewed from such a perspective, the conflict over the ECB presidency, for all the concern it generated in the heat of the moment, looks like a 'very ordinary crisis', unlikely to exercise a significant impact on the long-term evolution of the relationship (Rovan 1998). At no point in the 1990s have the problems and conflicts in Franco-German relations looked as numerous and as serious as, for example, in the mid-1960s, when Bonn and Paris were at loggerheads over the issues of British entry to the EC, the NATO and relations with the USA, the future of the integration process, relations with the Soviet Union and the Communist bloc, and the development of the CAP and President de Gaulle, far from free of blame for the parlous state of the relationship at the time, lamented that, on EU issues, the two governments almost always had opposing positions (*Akten* 1963: 615).

Arguably, geopolitical changes such as those brought about by the end of the Cold War do not themselves have a direct impact on states' foreign (or, in this case, European) policy orientations. Their impact is rather mediated by or filtered through the analysis of such changes, or rather the analysis of the implications, of such changes developed and held by states' political classes.[12] In the case of the France, the dominant, but not consensual, analysis within the political class is that, following the end of the Cold War and despite the fear that France might be degraded to Germany's 'junior partner', the European integration process and the special relationship with Germany are as much, if not more, in the interests of France as they were before 1990. That this analysis is more strongly contested on the French right than on the left certainly helps to explain why, during the first years of the the neo-Gaullist Chirac's presidency, the Franco-German relationship did not function as smoothly as under his predecessor Mitterrand and Kohl. In the case of Germany, although the public has grown more 'Euro-sceptical' during the 1990s and this has encouraged some politicians, such as Chancellor Schröder and the Bavarian premier Staber, to become more critical of the EU in their rhetoric, no relevant political force yet questions the importance of Germany being integrated into the EU or the indispensability of the Franco-German relationship, deemed by the Christian Democrats as having become not less, but rather 'more important' following the end of the East–West conflict and by the new Green Foreign Minister in 1998 as having an 'increasingly important significance' in the continuation of the European integration process (CDU/CSU Parliamentary Group 1994; Fischer 1998: 16).[13] France still wants to control Germany and Germany to control itself (cf. McCarthy 1993: 2), but Germany also wants to be controlled by its Western neighbours in such a way as to reassure them that the united Germany will not veer off, as it did before World War II, on a German *Sonderweg* and does not therefore need to be contained or 'balanced' by traditional inter-state coalitions. Of course, the affirmation of the significance of the Franco-German relationship by political leaders of both countries may in principle disguise a deterioration or impoverishment of the substance of the relationship and should not necessarily be taken at face value. But neither should the existence or occurrence of conflicts as such be taken as an indicator of the imminent demise or collapse of the relationship. Crises have – if not always, then at least very regularly – been a part of the relationship and, as argued above, the relationship draws its strength in the EU from the two states representing, but also being able to reconcile, opposed or contradictory interests and preferences. What is decisive is rather how, and especially how successfully, crises and conflicts are managed and mediated and that they are contained in such a way as not to imperil the overall relationship. Since the foundation of the EU, the two states' capacity for effective bilateral conflict management has certainly increased rather than diminished.[15]

Conclusions

The principal focus in the preceding contributions was on the influence of the Franco-German relationship on the EU. It would, however, be erroneous to suppose that the causal relationship between these two phenomena operates only in this direction. The contributions also suggest collectively that if, over time, the French and German governments have developed a stronger bilateral conflict management capacity, then this is attributable in large measure to the European integration process: the EU is as much the engine of Franco-German co-operation and co-ordination as the Franco-German relationship is that of the EU because it arguably constrains them to interact and to negotiate with each other, promotes the exchange of information about the states' respective preferences and intentions, monitors the implementation of multilateral decisions so as to discourage cheating or backsliding on agreements, facilitates conflict resolution by making possible inter-temporal and inter-spatial issue linkage and thus contributing to a roughly equal distribution of the benefits of co-operation, and fosters, although by no means makes inevitable, the development of mutual trust and confidence. The EU – the more so, the longer it survives the end of the Cold War – is a powerful verification of the optimistic view of international institutions that these can 'civilise' international relations.[14] The impact of the EU as a force for Franco-German co-operation has been strengthened by the Elysée Treaty with its provisions for mutual information and consultation; the treaty of which, soon after its entry into force, disappointed by the 'pro-Atlantic' preamble added to it by the German Parliament, de Gaulle, adapting Victor Hugo, said: 'With treaties the same thing happens as with young girls and roses … Oh, how many young girls have I seen die' (as quoted in Schwarz 1994: 858). The survival and consolidation of the Franco-German relationship supports rather the optimistic prognosis of the rose-grower Adenauer, who replied to de Gaulle: 'The rose … is, of all the plants we have, the one with the greatest stamina … It survives any winter' (as quoted in Schwarz 1994: 858). The evolution of both the bilateral relationship and the European integration process points to the integrative power, to the 'strength of institutions' (Mitterrand 1994). It vindicates the philosophy of the pioneer of this process, Jean Monnet, who, in 1952, told the Parliamentary Assembly of the Coal and Steel Community:

> The union of Europe cannot be based on goodwill alone: rules are needed … Men pass away; others will take our place. We cannot bequeath them our personal experience. But we can leave them institutions. The life of institutions is longer than that of men; if they are well built, they can accumulate and hand on the wisdom of succeeding generations.[16]

Notes

1 On the 'personal factor' in Franco-German relations up to 1984, see Simonian (1984: 366–73). Simonian, too, however, concludes his analysis by emphasising the high degree of institutionalisation of the relationship.

2 After the Socialist Party had strongly opposed the Stability Pact negotiated in the EU under German pressure as a concomitant to the single currency in 1996, during the 1997 Parliamentary election campaign, the Jospin government approved the pact with only minimal changes and flanking measures within about two weeks of its election. In the German election campaign in 1998, the SPD candidate Schröder emphasised his closeness to the new British Labour government and occasionally stated his intention to broaden the Franco-German 'tandem' to include Britain. However, he made his first post-election foreign trip to Paris and subsequently assured that any improvement in German relations with Britain would not be at the expense of the Franco-German relationship.The conflict between Bonn and Paris over CAP reform in the EU's 'Agenda 2000' destroyed premature predictions of a new 'honeymoon' in Franco-German relations, but the process by which the reform was negotiated – largely in bilateral talks between the two governments, with their accord subsequently being taken over by the other member states – and the outcome of the conflict – with the German government capitulating to French resistance to a more radical reform – conformed very closely to the historical precedents (see Chapter 7). The outcome of the talks, observed the *Financial Times*' correspondent at the March 1999 European Council meeting, 'confirmed Germany and France as the dominant powers in the EU' (Norman 1999).

3 The same is true of EU environmental and road haulage policies, analysed in a paper presented to the conference 'The Franco-German Relationship in the European Union: The Hard, the Rotting or the Non-existent Core?' (see preface) by Adrienne Héritier.

4 I am indebted to Patrick McCarthy for this insight and phrase.

5 Interview by the author of an official in the Federal Ministry of Economics, 23 February 1996.

6 Fraser (1996: 207–8), in his study of the EU 'television without frontiers' project, quotes an adviser to the French audiovisual minister in the late 1980s who describes the contrasting logics of foreign and 'sectoral' or technical ministries as follows: 'It's quite classic, this clash between diplomatic logic and technical logic. It occurs in virtually all domains. More often than not, the Quai d'Orsay [the French foreign ministry – DW] wants a dossier to be agreed and signed, while a technical ministry like the Ministry of Culture is interested more in the contents of an agreement or treaty. And those two orientations are not always compatible with each other. An adviser to the Culture Minister said of the Foreign Ministry: 'They want to sign, that's all. The diplomats always want to come to an agreement. That's why they are always busy telling us in the technical ministries: "Stop, make some concessions."'

7 Interview by the author of the permanent representative of an EU member state, 29 July 1997.

8 On a scale of 'Europeanisation' (ranging from 1 where all policy decisions are taken at the national level to 5 where they are all taken at the EU level), Philippe Schmitter and his colleagues (1996) have estimated that, in 1992, agricultural policy issues and issues concerning the free movement of goods and services inside the EU were highly Europeanised (value of 4 on the Europeanisation scale, meaning that most policy decisions were taken at the EU level), while most other issue areas analysed in the contributions to this volume – communications, industrial, research, energy, social, defence and security policies, for example – were only very moderately Europeanised (value of 2, meaning that only some policy decisions were taken at the EU level).

9 Remarks based on interviews with an official at the German Federal Ministry of Agriculture, 29 November 1996 and officials at the German Federal Ministry of Post and Telecommunications, 27 March 1997.

10 It is noteworthy that small and large member states could not agree on a redistribution of votes in favour of the large member states when, against the background of the prospective Eastern enlargement, this issue was discussed at the Amsterdam IGC in June 1997.

11 For a particularly alarmist, 'realist' analysis of the implications of the end of the Cold War for relations between West European states, including France and Germany, see Mearsheimer (1990).

12 By 'political class' is understood the upper levels of office-holders and public office-holding members of the political parties and the policy-making civil servants in government ministries.

13 A good indicator of the growth of 'Euro-sceptical' sentiment in Germany is the evolution of opinions as to whether Germany has benefited from being an EU member. In 1990, the proportion of Germans believing that Germany had benefited from EU membership outnumbered that believing the opposite by three to one. By 1997, more Germans (43 per cent) believed that Germany had not benefited from EU membership than the opposite (36 per cent) (European Commission 1998: 24). However, the increasingly critical popular mood towards 'Europe' did not have any sustained impact on the political parties and when, in 1996 and 1997, the SPD contested some state elections with a platform critical of the single currency, it performed poorly. The most important 'Euro-sceptical' forces in German politics were the federal states, in response to whose opposition to an extension of the powers of the EU Chancellor Kohl opposed an extension of qualified majority voting in the council to new policy domains at the Amsterdam IGC in 1997. There is already voluminous literature on the prospective future European policy orientationof the united Germany. For two contrasting analyses, the one predicting continuity and the other a diminution of Germany's commitment to the integration process, see respectively Katzenstein (1997) and Markovits and Reich (1988), especially 326–8.

14 Realist theorists of international relations attribute the post-World War II strength of the Franco-German relationship to the Cold War and the Soviet security threat (see, for example, Mearsheimer 1990). However, the longer both the bilateral relationship and the European integration process survive the end of the Cold War, the less credible this theory becomes. On realist and international-institutionalist predictions of the consequences of the end of the Cold War, see Mearsheimer (1990) and Keohane (1993).

15 For another, very balanced analysis of the post-Cold War Franco-German relationship and its prospects – one which comes to cautiously optimistic conclusions – see Szukala and Wessels (1997).

16 As quoted in Grant (1994: 273). See also Duchêne (1994: 238–9).

References

Akten zur Auswärtigen Politik der Bundesrepublik Deutschland 1963 (3 vols), Hauptherausgeber: Hans-Peter Schwarz; wissenschaftlicher Leiter: Rainer A. Blasius; Bearbeiter: Mechthild Lindemann and Ilse Dorothee Pautsch. Munich: R. Oldenbourg, 1994.

Armstrong, Kenneth and Simon Bulmer (1998) *The Governance of the Single European Market*. Manchester and New York: Manchester University Press.

CDU/CSU Parliamentary Group ('Schäuble/Lamers Paper') (1994) *Überlegungen zur Europapolitik*. Bonn: CDU/CSU-Fraktion im Deutschen Bundestag.

Duchêne, François (1994) *Jean Monnet: The First Statesman of Interdependence*. New York/ London: W.W. Norton.

Fischer, Joschka (1998) 'Vorwort: Von der Macht und ihrer Verantwortung', in: Andrei S. Markovits and Simon Reich, *Das deutsche Dilemma: Die Berliner Republik zwischen Macht und Machtverzicht*. Berlin: Alexander Fest, 7–16.

Fraser, Matthew (1996) ' *"Télévision sans frontières": décryptage d'un "grand projet" européen'.* Paris: PhD thesis, Institut des Études politiques.

Grant, Charles (1994) *Delors: Inside the House that Jack Built.* London: Nicholas Brealey.

Katzenstein, Peter J. (1997) 'United Germany in an Integrating Europe', in: Peter Katzenstein (ed.), *Tamed Power: Germany in Europe.* Ithaca and London: Cornell University Press, 1–48.

Keeler, John T. S. (1996) 'Agricultural power in the European Community: explaining the fate of CAP and GATT negotiations', *Comparative Politics* (January 1996), 127–49.

Keohane, Robert O. (1993) 'Institutional theory and the realist challenge after the Cold War', in David A. Baldwin (ed.), *Neorealism and Neoliberalism: The Contemporary Debate.* New York: Columbia University Press, 269–300.

McCarthy, Patrick (1993) 'Condemned to partnership: the Franco-German relationship, 1944–1983', in: Patrick McCarthy (ed.), *France–Germany 1983–1993: The Struggle to Cooperate.* Basingstoke and London: Macmillan, 1–26.

Markovits, Andrei S. and Simon Reich (1998) *Das deutsche Dilemma: Die Berliner Republik zwischen Macht and Machtverzicht.* Berlin: Alexander Fest.

Mearsheimer, John (1990) 'Back to the future: instability in Europe after the Cold War', *International Security* 15:1 (Summer 1990), 5–56.

Milesi, Gabriel (1998) *Le Roman de l'Euro.* Paris: Hachette.

Mitterrand, François (1994) 'L'Allemagne et nous' (interview), *L'Express*, 14 July, 36–52.

Moravcsik, Andrew (1993) 'Preferences and power in the European Community: a liberal intergovernmentalist approach', *Journal of Common Market Studies* 31:4 (December 1993), 473–524.

Norman, Peter (1999) 'Twenty-hour talk marathon ends in compromise', *Financial Times*, 27/28 March 1999.

Pierson, Paul (1996) 'The path to European integration: a historical institutionalist analysis', *Comparative Political Studies* 29:2 (April 1996), 123–63.

Rovan, Joseph (1998) 'Une crise bien ordinaire', *L'Européen*, 8 (13 May 1998), 14–15.

Schmitter, Philippe (1996) 'Imagining the future of the Euro-polity with the help of new concepts', in Gary Marks, Fritz W. Scharpf, Philippe C. Schmitter and Wolfgang Streeck (eds), *Governance* in the *European Union*. London/Thousand Oaks, California/New Delhi: Sage, 121–50.

Schwarz, Hans-Peter (1994) *Adenauer. Band 2: Der Staatsmann 1952–1967.* Munich: Deutscher Taschenbuch.

Simonian, Haig (1984) *The Privileged Partnership: Franco-German Relations in the European Community 1969–1984.* Oxford: Clarendon Press.

Szukala, Andrea and Wolfgang Wessels (1997) 'The Franco-German tandem', in: Geoffrey Edwards and Alfred Pijpers (eds), *The Politics of European Treaty Reform: The 1996 Intergovernmental Conference and Beyond.* London and Washington: Pinter, 74–9.

Védrine, Hubert (1996) *Les mondes de François Mitterrand: A l'Élysée 1981–1995.* Paris: Fayard.

Wessels, Wolfgang (1997) 'An ever closer fusion? A dynamic macropolitical view on integration processes', *Journal of Common Market Studies* 35:2 (June 1997), 267–99.

Westlake, Martin (1995) *The Council of the European Union.* London: Cartermill.

INDEX

Adenauer, K. 4, 167, 178; agricultural
   policy 114, 118, 126; foreign, security
   and defence policy 149–50
Administrative Supreme Court (le Conseil
   d'Etat) 160, 162
Aeschimann, É. 27
Africa 51
Agenda 2000 176
Agricultural Council 111, 113, 118, 119,
   120, 123, 126
Agricultural Ministry, German 114, 123
agricultural policy 15, 45, 62, 111–28,
   168–71, 173–4, 176; Blair House
   accord 120–4; Common Agricultural
   Policy 113–16; Common Agricultural
   Policy financing and 'empty chair' crisis
   116–18; Common Agricultural Policy
   reform 119–20; General Agreement on
   Tariffs and Trade 119
Aked, N.H. 95
Akten 118
Algeria 50, 51, 160
Allin, D.H. 137
Almelo case 69
Alphandéry, Finance Minister 32
Alter, K.J. 81
American Multilateral Force (AMF) 150
Amsterdam summit (1997) 54, 55, 144,
   148, 149, 151
Amsterdam Treaty 16
Anderson, P. 4
anti-trust commission 77
Argyris, N. 67
Armstrong, K. 4, 6, 173
asylum seekers 164, 165
AT&T 80, 86, 87
Atlantic Alliance 152, 153, 154, 156; see
   also North Atlantic Treaty Organisation

Atlas 86–9, 90
Attali, J. 12
Austria 52
autre politique, l' 48
aviation sector 95, 99

Badenwerk 63
Balkan wars 176
Balkhausen, D. 27
Balladur, E. 27, 32, 48, 49, 50, 51;
   agricultural policy 12–3; electricity
   industry 67; telecommunications
   industry 79
Baltic states 47
Bangemann, M. 63, 87, 106
banking 77, 133
Barnouin, B. 134
Barre, R. 24
Basic Law 161, 162, 165
Bauer, M. 100
Baur, J.F. 62
Bavarian administrative court 161
beef 124
Belgium 36, 81, 139, 143, 151, 164;
   agricultural policy 114, 115, 121, 123,
   124, 127; electricity liberalisation 60,
   65, 68, 70
Benelux countries 3, 5, 49, 163, 175
Benès, E. 41
Bérégovoy, Finance Minister 25, 36, 49
Berlin Atlantic Council summit (1996) 23
Berlusconi government 45
Beuve-Méry, H. 41
Bigo, D. 165
Bildschirmtext 84
Blair House accord 120-4, 125, 127
Blair, T. 55, 154–5
Blank, K. 7

Bloch-Lainé, A. 15–16, 148–58, 172
Blüm, N. 134, 138, 139, 140
BMFT 101
Bocquet, D. 3, 10
Boetsch, Minister 87–8
Bosnia-Hercegovina 16, 45, 51, 155, 156
Boyer, Y. 2, 11, 149
Brandt, W. 42, 118, 167
Britain 5, 12, 172, 175, 176; agricultural policy 114, 116, 117, 118, 119, 120, 124; electricity liberalisation 60, 62, 63, 64, 65, 66, 68; foreign affairs, security and defence 152, 154, 155, 156; intergovernmental conferences and Eastern enlargement 45, 46, 49, 50, 52, 53, 55; monetary union 21, 23, 24, 30, 32, 34, 36, 37; research and technology policy 97, 98, 101, 102, 103, 104, 105; social policy 131, 133, 137–44; telecommunications 80, 81, 86, 88, 89
BRITE 104
British Employer's Association 65
British Telecom 84, 85, 86, 87, 88, 90
Brittan, L. 65-6, 123–4
Brussels summit 30, 32
Bulgaria 45, 47, 50
Bulmer, S. 4, 6, 107, 173
Bundesbank 13, 42, 43, 44, 49, 53; monetary union 20–1, 24–7, 29–36
Bundespost 77, 81, 84, 85, 86, 89
Bundestag 31, 32, 33, 77, 150, 152
Burley, A.-M. 81

Cairns Group 119
Callon, M. 106
Canada 48
Cardoso e Cunha 66
cartel arrangements 77
Cartel Law 60, 67
Cartel Office 69
Carter, J. 24
Cauret, L. 59
Cawson, A. 99, 100
CDU/CSU 70, 115, 140
Central and Eastern Europe 23, 175; see also Intergovernmental Conference and Eastern enlargement
Centre européen des enterprises à participation publique (CEEP) 69–70
cereal price 115–16, 117, 120, 123, 124, 125
Chamoux, J.-P. 80
Chancellor's office 167, 169, 170, 171

Chirac, J. 167, 168, 174, 176, 177; foreign, security and defence policy 148, 152, 153; Intergovernmental Conference and Eastern enlargement 43, 48, 49, 51–4, 55; monetary union 23, 26, 30, 32, 33, 34, 35; telecommunications industry 77
Christian Democrats 1, 49, 77, 134, 160, 177
co-ordination 170
coal 60, 61, 63, 65
COGECOM 84
Cohen, E. 100
collective bargaining 133
Combined Joint Task Force 155
Common Agricultural Policy 15, 111–16, 123-6, 175, 176; financing 116–18; intergovernmental conferences and Eastern enlargement 45, 46, 54; reform 119–20
'common carriage' 61–2, 63
Common Foreign and Security Policy 171, 172; foreign affairs, security and defence 148, 149, 151, 154, 155–6, 157; intergovernmental conferences and Eastern enlargement 44, 45, 47, 50, 51, 53
concession agreements 60
Concorde 95
Confédération Générale du Travail (CGT) 134
Confédérations Française Démocratique du Travail (CFDT) 134
Conférence européenne des administrations des postes et telecommunications (CEPT) 76, 80
Connolly, B. 21
Conseil d'Etat 160, 162
Conservatives 47, 142
constitution-making issues 168
Contact Group for Bosnia 155, 156
Coopération Scientifique et Technologique (COST) 96
Copenhagen summit (1993) 47
Corbeau case 69
COREPER 169–70
Corfu summit (1994) 52, 142
Cornish, P. 23
corporate governance 133
Council of Agriculutural Ministers 170
Council of Economics and Finance Ministers 170
Council of Ministers 9, 10, 29, 138, 172; agricultural policy 113, 117;

Intergovernmental Conference and Eastern enlargement 43, 47, 52, 53; Qualified Majority Voting 54; research and technology policy 98, 103; telecommunications 80, 81
Couve de Murville, M. 3, 114, 116, 127
Cowles, M.G. 4
Cresson, E. 49
Croatia 44
Croft, S. 23
Cyprus 51
Czech Republic 41, 43, 44, 45, 52, 164

Datex-P/T-Data 88
Davignon, Commissioner 103, 104
de facto refugees 162
de Gaulle, C. 4, 167, 176–7, 178; agricultural policy 114, 115, 116, 117, 118, 127; foreign, security and defence policy 150; immigration policy 160; Intergovernmental Conference and Eastern enlargement 42, 48, 55
De Schoutheete, P. 2, 9
decision-making 16, 173
defence see foreign affairs, security and defence
Delapierre, M. 103
Delors, J. 15; electricity industry 66, 70; monetary union 25, 26, 28, 30, 35; social policy 130, 132, 134–9, 141, 142, 144
demarcation agreements 60
Denmark 47, 49, 60, 65, 119, 120, 124
DePorte, A.W. 107
Der Spiegel 53
Deubner, C. 3, 133
Deutsche Mark 20–1, 23-5, 26, 31–6, 55, 123
Deutsche Telekom 77, 81, 85, 86, 87, 88, 89, 90
Deutscher Bauernverband (German Farmers' Association) (DBV) 114, 115, 118
Deutscher Gewerkschaftsbund (DGB) 135, 138, 143
directorate-general (of the EC) IV 62, 66; XIII 80
diffusion-oriented approach 97
diplomacy 9
Directorate for Employment and Social Affairs (DG 5) 135
Directorate of Gas, Electricity and Coal 59
discordia 85–6

distinctive traits of Franco-German relationship 2–3
distributional conflicts 97, 98
Divine, R. 159
division of labour 169
dollar 21–2, 23, 24, 31, 32
Dominique, D. 22
Doumic-Doublet, F. 161
Dublin European Council meeting (1996) 34, 36, 174–5
Dublin summit (1990) 22
Duisenberg, W. 36
Dumas, R. 12
Dunkel Paper 121

Eastern Europe 42, 162, 163, 164; see also Intergovernmental Conference and Eastern enlargement
Ebbinghaus, B. 135, 138
Eberlein, B. 9, 14–15, 93–108
Eckoff, J. 142
Economic and Finance Council 27, 32
Economic and Monetary Union 152, 171, 174, 176
Economic and Social Committee 70
Economics Ministry 67, 69, 114
EC Treaty: Article 1 140; Article 2 140; Article 235 143
Ecu Banking Association 34
egalitarian selection 159
Egypt 51
Ehlermann, C.-D. 64
Eising, R. 69
Electricité de France (EdF) 59, 62, 63, 68, 69, 71, 72
Electricity Act 1989 65
electricity liberalisation 14, 58-72, 168, 172, 174, 176; entrenched national differences 59–60; and European Council 65–6; existing constraints: treaty provisions 64–5; first steps 61–4; negotiations 67–71
electricity supply industry (ESI) 60, 63, 64, 66, 67, 68, 69, 70, 71
Elysée Treaty 2, 9, 112, 148, 150, 151, 167, 178
Emminger, Governor 25
employers' organisations 132
employment rules 131
'empty chair' crisis 116–18
Energieversorgung Schwaben 63
Energy Management Act 1935 59
Environment Ministry 60

environmental issues 170
equal pay 133, 136
equal treatment 133, 136
Ergas, H. 97
Erhard, L. 3, 115, 116, 118, 167
ESPRIT 80, 94, 102, 103, 104, 105
Essen summit (1994) 43, 50–1
Esser, J. 94
Estonia 55
EUCOM 84–5
Eunetcom 85–6, 89
EURAM 104
EUREKA 9, 98, 101, 102, 103, 106, 168
Eurelectric 64
Euro 26, 33, 34, 35, 36, 37, 42, 49, 53, 55
Euro-Med Economic Area 50, 51, 52
Eurocorps 16, 148, 151, 154
European Agreements 47
European Atomic Energy Community 95
European Banking Federation 33
European Central Bank 21, 27–30, 32, 35,
    36, 49, 55, 176
European Coal and Steel Community 167
European Commission 4, 5, 7–8, 10, 13,
    14, 15, 171–4; Action Programme on
    Science and Technology 96; agricultural
    policy 114–24 passim; Competition
    Directorate General IV 62; electricity
    liberalisation 58, 61, 63–9, 72;
    intergovernmental conferences and
    Eastern enlargement 46, 47, 52, 53,
    55-6; monetary union 23, 33; research
    and technology policy 97–105, 107;
    social policy 130–2, 134, 136–41, 143–
    5; telecommunications 78–9, 80–1, 82,
    84, 86–90
European Community Treaty 61, 63, 64–5,
    70, 131, 137; Article 34 64; Article 37
    64; Article 85 64, 87; Article 86 64, 87;
    Article 90 64–5, 66, 72, 80; Article 130
    93; Article 213 62
European Council 3, 7, 10, 13, 14, 137,
    170, 171; agricultural policy 115–16,
    121–4, 126–7; electricity liberalisation
    58, 61, 63–71; foreign affairs, security
    and defence 148, 156; of Hanover 27;
    Madrid (1989) 28; Madrid (1995) 33;
    monetary union 23, 30, 36; research
    and technology policy 93, 96; Rome
    (1990) 29
European Court of Justice 6, 7, 13, 14, 15,
    171, 172, 174; electricity liberalisation
    64–5, 67, 69, 70, 71, 72; social policy

131, 141, 145; telecommunications 81,
    82
European Currency Unit 25, 29, 32, 34
European Defence Community 4, 150
European Free Trade Association 43, 47, 48
European Industry Committees 135
European integration theory 4-9
European Launcher Development
    Organization (ELRO) 95
European Monetary Fund 25
European Monetary Institute 32, 33
European Monetary System 3, 9, 10, 24,
    27, 45, 49, 123
European Monetary Union 21, 36, 144,
    157
European Parliament 5, 23, 29, 117, 124;
    electricity liberalisation 65, 66, 67, 70;
    intergovernmental conferences and
    Eastern enlargement 44, 52, 53;
    research and technology policy 96, 98,
    102
European Political Co-operation (EPC) 151
'European Reserve Fund' 27
European Round Table 4
European Social Fund 136
European Space Agency 95
European Space Research Organization
    (ESRO) 95
European Trade Union Confederation
    (ETUC) 134, 135, 138, 142
European Works Council Directive 140,
    141
Eurosclerosis 100
Exchange Rate Mechanism 25, 26, 27, 28,
    31, 32, 34
exchange rates 21, 23–4, 25, 26
'exporting mission' (vocation exportatrice)
    112

Fabius, L. 53
'family farm' (bäuerlicher Familienbetrieb)
    112
family reunification 162
Fauroux, R. 142
FDP 115, 119, 134
Federal Communications Commission 87
Federal Constitutional Court 152, 161, 162
Federal Ministry of Economics 60, 70, 101,
    106
Federal Ministry of Finance 101
Federal Research and Technology Ministry
    101, 105, 106
Federal Reserve 31

Federation of German Employers' Associations (BDA) 138
Fillon, F. 78
Finance Ministers Council (1993) 32
Finance Ministry 26, 27, 29, 30, 32, 33, 34, 35, 36
Finland 68
Fischer, J. 177
Fontainebleau European Council 11–12
foreign affairs, security and defence 9, 15–16, 22, 23, 45, 55, 97, 148–58, 176; Common Foreign and Security Policy 155–6; external constraints and North Atlantic Treaty Organisation 154–5, 156; operational credibility, lack of 151–4; political and institutional co-operation 149–51
Foreign Office 101
former Soviet Union 22, 44, 47, 48, 52, 114, 152, 155, 176
former Yugoslavia 11
Framework Programmes 93, 94, 98, 105
franc 32, 36
France, Banque de 26, 27, 31
France Télécom 78, 79, 83, 84–5, 86, 87, 88, 89, 90
Franco-German Defence Council 151
Franco-German Dijon summit (1996) 70
Franco-German Security Council 22
Franco-German summit (1989) 22
Franco-German summit (1994) 50
Franco-German summit (1995) 70
Franco-German Treaty 1963 22, 27
French Constitution 162
French Office for the Protection of Refugees and Stateless Persons 162
Friend, J.W. 107
fusion model 8

Garrett, G. 5, 71, 127
Garton Ash, T. 20
gas 61, 62, 63, 65, 66, 67, 70
Gaullists 47, 48, 50, 51, 55, 160, 164, 177
gender equality 136
General Affairs Council 121, 169, 171
General Agreement on Tariffs and Trade 15, 119, 124, 125; Kennedy Round 115; Uruguay Round 11, 48, 113, 122, 123, 124, 125, 127, 172
Geneva Convention 161, 162
Genschel, P. 76
Genscher, H.-D. 12, 22, 27
Gerbet, P. 4

Gerstenmaier, E. 115
Giscard d'Estaing, V. 2, 3, 4, 9, 11, 167; agricultural policy 126; immigration policy 160; monetary union 24
Global One 86–9, 90
globalisation 108
Goodwin-Gill, G. 161
Gorbachev, M. 42
Grand Confederation 44, 48
grand projet 58
Grande, E. 9, 14–15, 79, 80, 89, 93–108
Greece 36, 49, 65, 68, 81, 97, 124
Gros, D. 27
Groupe d'Information et de Soutien des Travailleurs Immigrés (GISTI) 162
Guérin-Sendelbach, V. 4
guest worker programme (Gastarbeiter) 160
Gummet, P.J. 95
Gunther, H. 140
Guzzetti, L. 93

Hancher, L. 65, 69
Hantrais, L. 136
'hard franc' policy 26
Häusler, J. 94
Haussmann, Minister 138
Havel, V. 44, 48
Hayward, J. 99, 137
Héritier, A. 8
historical-institutionalist models 6–7
Hitler, A. 52
Holloway, J. 136
Hooghe, L. 7
Hort, P. 27
Hungary 43, 45, 52
hydro power 59

ideological conflicts 96, 97–8, 99, 106–7, 108
IJsselcentrale case 65
immigration policy 15–16, 159–66, 171, 176; co-ordination despite divergence 163–5; normative constraints 159–63
industrial relations 131, 133, 134, 140
Industry Ministry 59, 67
Info AG 88
institutionalisation 16
Institut des Hautes Etudes de Défense Nationale (IHEDN) 51
institutional reform 11, 13–14
inter-sectoral variations in Franco-German relationship 168-71

inter-sectoral variations in influence of Franco-German relationship 171–5
Intergovernmental Conference and Eastern enlargement 8, 12, 13–14, 41–56, 168, 170–3, 174, 176; 1990–93: enlargement versus indefinite postponement 43–6; 1993–94: French parliamentary elections and German presidency 46–51; 1995–96: Chirac, J. and monetary union 51–4
Interior Ministry 165
interlocking politics 8
International Monetary Fund 21
Ireland 25, 53, 64, 65, 68, 119, 120, 121, 123, 127, 138
Israel 51
Italy 81; agricultural policy 115, 116, 117, 121; electricity liberalisation 60, 65, 68, 70; Intergovernmental Conference and Eastern enlargement 45, 46, 49, 50, 53, 55; lira 49; monetary union 23, 24, 25, 32, 33, 34, 36; research and technology policy 103, 105
ITU 76

Japan 21, 84, 87, 97, 99, 103; Kobe disaster 22, 32; Nippon Telegraph & Telephone Company 85
joint ventures 75
Jordan 51
Jospin, L. 54, 55, 142, 144, 168
Juppé, A. 34, 48, 51, 123

Kanstroom, D. 161, 162
Kartellamt 87
Kaufmann, I. 143
Keeler, J.T.S. 169
Keynesianism 26, 54, 100
Kinkel, K. 52
Klaiber, K.-P. 2, 3
Klaus, V. 46
Kohl, H. 2, 12, 167, 174, 177; agricultural policy 119, 120, 122–3, 124, 126; electricity industry 63; foreign, security and defence policy 148, 150–1, 152; immigration policy 164; Intergovernmental Conference and Eastern enlargement 42–4, 47, 49–50, 52, 54–5; monetary union 21–2, 26–33, 35–6; social policy 137–8, 142, 143, 144; telecommunications industry 77
Kohlepfennig (coal penny) 60
Kohler-Koch, B. 135

Kolboom, I. 11
Krige, J. 93
Kuhlmann, S. 94
Küsters, H.J. 4

La Rochelle summit (1992) 151
Labour government 144
labour markets 131, 132, 136
Labour Ministry 138, 143
Lafontaine, O. 144
Lahr, R. 114
Lamassoure, A. 48, 49
Lamers, K. 49, 50, 52
Länder 55, 143
Lange, P. 130
Larédo, P. 106
Lasserre, B. 78
Le Theule, F.-G. 120
Lebanon 51
Leblond, L. 3
Legras, G. 120
Leibfried, S. 141
Lellouche, P. 51
Lemaître, P. 120
Lequesne, C. 112
Lewis, J. 137
liberalisation 81–3, 169; *see also* electricity liberalisation
Liberals 77, 134
lignite 60
Litvan, D. 120
Longuet, Minister 67, 84, 88
Ludlow, P. 24
Luxembourg 114, 124, 139, 140; Compromise 116–17, 119; summit (1997) 144

Maas, C. 33
Maastricht Treaty 3, 10, 11, 12, 16, 93, 121, 151, 163, 172; immigration policy 163, 164; Intergovernmental Conference and Eastern enlargement 44, 45, 47, 48, 51, 53, 54; monetary union 22, 23, 29, 31, 32, 34; social policy 132, 137, 139-44, 145; telecommunications 81, 86
McCarthy, P. 14, 41–56, 107, 177
MacSharry, Commissioner 120
Maginot Line 41
Majone, G. 66
Major, J. 154
Malta 51
Mansholt, S. 115, 117

Markert, K. 69
market liberalisation 169
Marks, G. 7
Marqués-Ruiz, C. 156
Martin, D.A. 161
material conflicts 96, 97, 108
Mattli, W. 81
Mazzarelli, C. 3
MCI 86, 87, 88
Mediterranean countries 23, 24, 47, 50
Mega-Project 101
Mendes-France, P. 150
Meunier-Aitsahalia, S. 81
Mexican debt crisis 22, 32
Mez, L. 59
microelectronics 76, 95, 99, 101
Middle East 51
Middlemas, K. 2, 10–11
Milesi, G. 175
military policy *see* foreign affairs, security
    and defence
Miller, M.J. 161
Minitel 84
mission-oriented approach 97
Mitterrand, F. 2, 11, 12, 167, 168, 177,
    178; agricultural policy 120, 121, 122,
    124, 126; electricity industry 63;
    foreign, security and defence policy
    150–1, 152; immigration policy 164;
    Intergovernmental Conference and
    Eastern enlargement 42, 44–9, 52, 55;
    monetary union 21, 22, 25, 26, 28, 29,
    30–1, 35, 36; social policy 130, 136,
    137, 139, 142, 144
mobile services 78
Mollet, G.A. 4
monetary integration 42
monetary policy 9, 49, 55
Monetary Policy Council 31
monetary union 11, 13–14, 20–38, 44, 46,
    48, 51–4, 56; Atlantic context 21–3;
    France challenging the Deutsche Mark
    27–30; German primacy 23–7
Monnet, J. 178
Moravcsik, A. 3, 5, 8, 67, 127, 130, 165,
    173–4
Morgan, K. 79
Morocco 50, 51
Motomura, H. 162
Moyer, H.W. 118, 120
Muldur, U. 108
multi-led governance model 7
Mustar, P. 106

Mytelka, L.K. 103
National Alliance 45
National Assembly (1989) 22
National Socialism 161
Nazism 44, 160, 163
neo-functionalist theory 5–6
neo-institutionalist models 6–7
Netherlands 30, 49, 81, 155; agricultural
    policy 114, 116, 117, 119, 120, 124;
    electricity liberalisation 60, 62, 65, 68,
    69; research and technology policy 101,
    103; social policy 139, 141, 143
networked capitalism 133
Neuman, G.L. 162, 164
Nixon, R. 21
Nölling, W. 21
non-refoulement (non-repatriation) law 162
Norek, C. 161
North Africa 160
North Atlantic Treaty Organisation 16, 22,
    23, 176; foreign affairs, security and
    defence 150, 152–6; Intergovernmental
    Conference and Eastern enlargement
    42, 45, 47–8, 51–3, 55
Norway 47
nuclear sector 22, 59, 60, 62, 63, 65, 67,
    69, 95, 151
Nuremberg summit (1996) 148, 154

Odell, J.S. 119
Oder-Neisse boundary 44
oil 61, 62
Organisation for Security and Co-operation
    in Europe (OSCE) 50
Ostner, I. 137
Ostpolitik 42

Padgett, S. 63
Palestine 51
Parti Socialiste (PS) 54
Pasqua, C. 165
Paterson, W. 107
Peters, B.G. 7–8
Peterson, J. 7, 99, 102, 105
Petite-Entente 41
Petrella, R. 108
Peyrefitte, A. 114
Phoenix 86–9
Picht, R. 11
Pierson, P. 7, 141, 145, 173, 174
Pisani, Minister 126
Plan Fouchet (1962) 150
Pöhl, Governor 28

Poland 43, 44, 45, 47, 48, 52, 53, 164
policy networks 7
political refugees 162
political salience 168, 169
Pompidou, G.J.R. 118, 167
Poppe, M. 59
Portugal 34, 46, 49, 97, 138, 143;
   electricity liberalisation 60, 62, 65, 66,
   68
Post and Telecommunications Ministry 78
postal service 70, 77, 78
Postbank 77
Postdienst 77
President's office, French 169, 170, 171
Prime Minister's office, French 167
Prodi government 55
Programme d'action filière électronique 100
PTOs 83, 86, 88
PTT 80, 81, 83, 84
Puaux, F. 27
public ownership 133
Public Service Charter 70

Qualified Majority Voting 44, 49, 54–5,
   58, 98, 138–40, 143

RACE 80, 94, 104, 105
racialist selection 159, 160
Rapid Reaction Force in Bosnia 155
Rapport Mandil 67
Reflection Group 52
refugees 162
Reger, G. 94
regional policies 176
repatriation, forced 163
research and technology policy 9, 14–15,
   93–108, 168, 169, 170, 172, 174;
   co-operation: intergovernmental
   minimalism 99–102; co-operation:
   neo-functionalist logic 102–4; conflict
   96–9; convergence 104–7; role of
   European Union 94–6
reunification 16, 42, 45, 175–7
Rexrodt, G. 141, 142
Rhodes, M. 15, 130–46, 172
Rice, Condoleeza 22
Riché, Pascal 27
Risse-Kappen, T. 135
Ritter, K.L. 62
Romania 41, 44, 45, 47, 50
Rome Council (1990) 30
Ross, G. 135, 138
Roulet, M. 79, 85–6

Round Table 103
Rovan, J. 176

Sabatier, P.A. 103
Sandholtz, W. 4, 6, 67, 72, 80, 99, 100,
   103
Santer, J. 53, 143
Sauder, A. 153
Scandinavia 55
Scharpf, F.W. 8, 71
Schäuble, W. 49, 50, 52
Schengen agreements 16, 159, 163, 164,
   165
Schlesinger, H. 32
Schmidt, H. 2, 3, 4, 9, 11, 53, 167;
   agricultural policy 118, 126; monetary
   union 21, 24
Schmidt, S.K. 14, 58–72, 80, 172
Schmidt, V.A. 106
Schneider, V.G. 14, 75–91, 172
Schröder, Chancellor 168, 177
Schuman, R. 167
Schwarz, H.-P. 178
Schwarz, Minister 126
Schwarz-Schilling, Minister 77, 84
Secrétariat général du comité interminis-
   tériel (SGCI) 71
security *see* foreign affairs, security and
   defence
Séguín, P. 48, 49
semiconductors 101
Servan-Schreiber, J.-J. 95
service public 58, 59, 71, 79
Sharp, M. 95, 98, 99, 103
Shearman, C. 95, 98, 99, 103
side payments 5
Simonian, H. 107
Single European Act 3, 4, 5, 9, 10, 93, 132
single European currency 23, 35, 174, 175;
   see also Euro; European Currency Unit
Single Market for Energy 61
Single Market Programme 58
Slovakia 45
Slovenia 44, 45, 55
small and medium-sized enterprises 98, 106
Social Agreement 143
Social Charter (1989) 137, 172
Social Democrats (SPD) 36, 134, 144
social policy 130–46, 168, 169, 174;
   ideology 131–2; organised interests
   134–5; policy preferences 132–4; post
   Maastricht Treaty 139–44; pre
   Maastricht Treaty 135–9

social politics 15
Social Protocol and Agreement 132, 139–40
Socialists 46, 54, 78, 100, 137, 161, 164
SOG-T 80
Soisson, Minister 138
'Southern strategy' 50
space sector 95, 99
Spain 34, 49, 50, 53, 98, 138, 151, 155, 164; electricity liberalisation 62, 63, 65, 68
Sprint 87, 88, 89
stability pact 32, 34, 35, 48, 50, 54, 174–5
Stalin, J. 52
steel 45
Stone Sweet, A. 6
Story, J. 13, 20–38
Strasbourg summit (1989) 28, 138
strategic conflicts 96, 108
Strategic Defence Initiative (SDI) 100, 101, 102
Streeck, W. 134, 135, 136
Stürmer, M. 52, 55
sub-national actors 7
subsidies 112
supranational issues 7, 16, 171, 172, 173, 174
Sweden 53, 68, 155
'sweetheart deal' 31
Syncordia 85, 86
Syria 51

technology gap debate 99–100, 101, 102
Telecommunications Act 77
telecommunications industry 14, 66, 70, 72, 75-91, 99, 101, 168, 170, 172, 174; in an emerging political system 76; Atlas, Phoenix and Global One 86–9; conflict to co-operation 84–5; discordia and Eunetcom 85–6; Europeanisation 79–83; French policy patterns 78–9; German policy patterns 76–7
telecommunications terminal directive 65
textiles 45, 46
'third party access' (TPA) 63, 64, 67, 68, 69, 71, 72
Thygesen, N. 27
trade deficit 42
trade unions 15, 132, 133, 134, 135, 138, 140, 143, 160
transit directives 62–3, 64, 67
transnational exchange theory 6
Transpac 84, 88
transport 70

Treasury bonds 21, 26
Treaty of Paris 134
treaty revision conferences 7
Treaty of Rome 3–4, 14, 23, 58, 80, 117, 134, 135–6, 150; Article 118: 136; Article 119: 136; Article 121: 136; Articles 117–23: 136; Articles 123–8: 136
Trésor 25-6
Trichet, Governor 31
Tsebelis, G. 71
Tunisia 51
Turkey 48, 51
Turner, L. 135

unemployment 42, 54
Union of Industrial and Employers' Confederations of Europe (UNICE) 135
Union pour la Co-ordination de la Production et du Transport d'Electricité (UCPTE) 62, 64
United States 3, 5–6, 16, 176; agricultural policy 119, 120, 121, 123; foreign affairs, security and defence 150, 152, 154, 155, 156; immigration policy 159, 160; Intergovernmental Conference and Eastern enlargement 44, 47, 48, 50, 55; Justice Department 87, 88; monetary union 21–3, 25, 31; research and technology policy 97, 99, 101, 103; telecommunications 76, 77, 80, 81, 84, 85, 87, 89; Treasury bonds 21, 26
universal service 78, 79
universalistic selection 159
Uterwedde, H. 11

Val Duchesse European social dialogue 135, 137
value-added services 78
van Apeldoorn, B. 133
Van Miert, K. 67, 87
Vedel, T. 14, 75–91, 172
Védrine, H. 2, 11–12, 170, 171
Venturini, P. 134-5
Videotex 84
Visegrad four 50
Visser, J. 135, 138

Waigel, T. 32
Wallace, H. 9–10, 11
Washington Treaty 22
water 70

Webber, D. 1–17, 79, 108, 111–28,
167–80
Weil, P. 15–16, 159–66
Weiler, J. 64
Weimar triangle 44
Werle, R. 76, 89
Werner Report 23, 27, 28, 35
Wessels, W. 8, 11, 173
Western European Union 45, 47, 48, 55,
156
Westlake, M. 170

*White Paper on Growth, Competitiveness and
Employment* 140, 142
Willaert, P. 156
Wood, P.C. 11, 104, 107

Yugoslavia 41, 45, 152, 156

Zelikow, P. 22
Zerah, D. 25
Zwickel, K. 141
Zysman, J. 4, 80, 98